Faku

Rulership and Colonialism in the Mpondo Kingdom
(C. 1760–1867)

Timothy J. Stapleton

Wilfrid Laurier University Press

This book has been published with the help of a grant from the Humanities and Social Sciences Federation of Canada, using funds provided by the Social Sciences and Humanities Research Council of Canada. Wilfrid Laurier University Press acknowledges the financial support of the Government of Canada through the Canada Book Fund for our publishing activities.

Library and Archives Canada Cataloguing in Publication

Stapleton, Timothy Joseph, 1967–

    Faku : rulership and colonialsim in the Mpondo Kingdom (c. 1780–1867)

Includes bibliographical references and index.

ISBN 978-1-55458-593-9 (paper)
ISBN 978-0-88920-597-0 (PDF)

1. Faku, d. 1867. 2. Pondo (African people). 3. Pondoland (South Africa) – History. 4. Pondoland (South Africa) – Kings and rulers – Biography. I. Title.
DT2400.P66S72 2000   968.7'91   C99-932231-1

© 2001 Wilfrid Laurier University Press
        Waterloo, Ontario   N2L 3C5
        www.wlupress.wlu.ca

This printing 2013
Printed in Canada
Cover design by Leslie Macredie, using a photograph of a Pondo homestead with *imizi* scattered on ridges. Photograph courtesy of the Cory Library, Grahamstown, South Africa.

MIX
Paper from
responsible sources
FSC® C021996

Contents

Acknowledgements

A lthough this book has a single author, many people and institutions contributed, in a variety of ways, towards its creation. I would like to offer particular thanks to the staff of the William Cullen Library at the University of the Witwatersrand who were extremely helpful and friendly to a researcher who had much to do in a limited amount of time. The staff of both the Cape and Natal archives were also courteous and efficient. Cecilia Blight of the Cory Library for Historical Research at Rhodes University deserves considerable thanks for providing the photographs. The University of Fort Hare in South Africa, where I was a senior lecturer in history, generously provided a research grant which enabled me to conduct oral history fieldwork in Pondoland and to travel to the Natal Archives.

A number of individual colleagues deserve special mention for discussing various elements of this book with me. Professor Wellington Sobahle, of Fort Hare's Department of African Studies, raised important questions about Faku's ban on circumcision. Professor Mike Prins, of Fort Hare's Department of Afrikaans, translated several of Adam Kok's letters from Afrikaans into English. Professor Gideon Thom and Dr. Jacob Ndlovu, of Fort Hare's faculties of Theology and Education respectively, clarified the background of Methodism and the outlook of nineteenth-century Methodist missionaries, such as those who served in Pondoland during Faku's time. I owe a huge debt to Dr. Sean Morrow, a historian and dear friend who directs Fort Hare's Govan Mbeki Research Resource Centre, for his encouragement during the course of this project.

Special thanks go to the many people in Pondoland who helped me during fieldwork. Paramount Chief Mpondombini Sigcau and his wife Princess Lombekiso Sigcau, both of Eastern Pondoland, were incredibly hospitable to a complete stranger and permitted me to see the unmarked grave of Faku. Chief Mnakwa Mqabalaki, of Lusikisiki, took time out of his busy schedule to show me around the area. In Western Pondoland, the

Ndamase family was very helpful, and Mr. Arthur Lizo Luwaca, who lives near Libode, was exceptionally congenial, even when I inadvertently interrupted a family celebration.

I would also like to thank Sandra Woolfrey, former director of Wilfrid Laurier University Press, for suggesting improvements to the manuscript and guiding it through the process of evaluation.

My deepest gratitude goes to my wife, Mavis Ncube-Chinamora, who endured hours of neglect while I sat in front of a word processor and spent her vacation working as a research assistant driving throughout the dusty roads of Pondoland searching for oral informants.

List of Abbreviations

BK	British Kaffraria
BPP	British Parliamentary Paper
CA	Cape Archives
CO	Colonial Office
DSAB	Dictionary of South African Biography
FP	Fynn Papers
GH	Government House
JP	Jenkins Papers
NA	Natal Archives
Wits	University of the Witwatersrand, William Cullen Library
WMMS	Wesleyan Methodist Missionary Society

Mpondo Royal Genealogy from c. 1800

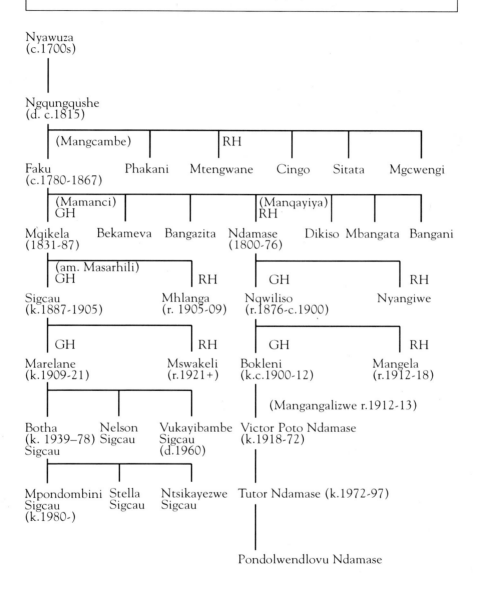

Nyawuza
(c.1700s)

Ngqungqushe
(d. c.1815)

(Mangcambe)   RH

Faku   Phakani   Mtengwane   Cingo   Sitata   Mgcwengi
(c.1780-1867)

(Mamanci)   (Manqayiya)
GH   RH

Mqikela   Bekameva   Bangazita   Ndamase   Dikiso   Mbangata   Bangani
(1831-87)   (1800-76)

(am. Masarhili)
GH   RH   GH   RH

Sigcau   Mhlanga   Nqwiliso   Nyangiwe
(k.1887-1905)   (r. 1905-09)   (r.1876-c.1900)

GH   RH   GH   RH

Marelane   Mswakeli   Bokleni   Mangela
(k.1909-21)   (r.1921+)   (k.c.1900-12)   (r.1912-18)

                                 (Mangangalizwe r.1912-13)

Botha   Nelson   Vukayibambe   Victor Poto Ndamase
(k. 1939–78) Sigcau Sigcau   (k.1918-72)
Sigcau   (d.1960)

Mpondombini Stella   Ntsikayezwe   Tutor Ndamase (k.1972-97)
Sigcau   Sigcau   Sigcau
(k.1980-)

                                   Pondolwendlovu Ndamase

Legend:
(c.1780-1867) = lifetime   k. = years of kingship   d. = died   r. = regency
(Mamanci) = mother of name below   am. = adopted mother
GH = Great House   RH = Right-Hand House

South Africa in the mid-1800s

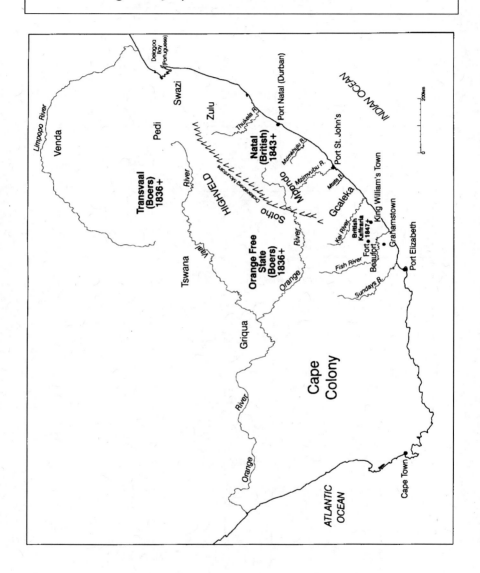

The Mpondo Kingdom and Its Neighbours

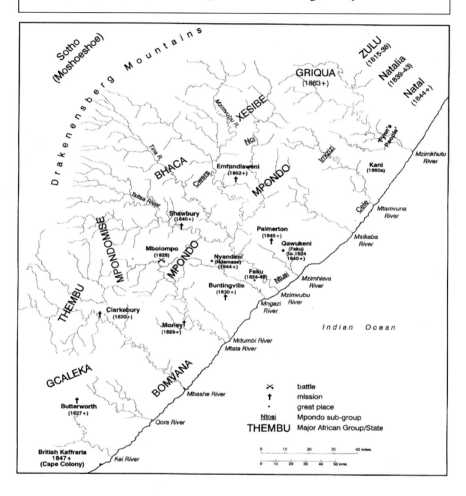

Centuries before the arrival of the first Europeans and the foundation of the country of South Africa that we know today, its indigenous peoples had formed complex states with sophisticated trade networks and dynamic Iron Age technological innovations. Geographically, South Africa is divided by the Drakensberg Mountains, which run parallel to its long Indian Ocean coast. North of these mountains, on the elevated grassland known as the Highveld, the ancestors of today's Tswana and Sotho people, by at least A.D.1000, had established large towns around the few available and reliable water sources. Below the Drakensberg water was more plentiful, so the Nguni-speaking people (ancestors of today's Xhosa and Zulu speakers) created more numerous but smaller communities along the many river valleys. Up to the 1600s, a typical chiefdom in this area might have consisted of a few family-based homesteads under a senior clan head. From around A.D.1000 to well into the 1700s, the Nguni people expanded west along the coast, but did not venture further than the area of annual summer rainfall in today's Eastern Cape. Although these Iron Age peoples, both of the Highveld and the coast, did cultivate millet and sorghum, the states which they developed were largely based on cattle herding economies as the vast grasslands of the subcontinent were well suited for this endeavour. In the Western Cape, the region of regular winter rainfall, numerous bands of Khoikhoi did not cultivate, but concentrated almost exclusively on raising livestock. It was through absorbing the Khoikhoi, along with the San (Bushmen) hunter-gatherers who were scattered throughout southern Africa, that three distinct click sounds were incorporated into what would become the Xhosa and Zulu languages. Today, in written orthography, these clicks, which are produced by sucking air into the mouth and then releasing it with the tongue, are represented by the letters c, q and x.

Note to the Preface is on p. 173.

This book focuses generally on a region to the south of the Drakensberg Mountains now within South Africa's Eastern Cape province, particularly the northeast section of this area, which is inhabited by the Mpondo people and commonly referred to as Pondoland. The Mpondo people, who speak a dialect of the Xhosa language, have a strong oral tradition which claims that their precolonial state originated somewhere up the coast in modern KwaZulu/Natal about twenty-two generations before c.1815, which might be as long ago as 1300. In addition, oral sources state that ten generations before c.1815, possibly as early as 1550, they crossed the Thukela River in modern KwaZulu/Natal and moved into present-day Pondoland. Since this time, the Mpondo people have inhabited most of the land along the Indian Ocean coast and its hinterland between the Mtata and Mzimkhulu rivers, just to the southwest of today's province of KwaZulu/Natal. This large strip of territory is characterized by many impressive river valleys originating in the Drakensberg Mountains to the north and running south toward the white sandy beaches and rocky cliffs of the coast. Along the large, rolling hills the vegetation is a mixture of lush forest near the sea and drier thorn bushes and open grassland beginning just a few kilometres inland. The climate is slightly warmer and more humid than the rest of the Eastern Cape.

Although there is not much evidence to reconstruct the lives of ordinary Mpondo people during this period, the basic foundation of Mpondo life seems to have been the homestead, called *umzi* (plural *imizi*) in the Xhosa language. Each *umzi* was dominated by a mature man who lived there with his wives and children as well as some of his brothers and sons and their wives and children. Usually built on the top of a hill or ridge overlooking a river, the Mpondo homestead was laid out in a circle with a semicircle of round huts facing a circular cattle enclosure (kraal) made of thorn bushes. The huts themselves were usually made of wattle walls, mostly dried mud and cow dung supported by an interlocking frame of branches, and a thatched grass roof. In this polygamous society, a husband and each of his wives had their own individual huts for living, and another, usually elevated on posts, for storing food. Cultivation was conducted on the slopes of the hills near the *umzi*; cattle and small stock like goats could graze nearby during the day, but were returned to the kraal at night. At times, a man, together with his wives, children and livestock, would leave the protection of his father or older brother to establish his own *umzi*. In 1829, missionaries visiting Pondoland observed that along the ridges of just one river valley there were around one hundred homesteads, each of which contained between twenty and forty huts. It would seem that Mpondo homesteads were somewhat larger than those of other Xhosa-speaking people in the area, and this trend continued throughout the nineteenth century. Spacing between homesteads varied a great deal, from fifty metres to several kilometres. The *imiẓi* of chiefs and even the king were not much different from those of common people, except that they often had more visitors such as the ruler's councillors, men gathering for a battle or emissaries from neighbouring states. However, rulers ensured control of their people by having a number of *imiẓi*, each administered by members of their immediate family, spread throughout their respective areas. Additionally, rulers' cattle tended to be spread among their subjects' homesteads, although at times the king did maintain special cattle kraals for larger portions of the royal herd. Politically, all the homestead heads in a given district would owe allegiance to a chief who was a vassal of the central ruler. As will be discussed in chapter 1, settlement patterns and political authority among the Mpondo changed significantly in the early 1800s. Socially, members of extended families (patrilineal clans in which intermarriage was forbidden) were scattered throughout many districts of the kingdom, with some clans dominating particular areas.

By 1800, the immediate neighbours of the Mpondo were mostly other southern Nguni-speaking (or Xhosa-speaking) groups such as the Xesibe to the north, the Mpondomise, with whom the Mpondo claim a common historical origin, to the northwest, the Thembu to the west and the Bomvana to the southwest. Further to the southwest were the two main splits of the Xhosa proper, the Gcaleka and Rharhabe. To the northeast were various northern Nguni-speaking (Zulu-speaking) peoples organized into states such as the Ndwandwe, Mthethwa and Ngwane. Around 1815, these northern Nguni states would begin to be amalgamated under the new Zulu Kingdom, which became the most powerful of the Mpondos' African neighbours. Later, in the early 1820s the Bhaca, originally a northern Nguni group, would move south across the Mzimkhulu River into Pondoland. Also in the early 1820s, various Sotho-speaking people on the interior Highveld would move up into the Drakensberg Mountains to form a centralized state, today's Lesotho, which would be a distant northern neighbour of the Mpondo kingdom further south on the coast.

Beginning in the 1490s, the Khoikhoi groups of the Western Cape were periodically visited by European seafaring merchants on their way to and from India. From 1652, the Dutch East India Company established a permanent station in Table Bay, the site of present-day Cape Town, to provide a reliable supply of food and water for their passing ships. Almost from the start of this settlement, Dutch settlers constantly expanding their holdings clashed with the Khoikhoi over cattle and land. Eventually, most Khoikhoi were either absorbed into Cape colonial society as subservient labourers or fled north across the Orange River to the

Highveld or east along the coast to the Xhosa states. On the Highveld, mixed groups of settler outlaws and Khoikhoi, eventually dubbed the Griqua and Korana, used horses and guns from the Cape to raid the local Sotho and Tswana speakers for livestock and forced labour. By the 1760s, Dutch settlers at the Cape who had adopted pastoralism had expanded so far east, usually without official support, that they made first contact with the western-most Xhosa-speaking people such as the Rharhabe. Throughout the 1780s and 1790s the Dutch trekboers and western Xhosa unsuccessfully attempted to drive each other off the rich grazing land between the Sundays and Fish rivers, the Zuurveld.

With the decline of the Dutch as a colonial power and the rise of the British, the latter seized the Cape Colony for the second and final time in 1806. With the firepower of a fairly large British army, Cape forces, in 1811 and 1819, were able to drive the western Xhosa off the Zuurveld and east of the Fish and Keiskamma rivers. In 1820, significant numbers of British settlers arrived in the eastern part of the Cape Colony and forts were built along the borders to keep the Rharhabe and other Xhosa groups from attempting to retake their land. As the settler population grew and demanded more African land and labour, the Cape would fight a number of wars of dispossession against the western Xhosa, primarily the Rharhabe but also the Gcaleka, throughout most of the nineteenth century. Of course, colonial expansion was often tempered by the reluctance of the British imperial government to finance expensive wars of conquest in the Cape which, at this time, had no value beyond the strategic position of its coast on the sea route to India. Although the Cape-Xhosa wars of the 1800s were mainly fought hundreds of kilometres west of the Mpondo state, they would become very important for the development of Cape-Mpondo relations in the same period.

For reasons discussed in chapter 3, in the late 1830s Dutch-speaking settlers (often called Boers[1]) left the Cape Colony to establish independent republics in coastal Natal and on the inland Highveld. This brought the reality of colonial conquest much closer to the Mpondo state as the Boers defeated the Zulu Kingdom and established the Republic of Natalia just north of the Mzimkhulu River. The British became worried that the Boers in Natalia would link up with another European naval power to block British shipping to India. Therefore, in 1842 and 1843 they seized the Boer republic and turned it into the British Colony of Natal, to which more British settlers would migrate. This meant that the Mpondo Kingdom now had British colonies to both its southwest, the fairly distant Cape, and northeast, the more immediate Natal. From the 1850s, the Mpondo state became a target for Natal's efforts to enlarge its borders.

North of the Drakensberg Mountains, the Boer republics, which emerged on the Highveld, dispossessed local Tswana-speaking and Sotho-speaking people. In 1848 the British annexed the Boer republics of the southern Highveld, but after suffering an embarrassing defeat at the hands of the Sotho, they realized that it was impractical to be involved in the affairs of the interior. Therefore, in the Sand River Convention of 1852, the British recognized the independence of the Boer republic in the Transvaal, and in the Bloemfontein Convention of 1854, they did the same thing with the Boers of the Orange Free State. Throughout the 1850s and 1860s, the Free State Boers engaged in almost constant conflict with the Sotho people of King Moshoeshoe and gradually pushed them off their best agricultural land.

Besides conquest of land and control of labour, another aspect of British colonialism in southern Africa was the activities of numerous mission societies. Spurred on by an evangelical revolution in England in the late 1700s, missionaries came to the Cape to spread Christianity and Western culture among African people. These missionaries were part of the colonization process, but were not always under the control of the colonial state. Throughout the nineteenth century, missions were set up within the territories of independent African states such as the Gcaleka, Thembu and Mpondo. There were many reasons why African rulers permitted these seemingly strange outsiders to work in their areas, including the desire to acquire European technologies such as firearms and to use them as quasi-diplomats with nearby settler colonies. However, the missionary enterprise did have limited success in this period; a small group of Westernized, Christianized Africans, many of whom had been outcasts from African society, developed around these scattered missions. In the interaction of colonial powers and independent African states, such as in the Mpondo case, these missionaries and their converts did play an often-decisive role.

Missionaries were not the only Europeans to live and work within independent African states. Various white frontiersmen, some of whom were fugitives from the Cape, travelled overland among the African people, trading luxury items like glass beads, cloth and firearms for local products such as cowhides, ostrich feathers and ivory. Some, in the early 1800s, may even have been involved in acquiring captives to sell as slaves to American and Brazilian vessels along the coast. As will be seen, these frontiersmen would also prove significant in the history of the Mpondo Kingdom.

It was in this increasingly complex milieu of competing African kingdoms, expanding settler colonies, proselytizing missionaries and ambitious white traders that Faku, around 1815, became ruler of the Mpondo state. Of course, the Mpondo Kingdom also had its own internal dynamics, political, economic and social, which influenced Faku's responses to these external forces.

Since there are many names and terms throughout this book which might be unfamiliar to readers without a background in South African history, the back matter includes three appendixes: a cast of characters, a list of terms and a chronology of major events.

Introduction

From roughly 1815 to 1867, Faku was ruler of the Mpondo Kingdom, which was located in what is now the northeast section of the Eastern Cape. After his father was killed in a campaign against the neighbouring Bomvana, Faku inherited power in a period of intense raiding, migration and state formation, the causes of which have stimulated an almost equally intense debate among historians. In order to survive the challenges of the early nineteenth century, Faku transformed the Mpondo polity from a loosely organized constellation of tributary groups into a more centralized and populous state with effective military capabilities and a prosperous agricultural foundation. Unlike most portrayals of the Mpondo in this period, they were not harried victims of the Zulu but a fast-growing and sometimes predatory regional power.

In 1830, Faku allowed Wesleyan missionaries to establish a station within his kingdom; they became his main channel of communication with the Cape Colony, and later colonial Natal, for the rest of his life. With the arrival of Boer trekkers in Natal in the late 1830s, Faku was now faced with two colonial neighbours and attempted, with a fair degree of success, to play one off against the other. This Mpondo king played a seminal, yet often understated, role in stimulating the British occupation and annexation of Natal in the early 1840s. This led directly to Faku enhancing his territorial claims and regional influence through official alliance with the Cape Colony in 1844. In return, the British, from the late 1840s and early 1850s, expected Faku to assist them in wars against the Rharhabe and Gcaleka Xhosa far to his west, but every attempt to mobilize the Mpondo failed. Instead, Faku concentrated his military resources on trying to dominate his close neighbours, such as the Thembu, Bomvana, Mpondomise and Bhaca.

Notes to the Introduction are on pp. 173–74.

1

Throughout the 1850s and 1860s, the British in both the Cape and Natal became less interested in Faku as a military ally and began to impose agreements on him which gradually removed more and more territory from the Mpondo Kingdom. However, even in his old age, Faku remained quite astute in diplomatic negotiations with colonial officials and used his missionary connections to optimum advantage. Splitting the state between his two principal sons, Ndamase and Mqikela, probably saved the Mpondo from the horrors of a civil war and served to stave off colonial annexation for nearly three decades after his death.

***

Many Europeans visited Faku throughout his life, but none of them seems to have made any sketch or painting or taken an early photograph of him. It is strange that Andrew Geddes Bain, at the time a trader and an amateur artist, met Faku in 1829 but only drew a picture of one of the Mpondo ruler's sons, Bangazita. Other African rulers of the period, such as Moshoeshoe, Ngqika and Shaka, were sketched by Europeans. Perhaps Faku did not want to be sketched. However, while this may not be academically significant, in reading this biography it would be useful, at least in terms of historical imagination, to visualize what the subject looked like. Luckily, some European visitors did compose written descriptions of Faku that might be useful for this purpose. After Bain's initial introduction to Faku, the former wrote:

> Faco [sic] was now pointed out to us among the bystanders. He is a tall good looking man, apparently not above forty, and in no way distinguishable from the rest of his people except by a bunch of red Lawrie's feathers which hung behind his head.[1]

In 1832, Andrew Smith, who was travelling through Mpondo territory on his way from the Cape Colony to Port Natal, noted that:

> Facu [sic] is almost always yawning, and when even in serious conversation is in the habit of looking all round him and even directly behind him as if he wished or expected to see something. His face is full and round, with a rather pleasing expression. He has tender eyes and cannot stand the light. His make is middling, his stature tall, and in his gait he has a stoop and motion somewhat like some of the men of fashion in England. His whole appearance indicates a superiority, and I think if a person not knowing him were to meet him they would consider him more than common. He is careless in the dressing of his hair, and had a fine ivory snuff spoon stuck in it.[2]

Certainly the most romanticized description of Faku was written in late 1834 by Captain Allen F. Gardiner, a former British naval officer who was on his way to the Zulu Kingdom:

> On this Faku rose from the assembly, and coming up, I dismounted to receive his usual congratulation, a shake of the hand, with which he now obliges his white friends. He was attired in a handsome leopard skin mantle, in this country the insignia of rank, which so remarkably became his tall and commanding person, that when he turned from me to resume his seat among the councillors, he looked the very beau ideal of an African chief.[3]

Observing Faku through their Western/colonial perspective, these writers certainly caste the Mpondo king in the typical mould of a "noble savage," which was popular in European literature at the time. However, some of the basic facts of their accounts, such as Faku's height and charismatic appearance, are substantially consistent and there is no reason to disbelieve them.

***

Despite guiding the Mpondo through half a century of profound change, Faku has never been the subject of a biography. There are many reasons for this. There are not many biographies of nineteenth-century African leaders in southern Africa, with some exceptions: Moshoeshoe of the Sotho, Maqoma and Sandile of the Xhosa and Shaka of the Zulu. In the few general works that mention Faku, he is frequently portrayed as a fairly unimportant and unexciting individual. Geographically, the history of the Mpondo area of the Eastern Cape is also somewhat neglected. Perhaps this is because it is situated between two comparatively well-studied parts of South Africa, the Eastern Cape's Ciskei/Border region, which was the scene of most of the Cape-Xhosa wars in the late eighteenth and nineteenth centuries, and the province of KwaZulu-Natal with the well-known Zulu Kingdom. Both these areas have tended to entice new historians. Today's Pondoland is a poverty-stricken, underdeveloped rural area, which attracts little popular, let alone academic, attention. There is no recent general history of the Mpondo as there are for other African groups such as the Xhosa, Zulu, Swazi or Pedi. It is hoped that this biography makes a contribution toward righting this omission, but at the same time it should be keep in mind that this is not meant as an "ethnic" history.

While there is very little literature on Faku, he has been mentioned in a few wider studies that tend to portray him in a variety of ways. Settler writers and historians of the late nineteenth and early twentieth centuries seemed either neutral or slightly positive about Faku. Charles Brownlee and George Theal, both former colonial officials, condemned many African leaders who resisted European conquest, but Faku, who protected missionaries and avoided war with the colonial powers, did not get similar treatment. Brownlee remembered that "our direct relationships with Faku, which were rather of a negative than positive character, were not unsatisfactory. He and his son Damas [sic], the chief of Western Pondoland, appeared to be desirous of living on friendly terms with the Government."[4]

Several African writers of the 1920s and 1930s, mostly products of mission education, saw Faku in a much more favourable light. For Victor Poto Ndamase, a direct descendant of Faku who wrote a book on the history and customs of his people, Faku had been one of the greatest rulers of the Mpondo. It is not surprising that Victor Poto Ndamase, paramount chief of Western Pondoland from 1918 to 1972, wrote his book at the same time that the South African government was implementing its retribalization policies which sought to emphasize traditional leaders and ethnicity in rural areas as a foil to developing class consciousness in urban centres. The memory of Faku represented the historical legitimacy of Victor Poto's own government-recognized chieftaincy in Western Pondoland.[5] John Henderson Soga, son of the famous Xhosa missionary Tiyo Soga and himself a Christian minister, wrote a brief biographical account of Faku in the first of his two books on Xhosa history and traditions. According to Soga, "The disposition of Faku was peaceable and tractable, always willing to live in friendly relations with all people in his country."[6] However, on the bottom of the very same page, Soga contradicts himself by describing how "On two separate occasions Faku led his army against the Bomvana."[7] Since Faku had supported missionaries, Soga, who was obviously biased towards mission endeavour, might have thought it ambiguous to describe the Mpondo ruler as anything but a pacifist who had been periodically forced into armed conflict.

The first professional historian to examine the nineteenth-century Mpondo Kingdom in any detail was D.G.L. Cragg, who wrote in the 1950s. Responding to the controversial polemic of Dora Taylor, which criticized missionaries as agents of colonial conquest, Cragg's doctoral thesis was a defence of Wesleyan missionaries who had operated in the Mpondo state during the 1800s. Although Faku protected Cragg's beloved missionaries, his portrayal of the Mpondo king is tempered by the fact that there were very few converts to Christianity during his reign. Describing Faku as a rather mediocre ruler, Cragg contends that the

Mpondo king's alliance with the Cape Colony "had rested more upon missionary influence and favourable political circumstances than upon his own skill. . . . Whatever his qualities as a traditional chief, his political dealings with the white man lacked the shrewdness of his contemporary, Moshoeshoe."[8]

In sharp contrast to the previous view, J.D. Omer-Cooper, working in the 1960s, produced one of the most overtly positive interpretations of Faku's career. Referring specifically to Faku's role in the intense state formation and raiding of the early nineteenth century, Omer-Cooper stated that:

> He is not usually thought amongst the great Bantu figures of this period but he deserves to be considered one of the most outstanding leaders of the Mfecane. By his diplomacy and military skill he held his people together in the face of wave after wave of invasion, dealt with his enemies one by one and prevented the tide of disturbance from flowing down the coast.[9]

Assessing the overall legacy of Faku's reign, Omer-Cooper maintained that "When the old chief finally passed away he left behind him a tribe which had successfully survived many hazards and which still remains one of the most important ethnic groups in South Africa."[10] A factor contributing to this assessment was that Omer-Cooper's book was written in Nigeria in the era when most African countries were receiving their independence from colonial masters. Omer-Cooper was certainly influenced by the African nationalist fervour of this period, and like other historians he bent over backwards to overthrow negative colonial stereotypes of African history by glorifying pre-colonial African states and their leaders.

William Beinart's materialist study of Pondoland mostly deals with the era after Faku's death in 1867 up to the 1930s. However, the first chapter, in providing a brief background on the changing material nature of the Mpondo Kingdom in the early and mid-nineteenth century, mentions Faku in many places. Since this period fell outside the scope of the study, Beinart's introductory chapter tended to rely on what others had written before him, and he appears to have accepted uncritically that the Mpondo had been ravaged by the Zulu in the late 1820s. Overall, Beinart offers the most objective portrayal of Faku while at the same time pointing out his many important contributions and innovations within the Mpondo state.

Beinart divides Faku's reign into two distinct phases. First, up to the 1840s, Faku led his people through a period of intense conflict in which the Zulu pushed them west of the Mzimvubu River and seized all their cattle. However, Faku attracted numerous refugees and eventually developed a powerful, centralized kingdom in the 1830s. Second, with the decline of Zulu raiding, Faku's subjects reoccupied their former land east of the Mzimvubu after 1840 and, as a result, the state became more spread out and decentralized. Economically, cattle raising once again became important and contact with colonial traders brought luxury goods to the Mpondo. Beinart claims that "Though Faku was able to exert some control over cattle and labour in the pastoral economy, partial reversion to older forms of subsistence and productive organization was accompanied by a decline in the immediate authority of the paramountcy."[11]

In the oral history of today's Mpondo people, Faku is generally remembered as "the founder of the present Pondo nation." The Mpondo state existed long before Faku, but no other ruler in its history is given the same credit in its development. His importance is illustrated by the fact that the name of the Mpondo royal clan shifted from Nyawuza, a king in the mid-1700s, to Faku. More generally, when Mpondo leave home they often refer to themselves as "Faku's people." In fact, among the rural Mpondo it is considered an honour to greet someone by saying "Faku."[12] However, as will be discussed below, some of the details of Faku's career have been forgotten.

Readers should note that the first chapter of this biography has implications for the so-called "Mfecane" debate within South African historiography. For many years historians of Southern Africa agreed that the wave of African state formation, population movement and intensified warfare in the early nineteenth century, termed the "Mfecane," or "crushing," had been caused by the establishment and expansion of Shaka's Zulu Kingdom in what is now KwaZulu/Natal. In the mid-1980s, however, this assumption was challenged by the revisionist work of Julian Cobbing, who claimed that the Zulu had been merely the scapegoats for violence caused by the interlocking activities of various colonial or colonial-sponsored raiders such as the British army from the Cape, mixed-race Griqua horsemen on the interior Highveld, the Portuguese and their African allies from Delagoa Bay (present-day Maputo) and British merchants with a private African army from Port Natal (now Durban). Cobbing also maintained that these activities were downplayed in the official record because they involved the acquisition of slaves and forced labourers, which was in contradiction to British imperial policy of the time. The Zulu state had not been at the centre of events, but was just one of a number of more powerful African kingdoms to emerge at this time in response to these new external pressures. For Cobbing, the term "Mfecane" is not an appropriate label for this period because it was selected to exclude whites from the process and to evoke images of so-called "black on black" violence. The conventional "Mfecane" theory was emphasized in apartheid-era history texts to justify white ownership of the best agricultural land, since Shaka had allegedly pushed black people into the areas that eventually became tribal homelands, and also to create fear by warning what might happen if Africans were ever to regain power in South Africa. While most historians now accept that Zulu expansion was not the sole cause of this "time of troubles" in the early 1800s, Cobbing's theory has been criticized for ignoring the role of drought in this process and for accusing missionaries of complicity in raiding without enough evidence. In addition, some have suggested that Cobbing set the start date of Portuguese slaving too early in order to portray it as the cause of the rise of the Zulu state, and that his theory denies African initiative in history by emphasizing external colonial forces.[13] Faku came to power at the beginning of this period, and evidence pertaining to the Mpondo state suggests that the fundamentals of Cobbing's theory, with some modifications, are essentially correct. However, this book is not only about the "Mfecane" debate; it is a much wider biography of a man who ruled an African state for over fifty years.

***

Why write a biography of Faku? As seen above, various authors have produced conflicting interpretations of this Mpondo king which certainly need to be sorted out. Was he a lacklustre ruler made great by circumstance and influential missionary friends as claimed by Cragg, or a skilled military leader and negotiator as supported by Omer-Cooper? Perhaps both of these descriptions are inaccurate. There is also a considerable literature on the impact of missionaries and Christianity on African societies. Since Faku had close contact with Wesleyan missionaries for over half his life, this might be a good opportunity to explore this terrain. Were Faku's missionaries covert agents of colonial conquest and what was the Mpondo king's personal reaction to their alien religion? Another much written about theme is African reaction to early colonial intrusion. While some Xhosa-speaking rulers in the same period – like Maqoma of the Rharhabe – resisted stubbornly, others – like Kama of the Gqunukhwebe – eagerly accepted colonial domination. How did Faku respond to the increased colonial presence around his borders from the 1830s? Faku's Mpondo never entered into armed conflict with a colonial power, and only on one brief occasion in the early 1850s did his warriors serve within the colonial armies that conquered other African groups in the region. Why did he adopt this policy? With reference to the internal affairs of the Mpondo Kingdom, what sort of a ruler was Faku? To what extent did he attempt to alter the nature of his state so it could better cope with the changing times?

In reconstructing Faku's career, there are certain problems with the available evidence. As this Mpondo ruler belonged to a non-literate society, he did not leave behind the type of personal papers or memoirs that form the basis of many biographies. Any existing record of what Faku said or did has been filtered through other individuals, whether missionaries who wrote letters on his behalf or Africans who narrated their memories of him years later in interviews recorded by Europeans. All these sources might have had their own reasons for altering or even inventing information about Faku. However, through comparing sources with different perspectives and subjecting each to careful scrutiny, it is possible to work towards a more balanced account of Faku's life.

Most of the detailed evidence about Faku comes from the papers of the Reverend Thomas Jenkins, a Wesleyan missionary in Pondoland from 1838 to 1868. He arrived in the kingdom when Faku was at the height of his power and died a few months after the African ruler he had known for nearly three decades. Letters to and from Jenkins cover the entire period of his mission with the Mpondo. Unfortunately, his diary, an extremely detailed account of day-to-day interaction with Faku and his people, was partially destroyed sometime before the 1930s, and the surviving portion only covers 1845 to 1852. As a result, this period can be reconstructed in much greater detail than other parts of Faku's life where there is comparatively less evidence. Accounts by other Wesleyans in the area, some whom had been there before Jenkins, help fill these gaps. However, it must always be kept in mind that these missionaries were biased in favour of their own culture and religion, which they were trying to recreate among the Mpondo. At the same time, the writing of Jenkins and some other Wesleyans shows obvious sympathy for Faku, despite his lack of serious interest in Christianity, perhaps because they were grateful for his protection over many years.

The papers of Henry Francis Fynn, who was a trader/raider in Pondoland in the 1820s and British Resident to Faku in 1835 and from 1848 to 1852, are problematic sources. Fynn was arguably Faku's greatest European enemy, and many of his statements about the Mpondo king were proven to be false by the Wesleyans. However, as Fynn played a significant role in Pondoland, it is important to at least consider the information which he left behind.[14]

For the period before the arrival of the Wesleyans in Pondoland in 1830, most of the evidence comes from scattered reports of European traders, raiders or nearby missionaries as well as Zulu oral histories mostly recorded by James Stuart, a Natal colonial official, in the early twentieth century. While Stuart may have edited the transcripts of his interviews with elderly Zulu men who had fought against the Mpondo, these informants do supply valuable, and sometimes surprisingly objective, testimony on Faku's military activities in the 1820s.[15] The books by Victor Poto Ndamase and J.H. Soga, although secondary sources, also contain valuable information as they almost certainly knew people who had lived in the Mpondo Kingdom during or just after the reign of Faku. On the other hand, as already stated, both these writers were also influenced by the biases of colonial and mission historiography.

As already mentioned, Faku occupies a central place in Mpondo oral traditions and these are very useful in examining particular periods of his life. However, as with most oral histories of events that took place so long ago, they have peculiar problems. As elsewhere in Africa, the spread of literacy has meant that Mpondo oral traditions have been influenced by written histories, especially the Xhosa language work of Victor Poto Ndamase, who collected some of his information from colonial sources. The natural fallibility of human memory has meant that there are many gaps and confusions in the oral history of Faku. In addition, the personal bias of informants seems to impact upon the stories they tell. For instance, people in Western Pondoland tend to concentrate on Ndamase, Faku's eldest son and a great military leader, in his movement west of the Mzimvubu River to create a new Mpondo Kingdom. In Eastern Pondoland, where the royal family still claims authority over both sides of the Mzimvubu River, this event is not seen in such a positive light, and the traditions which are related deal more with Faku and Mqikela, his heir. Fortunately, the praise songs of Faku are fairly well known, although they have certainly changed considerably over the generations, but they require an expert in that field to unlock their intricate symbolism. A broader study of oral history in Pondoland would be a useful and challenging project, but it is not the main focus of this work.[16]

An unfortunate problem with all these sources is that they reveal very little about the role of women in nineteenth-century Mpondo society. Documents authored by Victorian colonial agents and missionaries, with a very few exceptions, do not pay much attention to either European or African women. Similarly, Mpondo oral history tends to emphasize what is perceived as the important deeds of "great" men. It is therefore difficult to reconstruct the precise details of what Mpondo women were actually doing in the period of Faku's life and exactly what influence individual women had on him. However, there are rare pieces of information scattered here and there throughout most of the sources, nearly all of which have been included in this biography. Tantalizingly, these primarily illustrate some basic elements of Faku's relationship with his mother, sisters, wives and daughters, which is obviously a topic of great significance.

1

The Rise of Faku and the Centralization of the Mpondo Kingdom (C. 1780–1829)

lthough it is impossible to determine the exact date, Faku was born around 1780 at Qawukeni, the Mpondo great place, which is near the present-day town of Lusikisiki in the northeastern part of South Africa's Transkei region. His father, Ngqungqushe, was ruler of the Mpondo Kingdom, which had been an organized state since at least the 1500s. As the name Mpondo means "horn," it is likely that Faku's people had a long-established reputation for martial prowess. The Mpondo king had many wives and the ranking of his sons was determined by the status enjoyed by their respective mothers. Customarily, the king's first spouse, usually married before assuming power, became the right-hand wife whose eldest son had the privilege of eventually forming a semi-autonomous chiefdom. The paramount married his great wife, whose first son would become the heir, after he had taken power, and the bride price (iLobola) was paid for by a cattle levy from the entire kingdom. However, as Faku's mother, an Mpondomise woman named Mamgcambe, was an ordinary wife of the king, he was initially neither the right-hand nor great son.

During the late eighteenth century the Mpondo state, consisting of many vassal chiefdoms, was located near the coast along both sides of the Mzimvubu River. Though pre-colonial African polities did not have rigid boundaries, the Mpondo Kingdom extended along the coast roughly to the Mzimkhulu River to the northeast and the Mtata River to the southwest. At this time Dutch-speaking settlers had advanced east from the Cape Colony to meet Xhosa chiefdoms around the Sundays River, but they were still very far from Ngqungqushe's domain. The only Europeans seen by the Mpondo were either infrequent Boer hunters or helpless survivors of rare shipwrecks along their coastline. Most of these latter newcomers were incorporated into Mpondo society in the same way as

---

Notes to chapter 1 are on pp. 174–77.

various groups of Khoikoi pastoralists and San hunter-gatherers who were the earliest inhabitants of the region. Nevertheless, in 1782 Ngqungqushe ordered the execution of some survivors from the *Grosvenor*, a wrecked British vessel, but the circumstances around this incident remain unclear.[1]

Almost nothing is known about Faku's childhood in the late eighteenth century. Sometime in the late 1790s, when Faku was about eighteen years old, he went to the bush to experience a year-long initiation school, which culminated in circumcision. This signified his entry into adulthood. Around 1800 he married his first wife, Manqayiya, who was from the neighbouring Bomvana to the southwest. Within a short time she had given birth to Ndamase, who was Faku's first and ultimately right-hand son. Throughout his life, Faku would marry and have children with at least a dozen wives.[2]

Beginning in the late 1700s, the material basis of Mpondo society was experiencing significant development. Maize, an American crop introduced to southern Africa by Portuguese slave traders based at Delagoa Bay, had become the most important part of cultivation. Producing higher yields than the indigenous millet and sorghum, maize caused population growth and increased the power of chiefs who sought to control the new food surplus. Furthermore, more and more cattle were being brought under the authority of the king and lent out to subordinate rulers on an increase-sharing basis. Those who did not obey the paramount risked the repossession of most of their stock. Lastly, the Mpondo, like other African groups, did not live in isolation. Long-distance trade in items such as beads, iron, ivory and captives was becoming increasingly important. The Mpondo would trade with neighbouring groups such as the Bomvana to the southwest or the Mthethwa to the northeast, who would in turn trade with other groups until goods from Pondoland ultimately reached Dutch settlers in the Cape Colony or Portuguese seafaring traders at Delagoa Bay. Once again, the Mpondo ruler and his army exercised careful control over trade in their locality through taking a share of the merchandise in exchange for protection. These three factors, maize, cattle and trade, all served to enhance the power and prestige of the ruling elite.[3] However, the kingdom was fairly spread out and subordinate chiefdoms on its periphery enjoyed considerable autonomy.

Sometime in the 1810s, Ngqungqushe, the Mpondo king and Faku's father, intervened in a succession dispute between two Bomvana chiefs, the young Ngezana and his uncle Gambushe. It is important to note that Ngezana was allied to Ngqungqushe through marriage to one of the Mpondo king's daughters, and that Gambushe had been involved in previous disputes with the Mpondo. Therefore, the Mpondo king led his army southwest to combine with the forces of Ngezana, the younger Bomvana chief, in the hope of installing a friendly ruler in a neighbouring state. Subsequently, Ngqungqushe and Ngezana attacked Gambushe's great place forcing him and his warriors to retreat. Reorganizing his forces with surprising speed, Gambushe, the older Bomvana chief, then launched such an intense counterattack that the combined Mpondo-Bomvana army broke and fled. In the confusion of retreat, Ngqungqushe's personal bodyguard was overtaken by the enemy and the paramount was, as the historian J.H. Soga states, "sent to join his ancestors."[4]

At the time of his father's death, Faku was in his early to mid-thirties, but was not, as has been explained, the official heir. The son of Ngqungqushe's great wife, and therefore the legitimate successor, was the younger Phakani. Victor Poto Ndamase, a descendant of Faku who wrote a book in the 1920s on Mpondo history based partially on oral traditions, claims that while Faku's mother was skilful at cooking meat and generous to the late king's councillors, the other royal wives, including the great wife, were horrible cooks who were stingy when the councillors visited their houses. Consequently, "The councillors consulted together and said that she who resembled a chief's wife was the mother of Faku. A tribal meeting was summoned and it was announced that the appointment of the Great Wife was to be reversed."[5] In the following description of the event by Victor Poto Ndamase, the leopard's tail serves as a emblem of the late monarch's great house:

> Now there was a leopard's tail on a pole planted in the ground in between the huts of the Great Place. The councillors went to the mother of Phakani and said: "Listen to us: we are placing you below because you tie in knots this house." They went to the mother of Faku and said: "Listen to us: we are placing you above because you build up this house." The mother of Phakani said: "You are disgracing the leopard's tail by placing it below." The councillors were silent and said nothing. The mother of Faku said: "You are building up the house by raising the leopard's tail." The councillors said: "There is the woman who builds up the house." So they made her Great Wife.[6]

Another version of this story from a recent oral source is prefaced by the observation that "Phakani loved to work with cattle, he did not care about his subjects." After Ngqungqushe's death, the Mpondo held a ceremony where the great wife was supposed to secure her place by slipping the tail of a leopard over the end of a long stick. However, Phakani's mother was unable, or perhaps not allowed, to perform this task, which was then passed to Faku's mother who "put the tail on the stick to unite the people."[7] The result of both accounts is that Faku became the late Ngqungqushe's heir and was ultimately installed as the Mpondo king. Mamgcambe, Faku's mother, then took the name "Umkhulu," which means "the great one." It is likely that Faku was not appointed on the basis of his mother's cooking or her ability to perform a ceremony, but both stories seem to symbolize that Mamgcambe had considerably more influence with her late husband's councillors than the other royal wives. As a mature man who was married and had children, Faku himself must have been already established as an emerging leader within the kingdom. Phakani was young, probably an adolescent, and unknown. The transferral of the great house from Phakani's mother to Faku's mother legitimized Faku's succession. Furthermore, Faku seems to have enjoyed the support of a younger full brother, Cingo, and a half-brother named Sitata, who both eventually became subordinate rulers of large sections of the Mpondo state. Sitata was also from a relatively minor wife of Ngqungqushe and might have seen Faku's rise to power as an opportunity to displace the more prestigious houses.[8] Jeff Peires, a historian of the Xhosa who wrote mostly in the 1980s, claimed that Faku won a war of succession against Phakani who was backed by Gambushe's Bomvana.[9] However, there is absolutely no evidence for this, and the available sources indicate that the succession dispute was resolved without significant violence. After the usurpation of the original great house, Phakani and his mother became obscure figures and did not play a significant role in future Mpondo politics. According to Peires, Phakani and his mother later went to live among Hintsa's Gcaleka, who became rivals of Faku's Mpondo.[10]

Not everyone in the kingdom accepted Faku's succession. Mtengwane, the older right-hand son of the late king Ngqungqushe, expressed his dissent by moving to the neighbouring Bomvana chiefdom of Gambushe. However, Mtengwane had little popular support and not many people went with him. By the 1830s he had returned to live in the Mpondo Kingdom. In a more serious incident after Faku's succession, a significant section of the kingdom refused to accept him and fled to the Xesibe chief Sinama, who subsequently forced them to return as he did not want to risk jeopardizing his long-standing alliance with the Mpondo. After all, Sinama was married to a sister of the late Ngqungqushe.

Avenging his father's death, Faku's first major action as paramount was to launch a punitive raid against Gambushe's Bomvana. Another motive for this attack might have been that Faku wanted to dissuade his remaining rivals within the kingdom from defecting to Gambushe. Between 1815 and 1819, the Mpondo army forced Gambushe and his people west over the Mtata and Mbashe rivers and drove them as far as the Qora

River in Hintsa's Gcaleka Kingdom. Another successful counterattack by the Bomvana, however, sent Faku's exhausted men running home. Fearing repeated attacks from the Mpondo, Gambushe's group did not move back to their original area on the western edge of Pondoland, but settled between the Mtata and Mbashe rivers. An oral tradition condenses this process by stating that "Ngqungqushe was killed by the Bomvana. The Bomvana left Pondoland fearing that Faku would kill them. They went to Hintsa."[11] The attempt by the Mpondo royals to set up a satellite state among the Bomvana had failed, and conflict between the two groups would persist for some time.

In the 1810s, the indigenous societies of southern Africa began to experience much more concerted colonial intrusion. By 1819 the British had taken over the Cape Colony and had used the superior military power of their standing army to expel the Gqunukhwebe and Rharhabe Xhosa chiefdoms east of the Keiskamma River. North of the Orange River, mixed-race frontiersmen called Griquas and Koranas used their horses and guns to raid African chiefdoms for cattle and captives which were then traded further south to the labour-hungry settlers of the Cape. On the other side of Pondoland, Portuguese-sponsored slave raiding increased to the point where it began to destabilize the societies of the Delagoa Bay hinterland, and in the early 1820s mysterious British traders began to conduct seafaring commerce based from Port Natal (now Durban). Aggravating this situation, a protracted drought escalated competition for agricultural resources, which were suddenly becoming scarce. While the introduction of maize had caused population growth, in times of drought it was more difficult to feed such large numbers of people. African communities responded to these developments by either moving away from hazardous areas and/or forming larger, more centralized states for protection or raiding or both. Moshoeshoe's Lesotho, Mzilikazi's Ndebele, Sobhuza's Ngwane (or Swazi) and Shaka's Zulu represent some major examples of this process of migration and state formation which have been at the centre of recent academic debates.[12] Undoubtedly, Faku's Mpondo were not isolated from this process, but not much has been written on this area in the early nineteenth century.

Part of the intensification of colonial intrusion in the early nineteenth century involved the extension of European missionary activities beyond the Cape Colony and east of the Kei River. Directed by the Reverend William Shaw, who had arrived in the Eastern Cape with British settlers in 1820, the Wesleyan Missionary Society aggressively embarked on a plan to establish a chain of mission stations from the colony to Port Natal. As early as 1825 Shaw had founded Mount Coke station with Chief Ndlambe of the Rharhabe and had visited major African rulers such as Hintsa of the Gcaleka and Ngubencuka of the Thembu to convince them of the benefits of Christianity and Western education. Ignoring Hintsa's reluctance to accept a missionary, the Reverend William Shrewsbury, in June 1827, set up a Wesleyan station called Butterworth near the Gcaleka great place. Eventually, Hintsa sanctioned this mission out of fear of alienating his powerful colonial neighbour. In August of the same year Shrewsbury and Nicholas Lochenberg, an enigmatic Dutch fugitive who hunted and traded along the Transkei coast, rode to the east bank of the Mtata River to meet Chief Mdepa of the Tshomane which was a semi-autonomous sub-chiefdom on the periphery of the Mpondo Kingdom. In order to further secure his independence from Faku, who was in the process of centralizing royal authority, Mdepa requested a missionary. Shrewsbury recommended this on the basis of a rumour that Mdepa's mother had been a European who had survived the wreck of an unidentified ship in the 1740s and later married a Tshomane chief. However, the presence of Lochenberg indicates that this expedition was not simply interested in saving souls and must have also had a commercial motive. Ultimately, in 1829, the Wesleyans sent the Reverend William Shepstone to establish the Morley mission with Mdepa's chiefdom on the lower Mtata River.[13]

At roughly the same time Faku established himself as paramount of the Mpondo – in the mid 1810s – some of the states to his northeast amalgamated into the Zulu Kingdom under the famous Shaka. In order to protect themselves from Portuguese-sponsored raids from the north, the Zulu perfected a military system based on men of the same age grouped together in regiments and moved their state further southwest toward Pondoland. This put an extremely powerful and potentially hostile kingdom just over Faku's eastern boundary, the Mzimkhulu River.[14]

Around 1820 or 1821 Ngoza's Thembu, a group which had lived in the Thukela Valley of present-day Natal, fled southwest to escape incorporation into Shaka's Zulu state and sought to make a home for themselves by expelling the Mpondo from the eastern portion of their territory. In turn, Faku quickly organized his army and attacked the Thembu the day after they had crossed west of the Mzimkhulu River. Although the Thembu had not adopted a system of age-regiments, they had plenty of recent combat experience against the Zulu. As a result, Ngoza's force, which was divided into three major units, repelled the Mpondo onslaught. However, the following day, Faku, who had received reinforcements from other parts of his kingdom, redirected his attack on the Thembu. With superior numbers, the Mpondo soon overwhelmed their enemies and Ngoza was killed in the fighting. Tradition maintains that the Mpondo warriors then seized some Thembu women and cut off their hands in order to remove "the metal ornaments they wore on the arm."[15] Many of the surviving Thembu fled back to Zulu territory and others were incorporated into Faku's state.[16]

Sometime in 1824 Zulu regiments led by Mdhlaka, Shaka's premier military commander, moved west along the foot of the Drakensberg Mountains and then turned south into Mpondo territory where they seized some cattle. There are several Zulu oral traditions which seek to explain the motive for this campaign. The first claims that Shaka, the Zulu king, had sent this army to attack Hintsa's Gcaleka, but upon seeing European houses the Zulu regiments turned back and decided to conduct a livestock raid against the Mpondo. However, this story seems unlikely, as there is no other evidence that a Zulu army came that close to any colonial settlement. A more plausible account maintains that the army was in pursuit of Madzikane, a Bhaca chief who had fled southwest from present-day Natal to avoid Zulu raids. Failing to locate the Bhaca, Mdhlaka opted to seize Mpondo stock as he did not want to return to Shaka empty-handed.[17]

Describing Faku's alleged reaction to this intrusion, J.D. Omer-Cooper, a historian who wrote in the 1960s, claims that "The Pondo leader wisely restrained his people from engaging in any major battle with the Zulu. He offered his submission to Shaka and retained the fighting strength of his tribe virtually intact."[18] However, Zulu and Mpondo oral traditions tell a very different story. On this occasion, Faku delegated command of his army to his twenty-five-year-old right-hand son, Ndamase, who – the historian J.H. Soga describes as "a man of courage and resource."[19] Mobilizing his forces with amazing speed, Ndamase intercepted the invading Zulu and inflicted serious casualties on three of their senior regiments. The Mpondo warriors, with their distinctively long braided hair, watched as the older Zulu men, with their characteristic head-rings, ran from the fight. In turn, Mdhlaka, the Zulu commander, reinforced his beleaguered units with regiments composed of younger men, and the Mpondo were compelled to break contact. This gave the Zulus enough time for an orderly withdrawal. Interviewed in the first decade of the twentieth century, a Zulu oral informant maintained that as the Zulu warriors were moving along the coast toward their home: "Faku used supernatural powers to set hyenas of the forest on to them. The hyenas ate the Zulu cattle as well as the members of the force, and followed the force until it got. . .across the Tukela into Zululand."[20]

The hyenas are probably symbolic of Mpondo fighters – perhaps with hunting dogs – who pursued and harassed the retiring Zulu army. During the return journey Mdhlaka's Zulu raiders, who had lost all their cattle, were "obliged to eat melons [*amabece*] and wild plants." Consequently, the Zulu named this disastrous operation the *amabece impi*, or "melon army."[21] While this first Zulu attack was not very successful, Faku decided to be cautious and moved his great place, along with some of his people, west of the Mzimvubu River into the steep hills between the Great and Little Mngazi rivers. The width of the Mzimvubu would present a formidable obstacle to raiders coming from the east. However, Mpondo kraals did remain on the northeast side of that river throughout the 1820s.

At the same time the Zulu regiments were raiding Faku, Henry Francis Fynn and a few other British traders set up a station at Port Natal and entered into an alliance with Shaka, the Zulu king, in whose territory they were living. Soon after arriving in Natal, Fynn observed Zulu warriors returning from their foray into Mpondo territory.[22] Throughout September and October 1824, Fynn conducted a personal reconnaissance of Pondoland and then returned to his station to organize a larger expedition. Early in 1825, Fynn visited Faku, who initially suspected him of being a Zulu spy. However, as the Mpondo King did not want to provoke further attacks and probably wanted to promote commerce, he eventually permitted Fynn to travel as far west as the Mtata River to locate areas where elephants could be hunted for ivory. In addition, Faku allowed this British merchant to establish a temporary trading post with one of his sub-chiefdoms east of the Mzimvubu River. Fynn remained there for nine months before returning to Port Natal in October 1825. In the same year, another British trader, William Thackwray, travelled overland from the Cape Colony to trade with the Mpondo and make contact with Fynn's group.[23]

Although Faku may have been forced to abandon some of his eastern territory because of the Zulu threat, he gained more power as displaced people such as the ImiZizi, Nci, Cele and Cwera sought protection within the Mpondo state. In 1824, Madzikane, leader of the Bhaca, was killed in a battle with Ngubengcuka's Thembu, who were neighbours of the Mpondo to the northwest. After Madzikane's death, one of the late Bhaca chief's minor sons, Dliwako, took a section of his people to the Mpondo Kingdom for protection. Fearing loss of power, Ncaphayi, a more senior son of the late Madzikane, took the rest of his people into Pondoland and became ruler of all the Bhaca who settled in the northern reaches of Faku's area. In the late 1820s and early 1830s, Ncaphayi became an occasional yet important military ally of the Mpondo. According to Bhaca oral tradition, "Madzikane always had a feeling that in order for the Bhaca to get peace, they would have to go to Faku in Pondoland. . . . When they arrived in Pondoland, the Bhaca were warmly welcomed by Faku and they were given land on which to reside."[24]

With these new allies, Faku, around 1826, sought to expand his herds by launching another attack on his old enemies to the southwest, the

Bomvana, who had recently moved back into Mpondo territory by cross-ing to the east side of the Mbashe River. Organizing his force into two columns, Faku's Mpondo army headed directly toward the Bomvana great place while his Bhaca allies circled round to attack it from the north. Hopelessly out-numbered, the Bomvanas fled with their cattle towards the Mbashe River in the hope of receiving protection from Hintsa's Gcaleka, who lived to the west. The Mpondo army pursued the Bomvanas for a short distance, picking up stray cattle, but began to retire upon hearing that the enemy had crossed the river and were in Gcaleka territory. While the Bomvana were bringing their cattle across the Mbashe, the Bhaca warriors descended upon them and rapidly withdrew with a large amount of stock.

That night the Mpondo fighters, who were returning to their homes, stopped in a forest to feast on some of the captured animals. However, the Bomvana had quickly regrouped and stealthily approached the glowing fires of the Mpondo camp. In the subsequent attack, the Mpondo were taken completely by surprise and retreated in disarray. Notwithstanding the fact that the Mpondo raiders had been driven away, the Bomvana realized that it was far too dangerous to live in Faku's vicinity and they once again moved their kraals west across the Mbashe River into Gcalekaland.[25]

Throughout 1826, Fynn became a regular visitor to Pondoland, and in 1827 he established a station near the Mzimkhulu River which attracted around two thousand African followers.[26] Some of these people must have come from the outskirts of Faku's state. This private army hunted elephants for ivory, captured cattle to consume and trade, and possibly abducted people for a covert slave trade with American and Brazilian vessels calling at Port Natal. Since London had outlawed the slave trade in 1807, the Port Natal merchants had to conceal these latter activities while in their area the demand for slaves increased as slaving ships were driven from the West African coast by the British navy. In addition to the Zulu, Faku now faced another aggressive neighbour on his immediate northeast frontier.

There is considerable disagreement among historians concerning a large-scale attack on the Mpondo that originated from the northeast in 1828. The conventional view maintains that Shaka sent a Zulu army into Pondoland as part of a mourning ritual for his late mother, Nandi. During this invasion the Zulu supposedly drove all the Mpondo southwest of the Mzimvubu River and plundered all their cattle to the extent that, for years after, Faku's people were forced to live exclusively by cultivation.[27] However, recent revisionism claims that the raid was actually the work of British traders from Port Natal, such as Henry Francis Fynn, who did not succeed in totally ravaging the Mpondo state. In May 1828, Fynn, accompanied by a few other white traders with guns, led his private army into the Mpondo Kingdom and returned with a sizable herd of cattle. Since British officials in Cape Town and London would have disapproved of these warlord-like activities, Fynn wrote to the colonial authorities maintaining that it was Shaka who had attacked the Mpondo and warning that the Zulu would soon attack the colony. Two months after the incident Major W.B. Dundas, who was in charge of a colonial patrol from the Cape, visited Faku's great place, which had been burned to the ground. After stating that the Zulu army had been raiding his country for one and a half months, the Mpondo monarch claimed that "Fynn was present with the invading army" and that "there were other white people with Fynn." Faku identified Lieutenant Francis G. Farewell and Henry Ogle, colleagues of Fynn from Port Natal, as having been among the raiders. In fact, Faku showed Dundas an Mpondo man who claimed that it was Fynn who had shot him in both thighs during the raid. Understating his role in this affair, Fynn later admitted that some of his African employees had raided Mpondo cattle.[28]

It seems likely that both these versions are partially correct. While there is substantial oral evidence that Shaka did order an attack on the Mpondo in 1828, it also seems clear that Fynn's force was involved in the campaign. Rejecting the mourning ritual as the sole cause of the attack, John Laband states that Shaka's motive for this offensive

> was probably to muffle internal opposition by seizing sufficient cattle to redistribute to his most important chiefs. But it is also evident that he was egged on by an unscrupulous faction among the Port Natal traders. For they were in hope that a confrontation between the Zulu and the British authorities, which the Zulu armed presence so near the Cape frontier was calculated to induce, would expedite British intervention in the affairs of Natal. Thus the way would be opened for increased trade, for the loosening of Shaka's control over the settlement at Port Natal and, ultimately, for British protection.[29]

It is worth noting that Shaka had employed Fynn's gunmen as mercenaries in his 1826 campaign against the Ndwandwe, a rival state.[30] Since Shaka's attack on the Mpondo in 1824 had been a dismal failure, he probably supplemented his army in 1828 with Fynn's musketeers. Firearms offered a strong advantage. Shaka personally led his regiments as far as the Mzimkhulu River, where Fynn had a large post. It was here that Shaka based himself during this campaign, and here he may have once again enlisted the services of the white traders and their African adherents.

As he had done four years earlier, Mdhlaka, Shaka's veteran commander, took the Zulu army and its auxiliaries southwest into the Mpondo Kingdom. There are many versions of the subsequent events. In one Zulu account, Faku's warriors put up stiff resistance and inflicted heavy casualties on the Zulu Mkandhlwini regiment, which subsequently retreated from the battlefield. The Mpondo army then virtually annihilated the Zulu Mkandhlu regiment with "a shower of assegais – small assegais" [spears] which appeared to have been dipped in poison. Finally, the Zulu regiment called Nomdayana, "came to the rescue and the Pondos were repulsed." In turn, the Zulus were able to seize some cattle and return home, where Shaka had surviving members of the Mkandhlwini regiment executed for cowardice.[31] Another Zulu version of this campaign states that Faku directed his warriors not to oppose the advancing Zulu army. The Mpondo paramount took his royal herd to the Drakensberg Mountains and allowed the Zulu regiments to travel as far southwest as the Bomvana country, seizing cattle that belonged to subordinate chiefs. Apparently, only light-brown cattle were captured during this operation. If these traditions are correct, then it is doubtful that the Mpondo lost all their cattle to Shaka's Zulu. Additionally, there is nothing to indicate that the Mpondo abandoned all their land east of the Mzimvubu. After this campaign, Faku attempted to avoid any further attacks by sending peace envoys to Shaka with a few cattle as tribute.[32] Unfortunately, these oral accounts do not reveal anything about Fynn's role in the operation.

There are several very interesting Mpondo oral traditions about this Zulu attack. One informant relates that the Mtwa and Ntusi, sub-groups of the Mpondo led by Faku's son Ndamase, defeated the Zulu army somewhere around the Mzimvubu River. The Zulu then headed north, seized some cattle from the nearby Thembu and returned to Shaka, claiming that they had beaten the Mpondo. However, since the captured cattle did not have long horns like typical Mpondo cattle, the Zulu king knew that his army had been defeated and sent its dishonest commanders to campaign against the Shangaan people in what is now Mozambique. While Shaka had previously seen Faku as an unimportant ruler, he now understood the strength of the Mpondo Kingdom. Consequently, the Zulu monarch sent one hundred of his cattle to Pondoland and Faku sent back one hundred long-horned Mpondo cattle in return. This cemented an alliance between Shaka and Faku, and the former awarded the Mpondo with all the land up to the Thukela River, far northeast of Faku's domain. A second account maintains that the Zulu and Mpondo armies met on the east side of the Mzimvubu River near Qawukeni, the historic Mpondo capital, where the two commanders personally faced each other in combat. Because the Mpondo leader, who in this account was not Ndamase, had a huge shield that covered his entire body, the Zulu commander could not find a place to strike with his distinctive short spear. Eventually, the Zulu leader managed to stab his Mpondo counterpart in the nose and the latter fell to the ground, apparently dead. However, the Mpondo commander suddenly jumped to his feet and drove his spear into his unsuspecting enemy's stomach. With their leader lying dead, the Zulu were driven from the battlefield. From then on, the unidentified Mpondo leader was popularly known as the one with a scar on his nose.[33] While these oral histories certainly contain some exaggerations, such as Shaka granting Faku all the land up to the Thukela River, they clearly state that the Mpondo were not defeated by the Zulu.

Faku's military activities throughout the rest of 1828 demonstrate that the Mpondo state had not been seriously damaged by the Zulu assault. Shortly after this attack, Faku's old allies, the Xesibe, returned to Eastern Pondoland after temporarily moving west out of fear of raids from either Fynn or Shaka or both. While the late Xesibe chief Sinama had been an ally of both Ngqungqushe and Faku, their new ruler, Nogula, attempted to make an alliance with the Bhaca people against the Mpondo. The situation was complicated by the fact that Nogula was a regent for Jojo, the child heir of the Xesibe chiefdom, who was a nephew of Faku. Fearing that Nogula was planning to use his proposed alliance with the Bhaca to place Jojo in control of the Mpondo Kingdom, Faku directed one of his sons, Bangazita, to lead an attack upon the returning Xesibe. Despite the partial failure of this operation, Nogula had been given a taste of Mpondo power and abandoned his ambitions. Once again, the Xesibe chiefdom became a tributary state of the Mpondo Kingdom.[34]

In the early 1820s, the Ngwane of Chief Matiwane had fled west of Natal towards Moshoeshoe's mountain state, now Lesotho, only to be turned south by Griqua raiders. By 1826 or 1827 they had settled on the upper Mtata River on the northwestern edge of Mpondo territory. As Faku probably saw Matiwane's group as both a threat and a potential target, Mpondo warriors raided the Ngwane around 1827, but were driven off without much booty.[35] However, in 1828 the Ngwane were targeted by the British army as a possible source of forced labour and cattle that could be brought into the Cape Colony. In late July 1828 Major Dundas, a British officer who had just visited Faku to obtain intelligence on the area, led a mounted reconnaissance force of fifty armed settlers and many more Thembu allies against the Ngwane and seized 25,000 cattle plus an unknown number of female prisoners. The effectiveness of colonial firepower in this operation greatly impressed both Faku and Hintsa, the Gcaleka king. Faku saw an opportunity to launch another raid against the

Ngwane. Therefore, when Colonel Henry Somerset's main colonial army, which consisted of about one thousand mounted Khoikhoi riflemen and armed settlers along with several howitzers, attacked the Ngwane on 27 August, they were assisted by not only Ngubencuka's Thembu but also Mpondo and Gcakela warriors. It may be significant that around this time Faku was attempting to secure an alliance with the Thembu by sending his daughter, Nonesi, to become the great wife of their king. According to Victor Poto Ndamase, Faku "was requested by Ngubencuka to come and help him in the battle with Matiwane at Mbolompo."[36] An Mpondomise oral account from the late nineteenth century describes the rather one-sided engagement:

> The AmaNgwana [sic] made no stand, but fled and went into the bushes. The reports of the guns were very dreadful, none of the native allies fought, they just looked on in astonishment. The report of the cannon was fearful, it was directed into the bush; women and children screamed, and cattle bellowed, and all came out of the forest towards where the army was, and were captured.[37]

Over seven hundred Ngwane were killed, and the white farmers brought over one hundred women and children back to the colony. The Thembu, Gcaleka and Mpondo returned to their respective homes with many cattle and prisoners. A Zulu oral tradition indicates that a considerable number of Ngwane went to live under Faku. Interestingly, the Reverend Shrewsbury of Butterworth mission purchased a pregnant woman for two cows from a Gcaleka warrior who had participated in the raid. Just as Fynn had done, Somerset, the British commander, covered his actions by maintaining that he had heroically defended the colony and its African neighbours from an advancing Zulu army. Subsequently, this massive labour and livestock raid against the Ngwane was disguised as the "Battle of Mbolompo."[38]

In the late 1820s, increasing numbers of European traders and raiders, many of whom enjoyed missionary support, began operating in and around Pondoland. Sometime in late 1828 a British trader named Shaw visited Faku on his way to see Shaka, the Zulu ruler, on behalf of Colonel Somerset. Stressing that he was an agent of the colonial government, this trader demanded that Faku should prohibit any other Europeans from passing through his country. Shortly thereafter Faku attempted to turn back a group of Boer hunters who were on their way from the Cape colony to the Mzimvubu River. However, the fear of firearms and the goodwill of a few gifts convinced Faku to let them pass. Despite his failed attempt to gain a monopoly over the Pondoland trade, Shaw, the trader, continued to hunt elephants in the area for at least another year. Furthermore, Fynn's father and two brothers began taking wagon loads of unidentified trade goods back and forth between the Cape Colony and Port Natal via Pondoland.[39] It was in this period that a rough wagon trail began to develop through Faku's territory.

The September 1828 assassination of Shaka by his brother Dingane, who seems to have been in collusion with Port Natal traders such as the Fynns, sent shock waves throughout the Zulu Kingdom. Nqeto, chief of a section of the Qwabe who had supported the late Zulu ruler, took his followers southwest across both the Mzimkhulu and Mzimvubu rivers, but passed north of Faku's territory. However, Nqeto's people were blocked by the Mpondomise, northern neighbours of the Mpondo, and forced to turn south into Mpondo country where they settled along the upper Mzimvubu River. Early in 1829 Lochenberg, the frontiersman who had just been temporarily in charge of the Butterworth mission, organized a party of Mpondo to raid the Qwabe. There is no direct evidence to link Faku with this group, but the presence of Mpondo warriors in its ranks and previous Mpondo involvement with attacks on the Ngwane suggest that the paramount knew about the expedition and might have sanctioned it for a share of the loot. While the objective of this attack remains somewhat obscure, Lochenberg may have seen the Qwabe in the same way Somerset had seen the Ngwane and sought to replicate the Mbolompo raid, albeit on a smaller scale, in order to take cattle and captives for trade elsewhere. However, Lochenberg's plans were foiled, as Nqeto, the Qwabe leader, learned of the approaching marauders and personally organized an ambush against them. Although Lochenberg managed to shoot Nqeto in the leg, the large group of Qwabe warriors quickly overwhelmed the relatively small raiding party, killing the white gunman and many of his Mpondo henchmen.[40]

The destruction of Lochenberg's raiding party made Faku eager to seek an alliance with the Cape Colony through accepting a missionary into his kingdom. On the fifteenth of May 1829, the Wesleyan missionaries William Shaw, William Shrewsbury and William Shepstone, visited Faku's great place. As part of their plan to set up a chain of stations from the Cape to Port Natal, this group was in the process of establishing Shepstone's Morley mission with Mdepa's Tshomane, an Mpondo tributary state, on the Mtata River. Addressing the Mpondo king and his court, Shaw said, "We have frequently heard that you wish for a missionary to reside among you and we have come to hear for ourselves whether this is really the case. Therefore, speak Faku, we wait to hear". Faku then stated that "The reports you have heard are true. We wish missionaries to come and live amongst us."[41] Faku surely did not want the Tshomane, one of his vassal chiefdoms, to enjoy the possible protection that would come with having a white missionary while he did not. At the same time, Shaw and his Wesleyan colleagues knew about the death of Lochenberg, their close friend, and probably wanted to cultivate Faku as a potential ally against the Qwabe.

In early August 1829 Lieutenant Farewell, a Port Natal trader who had just accompanied a Zulu deputation to the Cape, set out from Grahamstown with a wagon train guarded by at least thirty armed and mounted Khoikhoi and Europeans. The wagons contained muskets and "a large supply of ammunition" meant for either Fynn's private army on the Mzimkhulu River or for trade to the new Zulu king, Dingane. Passing through Butterworth mission in early September, Farewell advised the Reverend Shrewsbury that it would be advantageous to establish a monthly communication between the colony and Port Natal

> which could be accomplished through the medium of Missionary Stations, providing a mission with the Amapondos, then in contemplation, should be commenced, which would extend the stations in a connected line along the coast, to within one hundred and fifty miles of Natal.[42]

In late September Farewell's party visited Faku at an Mpondo kraal on the banks of the Mzimvubu River. Although the exact details of Farewell's conversation with Faku are unrecorded, the Mpondo paramount informed him that Nqeto, the Qwabe ruler, would supply the traders with enough cattle to sustain them on their journey. As he had done with Lochenberg, Faku might have given Farewell permission to extort livestock from the Qwabe as long as Mpondo kraals remained unmolested. Faku certainly remembered that Farewell had been employed by the Zulu army, which had raided the Mpondo just a year before. The Port Natal party then rode north and halted about sixteen miles from Nqeto's kraal. Farewell led two white traders, Thackwray and Walker, and a few Khoikhoi bodyguards into the Qwabe great place to demand cattle. Initially negotiating with Farewell, Nqeto eventually became angry and complained about the wound he had received from Lochenberg's gun. That night he ordered his people to kill the visitors; only Farewell's Xhosa interpreter escaped to warn the wagon party. The following morning a large group of Qwabe warriors captured the gun-laden wagons, which had been abandoned by the remaining Europeans and Khoikhoi who were already riding speedily southwest towards the safety of Reverend Shepstone's Morley mission on the Mtata River.

Why did Nqeto order the death of Farewell and his party? One account maintains that Nqeto wanted to prevent Farewell from reaching Natal because he was afraid that the firearms in his wagons would be traded to Dingane, the Zulu king, who would then use them to attack the Qwabe deserters from the Zulu state. An oral tradition confirms that Nqeto ordered the traders to be killed because he thought that "Farewell would bring the Zulus against him."[43] This is not surprising considering that Nqeto knew that on several occasions the Port Natal traders, particularly Farewell, had been employed as mercenaries by the Zulu Kingdom. Additionally, Nqeto's reference to the Lochenberg incident illustrates that he was enraged by yet another attempt by Europeans to seize his livestock.

In October 1929, in response to both the Lochenberg and Farewell incidents, Nqeto's Qwabe followers began to attack Tshomane kraals around Shepstone's Morley station, which gave the missionary plenty of time to escape. By the end of the month, the Qwabe had destroyed Morley itself.[44] This was perhaps to be expected, as Lochenberg had helped establish this station, enjoyed a friendly relationship with the Wesleyan missionaries and used their missions as bases of operation. Similarly, Farewell had also been close to the Wesleyans, and the surviving gunrunners from his party had received sanctuary at Morley. Nqeto did not see Morley as a centre for Christianity but as a base for military operations against his people.

Faku now feared that Nqeto's actions would lead to an attack by either colonial soldiers from the west or the Port Natal traders and/or the Zulu from the east. Either one of these outcomes, as Faku knew from personal experience, could easily destabilize the region. Since the Tshomane paid tribute to the Mpondo Kingdom, the Qwabe attack on them was indirectly an attack upon Faku himself. Furthermore, the firearms captured by the Qwabe made them all the more dangerous, and probably convinced Faku that their complete destruction was vital to his security. He was also wise enough to realize that destroying the Qwabe would enhance his growing relationship with white missionaries and traders. Although Faku had maintained cordial relations with Nqeto, the Mpondo king began sending messengers to Dingane, the Zulu ruler, asking for advice as to what action to take against the migrant Qwabe. Learning that Faku was plotting against him, Nqeto dispatched his army to attack the Mpondo cattle kraals. Mpondo spies quickly informed Faku about the impending assault, and the king personally led his army to set up an ambush for the Qwabe, who were advancing southward along the banks of the Mzimvubu River. From his two previous encounters with the Zulu, Faku knew that if the Qwabe regiments, formerly part of the Zulu army, were given an opportunity to deploy in orderly formation, they could possibly defeat the superior numbers of the Mpondo. The paramount's plan hinged on catching Nqeto's army off guard in territory that was unfavourable to their usual tactics.[45]

There are two slightly different versions of the ensuing battle. The Reverend Shrewsbury of Butterworth was told that while Faku allowed Nqeto's Qwabe to take cattle from Mpondo kraals, the paramount concealed some of his warriors in a thicket of ten-foot high grass near a river crossing that had been previously used by the enemy. Once the Qwabe were returning home with the captured cattle

> Faku and his warriors pursued at a distance till they reached the heights of the Umzimvubu. The descent from those heights to the river is studded all over with trees (the Mimosa) and here the Mpondo poured down upon their adversaries. Unable to collect in a body, Faku's people fought them single-handed among the thorn-trees, and cut them off in great numbers, while those lying in ambush arose at the proper juncture and slew all that were rushing through the ford at the river.[46]

According to H.F. Fynn, who had also heard of the event second hand, Faku used his advance warning of the Qwabe offensive to organize his army near the bank of the Mzimvubu River. Ignoring a message from Nqeto to return home with their loot, the Qwabe army attacked the Mpondo ranks:

> But Faku, as it turned out, had been carefully manoeuvring for position. He at length succeeded in getting the Qwabes into a bend in the river, where, owing to his superiority of numbers and a more advantageous position (a position that permitted only one regiment to attack at any given moment), he completely defeated his rival. In addition to those killed in battle, many of Nqetho's men, unable to resist the pressure of their assailants, threw themselves into the river and were drowned in attempting to make their escape over to the other side; many others again were torn to pieces by the hippopotami that abounded in that part of the river.[47]

Years later, a missionary travelling through Pondoland was told that Ndamase, Faku's eldest son, served as "a leading warrior in the final engagement which utterly crushed the Zulu [Qwabe] invader and closed the war."[48] Faku's plan had been a complete success and it was later rumoured that the Mpondo army did not suffer a single fatality. This was Faku's greatest military victory, and in recognition Mpondo praise-singers dubbed their king *Jasele*, which means "him who destroys all." Furthermore, by defeating the migrant Qwabe, Faku endeared himself to the Wesleyan missionaries and white traders who had seen Nqeto as a serious impediment to their work.[49]

Shortly after this engagement, Faku sent a message to Ncaphayi, chief of the Bhaca people to the north, advising him to attack the Qwabe villages as they had little protection. In turn, the Bhaca wasted no time in burning the huts of Nqeto's remaining followers and seizing their cattle. It must be noted that Faku had not taken any of Nqeto's cattle as they had been previously claimed by the Zulu king, Dingane. This also makes sense because Faku had defeated an invading army, which probably had few animals with it, while the Bhaca raided the Qwabe villages and cattle kraals. As a result of these two serious defeats, Nqeto and his people fled northeast, where they were eventually killed by the Zulu.[50]

By the end of the 1820s, Faku's kingdom had experienced some fundamental changes. Geographically, the great place had shifted position southwest of the Mzimvubu River in order to avoid raids from Fynn's private army on the Mzimkhulu River and the main Zulu state further north. Simultaneously, the Mpondo population, which continued to grow as a result of immigration by refugee groups, became more concentrated in fewer but much larger communities. At the end of the decade the immediate area of Faku's great place had a population of around ten thousand people. This not only enhanced military mobilization for either defensive or offensive purposes but further centralized the authority of the paramount by allowing him to more effectively control the labour of his subjects. Comparing Faku to Xhosa chiefs closer to the colony, a missionary stated that:

> His authority is less limited, and he decides on matters of business chiefly on his own responsibility. His answers are given in plain and unequivocal language, so that it is possible for a person even not well versed in the intricacies of Caffer diplomatic phraseology to understand what he means by what he says, which is a rare case in this country.[51]

This caused a decline in the influence of the king's councillors and subchiefs. Because of the increased frequency of conflict, skilled military leaders, regardless of rank, became of greater importance in Faku's state. In May 1832 Andrew Smith, a European traveller who passed through Faku's great place on his way to Port Natal, observed that:

> Facu [sic] pays only deference to one man, a great warrior and he principal in that he is not a chief. When Facu is deciding foolishly according to the opinion of this man he will sometimes slowly say "What nonsense you are talking." Facu will sometimes alter his decision and sometimes say nothing in

reply but look sulky. Facu consults no one, answers everything from himself, quickly decides, is honest, will tell anything though against himself.[52]

Smith also observed that "Facu [sic] is in the habit of occasionally causing the virgins of the tribe to be assembled at his kraal and then he perhaps takes a part of them himself for a few days and distributes others amongst the young men composing his bodyguard."[53] This illustrates the authority of the Mpondo ruler and his dependence on fit men with military skills.

Although some historians have claimed that the Mpondo had no cattle after 1828 as they had been taken by the Zulu, this is doubtful, as the success of the two Zulu attacks has been exaggerated and any losses would have been at least partially replaced by raids on neighbouring groups such as the Bomvana and Ngwane. A year after the Zulu/Fynn raid of 1828, Faku's system of pastoral patronage was still operating, as he was known as "a person who makes presents of cattle." Additionally, the Mpondo king still demanded that sub-chiefdoms pay tribute in the form of cattle.[54] However, Faku must have been well aware that cattle, given their mobility, were a fairly unstable resource in a period of such intense raiding, and as a result he concentrated his people's efforts on cultivation. This was not because he lacked livestock; within the context of the time it was a rational improvement of the Mpondo economic system. These endeavours were facilitated by the exceptionally dense settlement of the population. Visiting Pondoland in 1829, the colonial trader Andrew Geddes Bain stated that "Faco's [sic] country may be considered the Granary of the eastern parts of Caffreland as they, the Amapondo, annually supply the inhabitants with great quantities of Maize and Caffre corn for which they receive in return hides, beads and cattle."[55] According to a missionary who visited Faku in 1830:

> Most of the land suitable for cultivation is occupied with corn-fields and gardens, upon which the inhabitants chiefly depend for food: they have two crops of corn in a year, and as the rains are more regular than in Cafferland, the harvest seldom fails.[56]

In fact, it became acceptable for Mpondo men to pay bride price in the form of produce rather than cattle. This was not because of an absence of cattle but because cultivation had become more important and prestigious. Another adaptation was that unlike other southern Nguni societies where cultivation was done primarily by women, Mpondo men began to work in the fields.[57] Nonetheless, outside Faku's kingdom "many hundreds of people are living in the bushes on roots, without any fixed habitation, and almost driven to desperation from distress."[58] Therefore, these agricultural adaptations attracted more people to the Mpondo state and further enhanced the power of its king.

The growing ivory trade with white merchants also became so important that Faku demanded one tusk for every elephant killed by his people.[59] Through this practice he acquired a large personal supply of ivory to exchange for luxury, colonial goods. In 1830, W.B. Boyce, the first missionary to live in Pondoland, observed that:

> My last visit this journey was to a party of Bushmen, living in some wretched sheds close to the Zimvooboo [sic]. They usually roam about between that river and Natal, shooting elephants, the flesh of which they eat, and exchange the ivory with Faku's people for corn and tobacco.[60]

According to Pieter Jolly, in a recent work on the San, this suggests that Faku was acting as a middleman in the ivory trade. The Mpondo king would obtain ivory from San hunters and in return provide agricultural products, of which he usually had a surplus, and then trade the ivory to Europeans.[61] In 1848, Henry Francis Fynn, by then the British Resident in Pondoland, reported that "for the last 20 years, he [Faku] has had buried about two tons of ivory to present at intervals to the Government as tokens of his good will."[62] Every trader operating in Mpondo territory was obliged to visit Faku and seek his protection through presenting tribute. Of course, these traders did not just acquire their merchandise through commerce but also engaged in periodic raids and served as mercenary gunmen for various African rulers. Using mission stations as resting places, frontiersmen such as Lochenberg often enjoyed a relatively close relationship with Wesleyan missionaries such as Shrewsbury and Shepstone. From Faku's perspective, white traders and missionaries must have been virtually indistinguishable in this period.

Sometime in the mid-1820s, Faku prohibited circumcision, which was the customary initiation for young men in Xhosa-speaking societies. The fact that Faku was able to stamp out such a popular practice illustrates the centralization of his authority. Those who were discovered conducting secret circumcision rituals were punished by cattle fines. While the motivation for this prohibition remains somewhat unclear, there are two possible explanations which may not be mutually exclusive. First, it may have been a military innovation inspired by similar changes made by Shaka among the Zulu as part of the development of their regimental system. Although Faku did not develop age regiments and Mpondo military units remained based on specific communities, the ban on circumcision schools could have been initially intended to keep males unmarried for a longer period and therefore prolong their availability for service to the king. Additionally, the circumcision ritual usually removed the young men from the community for up to a year, thus leaving it vulnerable to attack as well as reducing the accessible workforce for the fields and herds. The ban on circumcision was not only for defence. Without the burden of going to circumcision school, young Mpondo men were also more available for raids on neighbouring states. Since Mpondo tactics relied mostly on superior numbers, Faku had to maximize the number of men who were ready to fight on short notice. The second explanation centres on the health risks associated with the circumcision ritual. Oral informants in the early twentieth century stated that circumcision frequently made the initiates ill, probably through infection. Oral tradition claims that since one of Faku's sons, often identified as the great son Mqikela, was not well enough to endure initiation, the paramount banned the entire custom. It would have been unacceptable for Faku's son to remain a minor while his age-mates and even juniors attained adulthood. However, it is unlikely that the son in question was Mqikela as the prohibition began in the 1820s and he was not born until October 1831. It is possible that this account may be confusing Mqikela with an older son of Faku, possibly Ndamase, Bangazita or Bekameva. A compromise view, from an oral source, suggests that the initiation was banned because part of the Mpondo army died while being circumcised. A similar version claims that Faku outlawed the practice as "he thought that the people who were circumcised become very weak in fighting."[63]

Nevertheless, there are still some unanswered questions about Faku's ban on circumcision. For instance, if the reasons for this were mainly military, why did the Rharhabe Xhosa, who were constantly at war with the advancing Cape Colony throughout the mid-1800s, strictly adhere to the circumcision ritual?[64] Perhaps they were reacting to the intrusion of an alien culture by retaining their own customs. Additionally, if health problems represented a reason for the abandonment of this initiation, why did other Xhosa-speaking groups not follow suit as post-circumcision infection must have also happened outside Pondoland? Perhaps other rulers did not have enough power to enforce such a ban. It seems logical that a combination of factors, including military preparedness, influence from the Zulu and health concerns, caused Faku to want to crush this practice, and the increased centralization of the Mpondo state gave him the authority to do it.

Despite the common historical portrayal of Faku as a victim of Shaka's Zulu, the Mpondo Kingdom of the 1820s developed as both a successful defensive organization and an aggressive, even somewhat predatory, raiding state. Looking at defensive capabilities, the Mpondo completely destroyed Ngoza's Thembu who invaded around 1819, repelled a Zulu raid in 1824, put up stiff resistance to another Zulu attack in 1828 (which was augmented by white gunmen from Port Natal) and completely annihilated the intruding forces of Nqeto's Qwabe in 1829. Therefore, effective protection along with agricultural improvements encouraged more people to rally around Faku's great place and gave the Mpondo the military advantage of superior numbers. In terms of offense, throughout the 1820s Faku's followers attacked Nogula's Xesibe as well as the Qwabe, and twice raided both Gambushe's Bomvana and Matiwane's Ngwane. Although the Mpondo had been attacked by European mercenaries working for/with the Zulu, Faku had no reservations about cooperating with white gunmen such as Somerset, Lochenberg and Farewell when it suited his interests. Fear of firearms may also have convinced him to avoid alienating Europeans. Although Faku was responsible for important agricultural innovations within his state, his people certainly did possess cattle in this period as the success of the Zulu raids against them have been greatly overstated and they made up any losses by seizures from neighbouring groups. In addition, Faku did withdraw his great place southwest to the Great and Little Mngazi rivers, but continued to maintain a presence on the other side of the Mzimvubu River throughout the 1820s. Rather than hiding away during this period to emerge later in the 1830s, as soon as Faku inherited power in the mid-1810s he began to develop the Mpondo Kingdom into a major force along South Africa's Indian Ocean coast. Interviewed in 1883, an elderly Mpondomise chief claimed that "They (the Pondos) were the people that scattered the country, the Mfecane did not do much."[65] By 1829 Faku, who was then in his late forties, ruled a much more powerful and centralized kingdom than had existed during his father's or any previous generation.

These revisions have significant implications for the ongoing debate about the nature of state formation and population movement in early-nineteenth-century southern Africa. Besides reinforcing the concept that the Zulu were not the root cause of the major upheavals of this time, this chapter shows that the Mpondo were one of a number of super-states, such as Moshoeshoe's Lesotho in the Drakensberg Mountains or Mzilikazi's Ndebele on the interior Highveld, to emerge as a response to various external pressures and opportunities. However, this certainly does not negate African initiative as Faku himself was behind many of the innovations and strategies that enhanced Mpondo power.

2

Missionaries, Colonial Officials and Mpondo Power (1830-36)

There is an engaging Mpondo oral tradition about European missionaries coming to live in Faku's kingdom. Allegedly, Faku's mother advised him to fetch missionaries to pray for peace in Eastern Pondoland where there had been war with the Zulu. As a result, Faku sent ten men to Grahamstown with elephants' tusks as presents for the missionaries whom he hoped would come to his territory. During their journey, the safety of these envoys was ensured by an escort of fierce lions. After arriving at Grahamstown, the Mpondo men met with William Shaw, the missionary leader, who told them he wanted to work in "a place with many heathens" and agreed to send teachers to Pondoland. The missionaries who subsequently arrived in Faku's country were first given land west of the Mzimvubu River where they built what is now called the Old Buntingville mission; eventually they moved east of that river and established Palmerton.[1] It is obvious that not all the aspects of this story actually happened. Faku might have sent envoys to Grahamstown, but the reference to an escort of lions is probably symbolic of the importance of his request for missionaries. Interestingly, Faku's mother did eventually become a Christian, but her role in the initial invitation of missionaries to the area is not confirmed by other evidence.

In 1830 the colonial border was still far away from Faku's territory, but the activities of white traders and raiders, along with their Wesleyan missionary associates, had made a strong impression on the Mpondo ruler. Fortunately, Faku's defeat of the Qwabe in 1829 had solidified his developing alliance with the Wesleyans, and the king hoped that a white missionary near the Mpondo great place would discourage raids by colonial armies, white frontiersmen and neighbouring African states. As a result, in late April 1830 the Reverend William Shaw, director of the Wesleyan society in South Africa, travelled to the Mpondo Kingdom to

---

Notes to chapter 2 are on pp. 177–79.

introduce Faku to his new missionary, the Reverend William B. Boyce, who had just arrived from England. Since Faku had sent messages of complaint to the Wesleyans about the length of time it was taking to send him a missionary, Shaw pointed to Boyce and said, "You said last year that I did not intend to bring you a teacher; here is the proof of my truth, see him." Faku replied by stating that Boyce "must come soon," and it was agreed that the location of the mission would be determined by the Mpondo king and that it would be established in three months. Shaw and Boyce then returned to Grahamstown, where the latter began receiving instruction in the Xhosa language and gathered supplies.[2]

On the twenty-second of November 1830 Boyce, accompanied by the Tainton family, returned to the Mpondo Kingdom and was directed to a ridge overlooking the Dangwana stream, which was near, but not in sight of, Faku's great place between the two Mngazi rivers. Two days later, Faku and fifty of his subordinate rulers visited their new missionary. After slaughtering a cow in the king's honour, Boyce presented Faku with a number of gifts, including a blue cloak, an iron cooking pot, a black ox and numerous beads and buttons. The Mpondo ruler then promised that he would establish a cattle kraal near the mission so "that we may be one house and our cattle graze together under the same herders." With this meeting the Wesleyan mission was officially recognized by Faku; Boyce named it Buntingville, in honour of the Reverend Doctor Bunting who had been a founder of the Wesleyan Society. At this time Faku was particularly relieved to have a missionary living within his territory, as earlier in the year Dingane's Zulu had unsuccessfully raided Ncaphayi's Bhaca, Mpondo allies who were living on the upper Mzimvubu River, in search of the cattle which had been captured from Nqeto's migrant Qwabe.[3]

Faku wanted to gain accurate information on the powerful Cape Colony that had so easily dispossessed the Xhosa chiefdoms on its borders and destroyed Matiwane's Ngwane on the upper Mtata River. Consequently, around the beginning of December 1830 Faku directed Jiqwa, one of his "confidential servants," to accompany Boyce's wagon back to Grahamstown, where it was to pick up more supplies for the new mission. Returning to the Mpondo great place in late March 1831, Jiqwa must have informed Faku about the nature of settler society and the constant raids that the colonial army was conducting against the Rharhabe Xhosa. Several days later Faku and five hundred of his people visited Buntingville to obtain a tributary share of the wagonload of goods from Grahamstown. Boyce presented the king and his wives and councillors with various gifts such as beads and buttons, blankets and a looking glass.[4] Faku's attention now turned west.

Since Faku's primary motive for accepting a missionary was protection, his relationship with Boyce remained cordial, but the king refused to accept Christianity or Western education. This would have angered conservative elements within Mpondo society. Throughout February and March 1831 at least ten Mpondo were tortured and burned to death on charges of witchcraft relating to the death of Faku's sister-in-law and one of his sub-ordinate rulers. Realizing that this practice of "smelling out" witches was jeopardizing his relationship with Boyce, Faku and about one hundred and twenty followers visited Buntingville in mid-March. After Boyce had expressed his disapproval of the witchcraft executions, Faku presented the missionary with a cow on behalf of one of his brothers, whose wife had been executed because of alleged sorcery. According to Boyce, the Mpondo ruler "and his great men attempted to justify what had been done on the plea of ancient usage." In fact, later missionaries observed that the "smelling out" ritual could only be performed with the "express sanction of the chief." Furthermore, "the chiefs, therefore, find this a very convenient and powerful state engine to support their power, and enable them to remove individuals whom they would otherwise find great difficulty in getting rid of." Boyce failed to realize that witchcraft accusations had an important role in Mpondo society. Although some Mpondo periodically attended religious services and Sunday school at the embryonic mission, conversions were not forthcoming, and Faku constantly refused to have his children learn to read as "he is pained at knowing it is possible to express the sound of his name upon paper, being probably influenced by a superstitious dread of our having it in our power, by this means, to bewitch him."[5]

In the first half of 1831 Faku decided to deal decisively with the Tshomane, an Mpondo vassal chiefdom – now under both Mdepa and his brother Ngcetane – which had taken a step toward independence from the Mpondo Kingdom by accepting the Reverend Shepstone's recently built Morley mission. Faku and his warriors left the great place without telling Boyce, the Buntingville missionary, as the Mpondo ruler knew that the missionaries were in communication and that if Shepstone learned of this movement, he would warn the Tshomane. Dividing his force into three large raiding parties, Faku personally led an attack on the Tshomane kraals around the Morley mission. Faced with superior numbers, Ngcetane and the other Tshomane chiefs quickly sent their cattle to Shepstone for safekeeping and fled west over the Mtata River. While Faku did not dare to seize the cattle from Morley because of fear of colonial retaliation, the Mpondo army did kill six of Ngcetane's men and destroyed the Tshomane maize fields. After returning to his great place, Faku informed a very anxious Boyce that Ngcetane had insulted the Mpondo ruler by naming his dog "mother of Faku" and assuming Faku's praise-name, "Him who destroys all."[6] These seemingly trivial reasons may symbolize the Tshomane's increasing contempt for Faku's rulership. The Mpondo king's personal leadership of this attack seems to indicate that it was considered an extremely important operation aimed at securing royal authority.

At the beginning of May 1831 Zulu envoys arrived at Faku's great place to inform him that Dingane, the Zulu king, wanted peace with the Mpondo and that they were welcome to take the Zulu royal cattle which the Bhaca chief Ncaphayi had captured from Nqeto's Qwabe in 1829. Indirectly, the Zulu were asking Faku to recover their lost cattle. On Faku's request, the Reverend Boyce attended a meeting with the Zulu ambassadors in order to impress upon them that the Mpondo were allies of the Europeans.[7]

Since Boyce's presence was now required to prevent a Zulu attack, Faku began to more openly placate the missionaries. When Boyce and Shepstone visited the Mpondo great place on the twentieth of May to arrange a settlement between Faku and the rebellious Tshomane chief Ngcetane, Faku declared that the quarrel was over. The next day Faku went to the Buntingville mission to give Shepstone an ox as a symbol of good faith. Boyce then told the king that one of the mission's Mpondo servants, a young woman, had been accused of witchcraft and abducted by the headman of her kraal. Faku then informed Boyce that any of his people living at the station and employed by the missionaries were outside the jurisdiction of their former homestead. This was a major concession. That very evening, after Faku had left the station, the woman was returned to Boyce. Subsequently, those who were accused of witchcraft began to seek protection at Buntingville, where anyone who approached at night risked being shot by the missionary.[8] Gradually, a small community of Mpondo outcasts began to develop around the station.

With the beginning of the winter in June 1831, the Dangwana stream dried up and the Reverend Boyce began to realize that the location of his mission was too far from a reliable source of water to facilitate year-round cultivation. In turn, Boyce rode to Faku's great place to seek the king's approval for the removal of Buntingville to a more suitable place near the western Mngazi River. Initially, Faku complained that horses rumoured to belong to the Reverend Shepstone had been heard around the great place on several nights. This indicates that the Mpondo king was worried about a possible counterattack by the troublesome Tshomane tributary state, whose attempted defection he blamed on Shepstone. With a hint of sarcasm, Faku asked Boyce:

> Why don't you make rain? I know the Dangwana is a dry place, and I put you there thinking you would make rain for yourself, and then we would get some at the same time. . .Why do you talk to me about God? You yourself are God: do give us rain.[9]

After some discussion, it was agreed that the mission would move to the new location. Faku may have believed that the missionaries could induce rain, but he was also not eager for the station to move to the new site as it was farther from the great place and, therefore, less likely to offer immediate protection.

Dingane began to think that his Zulu Kingdom should exercise close control over the British traders at Port Natal, as they were within his territory. Alarmed by a rumour that the British government at the Cape was going to send a military force to occupy Port Natal and its hinterland, Dingane, in April 1831, drove most of the white residents of the port southwest toward Mpondo country.[10] By June, the Fynn family, along with 150 of their cattle and about seventy of their African employees, had sought refuge with one of Faku's subordinate chiefdoms on the east side of the Mzimvubu River. In early July, William Fynn, H.F. Fynn's younger brother, visited the Reverend Boyce, who was preparing to move his Buntingville mission to its new location on the Mngazi River. That same day Faku's mother, Mamgcambe, arrived at the mission with several of the king's wives and about fifty attendants. Addressing both the missionary and William Fynn, Mamgcambe stated that she would stay at the station for a few days and announced that:

> I want no presents; beads are of no use to an old woman like me; I wish to hear the great news, that I may make my son hear it, and that I may set the people a good example before I die. I am the god of the Amapondos, and perhaps they will listen to me. I am confident you have come into the land for our good, as there is nothing here to tempt white people with the prospect of gain; for ever since I can remember, there has been nothing here but sickness, and war, and famine. I pray to God everyday, and Oh! how I shout and cry to him! and if it were not for the great fear that comes over me when I pray, I think I should be more easy after prayer.[11]

It was certainly no coincidence that this partial conversion happened in the presence of Fynn. While Faku's mother may have been genuinely moved by the Christian message, she was certainly attempting to enlist Boyce's support against any possible aggression from the notorious gunmen from Port Natal. It may have been easier for the king's mother, rather than for the king himself, to avoid criticism from Mpondo traditionalists by pleasing the missionaries.

On the very day that William Fynn left the Buntingville mission with a supply of food for his party east across the Mzimvubu River, both Faku's foster father and personal healer arrived at Buntingville to deal with any of Boyce's grievances. Seizing this opportunity, Boyce stated that he was displeased by Faku's hostility toward the chiefs around Morley mission and his accusations against the Reverend Shepstone as well as the delay in purifying the station after the witchcraft accusation against his female servant. After promising the missionary that the king would deal with all these issues, the two Mpondo men asked Boyce how he "felt towards the Englishmen from Natal, whom Faku was inclined to consider his enemies and also what news they had told." The missionary then stated that:

> They are my countrymen and in distress, therefore I should help them as much as I could; for it was not our custom when people were in trouble to talk of their faults; but to assist them. Faku must take care they are not injured while living under his protection; they ask nothing of him but liberty to remain a short time to rest; with any future arrangements between Faku and them, as to their removal or remaining in his country, I had nothing to do, as it was a matter of perfect indifference to me whether they remained or went away, only they would not be allowed to remain on the station, as none but those concerned in the mission could live there.[12]

Boyce did not want to alienate his Mpondo hosts by appearing to be overly friendly with the Fynns. Realizing that he had satisfied his visitor's curiosity, the missionary took the opportunity to complain about the practice of witchcraft executions. Not wanting to irritate Boyce at this critical moment, Mamgcambe, Faku's mother, along with three of his wives and his foster father, promised to use all their influence to eliminate the "smelling out" ritual.[13]

On 1 August 1831 a wagon train, led by a trader named Mr. Collis and accompanied by two Englishmen and several Khoikhoi, passed through Boyce's old station on their way from the colony to the Zulu Kingdom. Collis carried a letter from the colonial governor to Dingane, the Zulu king, which requested the him to let the Fynn family return to Port Natal. Within ten days Dingane gave his permission for the Fynns to return, and they left Faku's territory. The Mpondo paramount must have been greatly relieved, as the Fynns were not only a threat themselves but their mere presence might have prompted a Zulu attack.

In late September 1831, Faku visited the new site of Buntingville, where Boyce had recently constructed a house and school. The Mpondo king brought the missionary a cow from the kraal head who had been responsible for the "smelling out" of one of Boyce's servants. Accepting this apology, the missionary then urged Faku to prevent any future attacks on his Tshomane vassals around Morley mission. While Faku's mother and some of his older councillors were against war, the Mpondo king was under tremendous pressure from his younger warriors to keep subordinate chiefdoms in line and to engage in cattle raids on neighbouring groups. To some extent, the monarch retained the loyalty of sub-rulers by distributing captured cattle. Therefore, while Boyce knew that Faku had accepted missionaries "as he hoped by their means to live unmolested by his much dreaded enemies," he also realized that "should the next news from Natal remove all apprehension from that quarter, I should not be surprised if the whole country from the Zimvooboo [*sic*] to the Bashee [*sic*] be involved in war."[14]

As soon as the threat of the Fynn party was removed, Faku became less concerned with offending the Reverend Boyce's alien sensibilities. Once again, various individuals were accused of witchcraft and executed.[15]

Sometime in 1830 Faku, apparently under pressure from his older sons Ndamase and Bekameva to clarify the issue of succession, had married a great wife, Nomandi, who was given the new name of Mamanci because she was from the Manci clan. In October 1831 Mamanci gave birth to a baby boy who was named Mqikela, which means "to predict," as Faku's older sons had arranged their father's marriage to Mamanci and thus predicted the birth of the heir. Immediately, Mqikela became recognized as heir to the Mpondo monarchy.[16]

An ancient ritual demanded that a subordinate chief be killed and his skull used as a vessel for washing the infant great son. Several chiefs who had displeased Faku fled with their cattle, while another left his livestock at the new Buntingville mission for safekeeping. When the Reverend Boyce visited the Mpondo great place to express his outrage over this custom, Faku simply ignored the missionary and his councillors feigned ignorance of the matter. It is not known whether this ritual was actually performed. However, Faku's attitude to the missionaries changed when, in December 1831 and January 1832, several parties of Europeans passed through the Buntingville mission on their way to Port Natal. With the growth of the potentially hostile colonial outpost to his northeast, Faku once again attempted to win Boyce's favour so the missionary might prevent any future attacks. In late December 1831, Faku and a large group of followers arrived at Buntingville to discuss the missionaries' disapproval of Mpondo customs. Responding to Boyce's criticisms of witchcraft accusations, Faku claimed that "it is our custom, and your laws are too hard for us." A month later, Faku intervened in the impending witchcraft execution of two headmen by "ordering their lives to be spared, but their cattle to be taken."[17] What Boyce did not understand is that punishment for witchcraft was one method used by the Mpondo king and his aristocracy to control their society. If a minor figure was becoming too powerful or flouted royal authority, he would be killed and his cattle taken under the pretext of his practising witchcraft. In addition, since Mpondo people did believe in sorcery, one of the ruler's most important religious duties was to protect his subjects through sanctioning the "smelling out" of malevolent supernatural forces.

In May 1832 Dingane, the Zulu paramount, once again sent messengers to Faku's great place. Before hearing the news, the Mpondo ruler invited Boyce and Andrew Smith, a colonial official who was returning from a trip to Natal via Pondoland, to attend the meeting with the Zulu envoys. Subsequently, the Zulu messengers stated that Dingane wanted to maintain open and friendly relations with the Mpondo. To facilitate this alliance the ambassadors asked Faku to send one of his daughters to marry Dingane and promised that the Zulu king would reciprocate. Since Dingane had failed to recapture the Zulu royal cattle that Ncaphayi's Bhaca had taken from the Qwabe in 1828, the messengers suggested that Faku should seize these animals from the Bhaca and keep most of them. However, Dingane demanded a portion of the cattle as proof that Faku had carried out the instructions. After the meeting the envoys rested at the Mpondo great place for three weeks before returning home.[18]

Faku rejected these overtures, as it would have been unwise to discard his longstanding alliance with the nearby Bhaca in favour of the more distant Zulu who had raided him in the past. After all, in April 1832 Ncaphayi, who lived northeast of the Mzimvubu River, moved closer to Faku and paid him fifty cattle for "a place to sit."[19] Reflecting on the events of 1833, the Reverend Samuel Palmer, Shepstone's replacement at the Morley mission, described the relationship between Ncaphayi and Faku:

> Capaai [sic] is a marauding Chief, as his father was before him. He is a man of great power; and from making attacks in the night, and putting all to death, is the terror of the country. For some time he has lived on the other side [east] of the Zimvooboo River, and Faku has been constantly watching his movements; for though his power is small, when compared to Faku's, yet, from the character of the man, Faku deemed it prudent to be on his guard.[20]

Frustrated by Faku's unwillingness to move against Ncaphayi, sometime in 1833 Dingane launched unsuccessful attacks against both the Mpondo and Bhaca.[21] Unfortunately, the details of these campaigns are not known.

In late 1833 Myeki, an Mpondomise chief who had become a vassal of the Mpondo Kingdom, became embroiled in a dispute with Faku and sought to move west of the Mtata River to settle near the Morley mission. Since Myeki had participated in Faku's attack on the Tshomane people around Morley just two years before, Palmer, along with Mdepa and Ngcetane, the Tshomane chiefs, refused Myeki's request and told him to settle his conflict with Faku. In early January 1834, Faku's army attacked Myeki's kraals and seized some of his cattle. In turn, Myeki ignored Palmer and moved west of the Mtata River to establish his kraals in close proximity to Ngcetane's Tshomane. Palmer became worried that the presence of Myeki would cause Faku to see Morley as a rallying point for rebels from his kingdom, which indeed it was, and launch an attack on the communities around the station. However, Myeki won the favour of the missionary by returning several prisoners whom he had taken from the Tshomane in the attacks two years before. Just as Palmer feared, in early March Faku, who intended to subdue Myeki, led his army to the Mtata River, but he was prevented from crossing as heavy rain had caused flooding.[22] Missionary threats of colonial intervention prevented Faku from making any further attacks against Myeki or the other people gathered around the Morley mission.

Since the Thembu to the northwest had observed Bhaca scouts in their area, the chiefs of the former visited Morley in late February 1834 to ask the Reverend Palmer to call upon Colonel Somerset, the British military commander at the Cape, to protect them. The missionary complied. In early May, Palmer received a letter from Somerset which warned Ncaphayi, the Bhaca ruler, against attacking the Thembu near Morley; a few days later the missionary set out to deliver it. Visiting the Mpondo great place, Palmer informed Faku that a colonial army would be sent out to punish the Bhaca if they raided the Thembu near Morley. Indirectly, this was also a threat against Faku, who had attempted to advance against Myeki several months previous. The next day Palmer crossed east of the Mzimvubu River, stayed for a night at the post of an unidentified Port Natal trader and then arrived at the Bhaca great place. Once the missionary had read Colonel Somerset's threatening letter, Ncaphayi claimed that:

> I have put myself under Faku. I am sitting still and building, nor shall I go out to war again unless called by Faku. I am still, and wish you to send a teacher to live with me, and then he can himself see what I am doing.[23]

Just as Faku had done, Ncaphayi was requesting a missionary as a way of preventing colonial attacks on his chiefdom. On his return journey to Morley mission, Palmer informed Faku about the Bhaca chief's statements and the Mpondo king maintained that "the Amatembu [*sic*] should not have run away; tell them to sit and build."[24]

The increased aggression of Cape forces against neighbouring Xhosa chiefdoms such as the Rharhabe throughout 1834, and Governor Benjamin D'Urban's subsequent invasion of Gcaleka territory in 1835, brought Faku into much closer contact with intrusive colonial authorities. As early as March 1834, the Reverend Boyce of Buntingville suggested to D'Urban that British officers should visit the Gcaleka, Thembu and Mpondo rulers at least twice a year in order to make them more submissive.[25] In early December 1834 Henry Francis Fynn, who had left Port Natal that September and moved to Grahamstown in the eastern Cape Colony, briefed Captain Allen Gardiner, a former British naval officer turned missionary, who was about to embark on an overland journey to Port Natal and the Zulu Kingdom. When the Rharhabe Xhosa launched retaliatory raids against the Cape Colony in late December 1834, D'Urban appointed the infamous H.F. Fynn as headquarters' interpreter for the colonial army. A few years later, James Read, a well-known humanitarian missionary, described Fynn in the 1835 conflict as "Sir Benjamin's creature and did his dirty work during the war."[26]

In mid-January 1835, as D'Urban was heading from Cape Town to Grahamstown to personally direct the campaign against the Xhosa chiefdoms, Gardiner arrived at Buntingville on his way to the Zulu. Faku, who was in the process of seizing the cattle of a rainmaker who had failed to produce rain, held several meetings with this visitor. Although Gardiner's journal is vague on the subject of his conversations with the Mpondo ruler, it does reveal that Faku warned the missionary that the Zulu were "an angry people – that they would kill me – and that I had better not enter their country."[27] With the Cape Colony expanding rapidly and violently to his southwest, the Mpondo king was uneasy about a British missionary seeking an alliance with his old enemies to the northeast, the Zulu. However, Gardiner, who had been extremely impressed with Faku, carried on with his journey.

Mobilizing and preparing his forces for an invasion of Rharhabe territory and a massive raid east of the Kei River, Governor D'Urban, in late February 1835, directed the Reverend W.J. Davis, a Wesleyan missionary at Clarkebury in Thembu country, to take a message to the Mpondo great place. Davis passed through Buntingville, now operated by the Reverend William Satchell and the Tainton family, and appeared before Faku expressing the governor's "feelings of friendship towards him and. . .

wishes for his prosperity." Reminding the Mpondo king of his involvement in the Mbolompo campaign of 1828 where the Ngwane were destroyed by the British, Davis told Faku that D'Urban expected cooperation in preventing the Rharhabe and Gcaleka from fleeing through Pondoland with their cattle. In turn, Faku used Satchell's messengers to forward the governor a favourable reply along with an elephant's tusk as a form of tribute.[28]

Just prior to launching his invasion, Governor D'Urban sent his interpreter, H.F. Fynn, by ship to Port Natal from where he travelled overland southwest to the Mzimvubu River and took up residence just one mile from Faku's great place. The purpose of Fynn's expedition was the "opening up of communications with the Thembu and Mpondo paramount chiefs, who lived to the east of the Xhosas, and securing their neutrality, and, if possible, active assistance against the belligerent." In his negotiations with Faku and Vadana, the Thembu regent, Fynn threatened that if he did not get their cooperation, he would call upon the Zulu to advance southwestwards. Subsequently, Faku agreed to remain neutral, but would only assist the colonial forces by preventing the Gcaleka from withdrawing east into his area and seizing any cattle they brought with them. On the other hand, Vadana, who saw this as an excellent opportunity to enhance his temporary power as regent, declared that he would assist the colonial forces by joining in their war against the Gcaleka.[29]

Around the same time that H.F. Fynn took up his post with Faku, Ncaphayi led his Bhaca warriors in a daring night attack against numerous Thembu kraals, capturing two thousand cattle and inflicting serious casualties. Since the Bhaca had passed within only four miles of Clarkebury, the Wesleyans decided to call upon Governor D'Urban, who was busy subduing the Rharhabe in the Amatolas Mountains near the Cape, to use his upcoming raid into the Transkei to withdraw the missionaries. The Reverend Shrewsbury, who had advised the governor to use Xhosa prisoners as forced labour, stated that "though Faku, the Amapondo [sic] chief, was well disposed towards the missionaries, he would have enough to do to take care of himself, and could not be relied upon for preserving them."[30] This call from the Wesleyans gave D'Urban added justification to send a military detachment to the Thembu in order to lead them against the Gcaleka. Hintsa's people would then be caught in a classic pincer movement.

When colonial forces crossed east of the Kei River in late April 1835 and began seizing cattle and captives from Hintsa's Gcaleka, Faku became particularly concerned for the security of his chiefdom. This became worse when Captain H.D. Warden led a mounted colonial patrol to the Clarkebury mission to remove the Wesleyan missionaries and enlist military assistance from the Thembu. The Reverend Satchell received a message to leave Buntingville with his staff and meet Warden's patrol at Clarkebury. However, when Satchell informed Faku of these orders, the Mpondo paramount objected strongly and according to the missionary, "used every means in his power to detain me permanently in his country." It took the intervention of Fynn, Faku's old adversary and now the resident colonial diplomat, to persuade the king to let Satchell leave Pondoland. Nevertheless, Satchell reported that "Faku would detain either me or my assistant, as he said he would not be without a representative." The king's councillors then intervened and strongly advised Faku to let the missionary depart, as they probably thought that the colonial forces would attack if they suspected that Satchell was detained against his will. Therefore, the missionary's assistant, Mr. Hamilton, along with his family, volunteered to stay at Buntingville in order to allay Faku's fears. In turn, the paramount entrusted Satchell with an elephant tusk to present to the governor, "certifying thereby that he has not detained my assistant from any hostile intention."[31] Faku might have been worried that if his more-sympathetic colonial representatives, the missionaries, left his territory, the Mpondo kingdom would be at the mercy of the notorious Fynn, who had participated in a Zulu raid against it seven years before. The presence of Warden's patrol with the Thembu exasperated these anxieties.

In early May 1835, after Satchell's party had rendezvoused with Warden's patrol, which had just led five thousand Thembu warriors against the Gcaleka, Governor D'Urban sent a confidential order to Fynn, accompanied by a letter which he was to read to the Mpondo paramount. The governor's letter to Faku thanked him for his willingness to "act vigorously against Hintza (the Gcaleka king), provided I should wish you to do so," informed him that Hintsa had been taken prisoner and warned him that "you will not commit any hostility upon the people or cattle of Hintza, but that you shall abstain from any attacks upon them unless I shall hereafter signify to you that Hintza has failed to fulfil his promises."[32] Obviously, D'Urban was concerned that Faku would use the opportunity of Hintsa's defeat to seize Gcaleka cattle which had already been targeted by the colonial army. In secret instructions to Fynn, D'Urban wrote that "Whenever, Mr. Fynn leaves Faku's residence he must contrive to bring away this Englishman [Hamilton] and his family with him." Praising Vadana, the Thembu regent, for his cooperation in the campaign against the Gcaleka, the governor continued to state that "Mr. Fynn must, by every practicable means, prevent Faku and Capaai from doing any harm to him and his tribe."[33] Realizing that the Mpondo could easily follow the lead of their Bhaca allies by raiding the pro-colonial Thembu, the governor was prepared to abandon his tenuous link with Faku in order to protect Vadana, his more reliable ally. A few days later, on 12 May, Hintsa was shot in the head by colonial soldiers who then mutilated his corpse. Despite the fact that the Gcaleka and Mpondo had not enjoyed a close relationship, Faku must have heard about this and been extremely worried that the Europeans could kill such a powerful ruler. It became obvious that a king's life meant nothing to the whites.

Around October 1835, after the victorious colonial army had withdrawn west of the Kei River with great herds of cattle and 16,000 Gcaleka captives and collaborators, several minor Mpondo chiefs conducted cattle raids against the Thembu. Interestingly, these attacks were organized without Faku's knowledge by his brother Mtengwane, who had been the right-hand son of the previous Mpondo king Ngqungqushe. During the mid-1810s Mtengwane had protested against Faku's succession by moving southwest to live among the Bomvana people, but was now back in the Mpondo Kingdom. In retaliation for the raids led by Mtengwane, the Thembu mounted counterattacks against Mpondo kraals and stole several horses from the Buntingville mission. Faku, who had recently strengthened his alliance with the Bhaca by sending one of his daughters to marry their chief Ncaphayi, became determined to exercise more control over Mtengwane, but at the same time punish the haughty Thembu.[34]

In early November 1835, Captain Gardiner passed through Pondoland on his return journey from Port Natal to the Cape Colony. In exchange for the return of Zulu dissidents from Port Natal, Dingane, the Zulu king, had proclaimed Gardiner chief over all the territory between the Thukela and Mzimkhulu rivers and granted permission for missionary activity in the Zulu Kingdom. Gardiner and D'Urban, the Cape governor, considered this a preliminary step toward the British annexation of Port Natal and its hinterland. While on the eastern side of the Mzimvubu River, Gardiner procured guides from an Mpondo village and visited H.F. Fynn, who had moved further east of Faku's great place after the end of D'Urban's campaign. A day later, after Gardiner had crossed west of the Mzimvubu River, he "found Faku in a grand consultation in the midst of a large assembly, seated on the ground." Standing up to shake his visitor's hand, the king, according to Gardiner, appeared "apparently highly amused at my unexpected return."[35] Since Gardiner had been travelling through Mpondo territory for a few days, it is more likely that Faku knew of his presence in the country and was trying hard to flatter the new ruler of Port Natal who seemed to be an ally of both Dingane and D'Urban. Faku may not have been aware that the Port Natal traders had repudiated Gardiner's treaty with Dingane by refusing to return Zulu dissidents who worked for them.

Staying for about two weeks with the Tainton family, who had recently returned to the Buntingville mission, Gardiner held a longer meeting with Faku in the middle of November. It was here that Gardiner learned that the gathering he had observed upon arriving at the great place had been planning an offensive against the Thembu and conducting religious ceremonies required before warfare. Faku told Gardiner that both the Mpondo and Bhaca armies would soon conduct a simultaneous attack upon not only the Thembu but "all the tribes on the sea coast" up to the Mbashe River. Later that day, the Reverend Davis and a small party of armed African horsemen rode into Buntingville to inform Gardiner that the war to the west was over, a fact he already knew from Fynn, and offered to escort Gardiner back to Grahamstown.[36]

There were many reasons for Faku to plan a major westward offensive at this time. First, while the Mpondo paramount certainly wanted to reassert his dominance over this area after the departure of the colonial army, his people's crops had been damaged by locusts and captured cattle would serve to prevent hunger as well as reinforce the loyalty of subordinate chiefs. Second, Faku certainly did not want to lose popularity among the younger warriors to Mtengwane, his old rival and half-brother, who had led successful stock raids against the Thembu some months before without colonial retribution. Third, Faku had never attacked the Thembu before because his daughter Nonesi had been the great wife of Ngubencuka, the Thembu paramount and an ally of Faku at the Battle of Mbolompo in 1828. However, as Nonesi had no children with Ngubencuka, she was eventually replaced as the king's great wife; when her husband died in 1830 she acted as regent for a portion of the Thembu, but within a short time she was overshadowed by Vadana who helped the British in their 1835 campaign. With the demotion of his daughter within the Thembu royal family, Faku may have felt insulted by that group and certainly had no reason to refrain from raiding them.[37]

The arrival of Davis, missionary to Vadana's Thembu around Clarkebury, made Faku reassess his ambitious military plans. Two days later, as Captain Gardiner was preparing to leave the Buntingville mission with Davis, the Mpondo monarch visited the station where an ox was slaughtered in his honour. After holding a private conference with the Reverend Palmer, the Morley missionary who was visiting Buntingville, Faku bide farewell to Gardiner who recorded that:

> He [Faku] gave me his hand with great cordiality, requesting me to inform the Great Chief [governor] that he should certainly make an attack on all the tribes between him and the coast, as far as the Bashee; but that he should not molest Ferdana [Vadana], as he had originally intended.[38]

Remembering the murder of the Gcaleka ruler Hintsa by the British, Faku was concerned that his forthcoming attack on the Thembu might result in a highly destructive colonial raid on his kingdom. This had to be avoided at all costs. However, the Mpondo paramount must have felt fairly confident as he openly admitted that he would attack the coastal communities to the southwest. In fact, at this time Vadana's Thembu were in constant fear of raids from the Mpondo and Bhaca.[39]

Another deputation from the Cape Colony caused Faku to further post-pone his attack against the chiefdoms across his western boundary. At the end of 1835 Colonel Harry Smith, commander of British forces in the Eastern Cape and administrator of the newly conquered colonial province of Queen Adelaide, had been briefed by Gardiner and the Wesleyan missionaries on Faku's plan to attack the pro-colonial Thembu of Vadana. In January 1836 Captain Delancy, under orders from Smith, led a party of eighty British soldiers, who were "intended to make an impression upon the native mind," and thirty support staff east of the Kei River to conclude a treaty with Sarhili, the new and inexperienced Gcaleka ruler. Accompanying the expedition were the Reverend Palmer and William Fynn, Henry Fynn's brother, who was working as an inter-preter. Subsequently, Delancy's patrol visited Vadana to assure him of their continued military alliance with the Cape. On the fifth of February, the expedition reached the Buntingville mission, where it was met by Faku, his councillors and a group of roughly 1,200 followers. Since the colonial boundary had advanced east to the Kei River, and the British seemed to be making a show of force, Faku and his people greeted Delancy "with every possible demonstration of pleasure and satisfaction." According to the captain's report:

> Faku promised to keep his word, and as far as regarded himself would remain at peace with Vadana, Kreli and Buku. At his request, my party manoeuvred on horse and on foot, and fired a few shots. This tribe is not so much acquainted with firearms as the others, and the effect was greater than I expected. Faku, after receiving the presents, gave me an elephant's tusk for the governor, one for Colonel Smith, and three for myself.[40]

During his conference with Faku, Delancy also met three councillors from Ncaphayi, the Bhaca ruler, who said that their chief could not attend the meeting because of flooded rivers and made a similar declaration on his behalf. The Bhaca councillors then confirmed that Ncaphayi was "an ally and subject of Faku."[41] After Captain Delancy's patrol had returned to King William's Town, the capital of the new colonial province between the Keiskamma and the Kei rivers, Colonel

Smith wrote to Governor D'Urban that "Faku for these last two years has only waited for an excuse to wage war on Vadana, and had not the embassy thus proceeded he would have done so. A mutual peace is established."[42]

By the middle of July 1836, Faku must have become aware that the colonial forces were withdrawing west of the Fish River, their former border from 1811, abandoning their newly conquered territory. While the Mpondo king may not have known that Governor D'Urban's empire building had met with disapproval in London, he was well aware that the colonial army was now much farther away from his country and that colonial officials were not supposed to interfere with the chiefdoms beyond their border. Therefore, Faku resuscitated his ambition of conducting a massive offensive against all the chiefdoms to his west, including Vadana's Thembu who no longer seemed to enjoy colonial protection. In October 1836, Faku's Mpondo and Ncaphayi's Bhaca warriors swept a wide area west of the Mtata River seizing cattle and driving away the Thembu, Bomvana and others. Ndamase, Faku's eldest and favourite son, directed the Mpondo army with great success. Beleaguered by Mpondo and Bhaca attacks, Vadana appealed to Andries Stockenstrom, the new lieutenant-governor of the eastern districts of the Cape Colony, for military assistance, but only received a meaningless letter of friendship in return.[43] With the withdrawal of intrusive colonial forces, Faku once again became the dominant ruler between the Mzimvubu and the Mbashe rivers, with his influence extending much further to the west than it ever had. This was facilitated by the cohesion and centralization of the Mpondo state. In mid-1836, the Wesleyans reported that Faku "governed a people composed of the fragments of many different tribes. . . held together and harmonised in a surprising manner by his influence."[44]

During the early to mid-1830s several important factors combined to cause Faku, now in his fifties, to direct more attention toward the western reaches of the Mpondo state. First, to the northeast he enjoyed a relative balance of power with Dingane's Zulu Kingdom, which was embroiled in its own conflicts with both the British at Port Natal and the Portuguese at Delagoa Bay. Faku gained confidence from the fact that on several occasions the Zulu had tried and failed to recover their cattle from outlying Bhaca and Mpondo kraals. The permanent presence of a missionary with Faku also served to prevent a concerted Zulu attack, and ruled out Dingane's use of white mercenary gunmen in that area. Contrary to most histories, which claim that the Mpondo remained west of the Mzimvubu during this period out of fear of the Zulu, Faku had several subordinate chiefdoms northeast of that river. Second, with the northeast relatively secure, the Mpondo king could easily concentrate on critical developments to his west, such as the advance of the Cape Colony to the Kei River in 1835 and the increased number of visits of colonial officials to his great place. Throughout his dealings with colonial officers and missionaries, Faku's overriding concern was to secure the safety of his subjects from European firepower. The only way to do this was to become a somewhat reluctant ally of the British at the Cape. However, the Mpondo paramount did not see the common threat that colonial conquest represented to all African rulers and as soon as the British withdrew from Transkeian affairs, Faku re-established and extended his influence over the region between the Mtata and Mbashe rivers. In fact, Mpondo power in this period must have been significantly magnified by the damage that the Europeans had inflicted upon both the Gcaleka and Bomvana as well as their abandonment of the Thembu.

3

CTrekkers and CTreaties
(1837-44)

A t the same time that Faku was conducting large-scale raids against the Thembu and Bomvana in 1836, considerable numbers of Dutch-speaking settlers were leaving the Cape Colony and moving northeast into the interior. Historians have offered many explanations for this movement. Describing it as the "Great Trek," Afrikaner nationalists of the twentieth century maintained that their ancestors left the Cape in order to escape from oppressive British rule and seek self-determination by founding independent republics in a land that had been supposedly depopulated by the wars of Shaka, the first Zulu king. Conversely, English-speaking liberals point out that since the Dutch settlers of the Cape had missed the European "Enlightenment" of the eighteenth century, their "trek" constituted a reaction against so-called progressive British policies such as the emancipation of slaves. Materialist historians of the 1980s maintained a similar argument, but dressed it up in new language. With the British-inspired development of capitalism at the Cape in the early nineteenth century, the Trekkers fled into the interior in order to retain their pre-capitalist economy, which involved slave labour. Recently, historians have recognized that the interior was not depopulated and that the "trek" was probably not such a backward-looking movement. Aware of the increased commercial opportunities caused by the growth of population in Europe and increased demand for agricultural goods which were prompting similar settler expansions in North America and Australia, the Trekkers set out to engage in large-scale land speculation. This process had been initiated by the Griqua, Dutch-speaking mixed-race frontiersmen, but was rapidly accelerated by the Trekkers who used their firepower and horses to drive Mzilikazi's Ndebele off the Highveld. Since the annexation of the Port Natal area had been desired by entrepreneurs at the Cape from the 1820s, in late 1837 a group of

---

Notes to chapter 3 are on pp. 179–80.

Trekkers made a "pre-emptive strike" by crossing south of the Drakensberg Mountains and settling between the Zulu Kingdom and Port Natal. The British at the Cape, including missionaries, disapproved of this as they thought that London would eventually take over Port Natal in order to supervise its orderly economic development.[1]

The arrival of Trekkers south of the Drakensberg Mountains was to become extremely important for Faku's future as the Mpondo king. In October 1837 the Reverend Boyce, who was about to leave the Buntingville mission, advised Faku that as soon as the Trekkers arrived in Natal he was to inform the colonial government that his northeast boundary had always extended to the Mzimkhulu River.[2] Faku did not follow through on this advice immediately, as he may have been glad that the presence of Trekkers in Natal seemed to further distract Dingane's Zulu. It is also worth noting that soon after the arrival of the Trekkers, probably in early 1838, they sent a message to Faku through the Reverend Thomas Jenkins, a new missionary at Buntingville whom they seemed to know from his short stay among the Tswana on the Highveld, proposing "peace and amity." On behalf of Faku, Jenkins drafted a favourable response, the details of which are not known.[3] As a result, throughout 1838 Faku felt confident enough in the security of his northeastern frontier to organize another series of raids against the Thembu and other groups to his west. Once again, Ncaphayi's Bhaca, a group who were located even closer to the Trekkers, assisted the Mpondo warriors. In the face of such attacks, large numbers of Thembu refugees flocked to the Clarkebury and Butterworth missions, which Faku had instructed his armies not to attack. However, Ndamase, Faku's son who was leading a large Mpondo raiding party, did seize some cattle from Thembu villages around Clarkebury, which displeased the Wesleyan missionaries.

By the middle of 1838, Faku learned that the Trekkers, who were using their firepower to push the Zulu off their land, were claiming all the territory from the Thukela River southwest to the Mzimvubu River. The basis for this was a dubious treaty supposedly concluded between Dingane, the Zulu king, and Piet Retief, a Boer leader who had been killed by the Zulu. The Mzimvubu River was roughly in the middle of the Mpondo state. Another worrying fact was that in April, Dingane's regiments sacked Port Natal after they defeated a large raiding party led by the British traders who had allied with the Trekkers. At this point Faku directed his scouts to proceed to the northeast bank of the Mzimkhulu River to give advance warning of raids from that direction. One evening Mpondo scouts ambushed a fleeing party of Port Natal traders led by D.C. Toohey, which they mistook for "Zulu spies in advance of the army."[4] Faku used his new missionary at Buntingville, the Reverend Jenkins, to write a letter of friendship to the colonial governor, confirming Mpondo claims over the land between the Mzimvubu and Mzimkhulu rivers and expressing worry over the potential threat of the Trekkers to that area. After sending the Mpondo king's message on to Cape Town, William Shaw, the Wesleyan director who was based in Grahamstown, wrote to Faku through Jenkins. "I am sorry you have been making blood in the land. Why cannot you sit still?" asked Shaw, who then complained about Ndamase's cattle seizure from Clarkebury. However, the most important part of Shaw's message was that "The English Governor is sending soldiers to Port Natal. The English will not have war; it is bad; and now they send soldiers by sea to Port Natal to stop the fighting that the land may have rest. Let Faku and Capai [sic] give over fighting and sit still."[5] Shaw was referring to the British contingent led by Major Samuel Charters, which would occupy Port Natal in early December 1838 in order to stop fighting between the Boer Trekkers and the Zulus. George Napier, new governor of the Cape Colony, hoped that the occupation of Port Natal would "have the effect of dispelling any uneasiness which Faku may have on the subject of the violation of his boundaries."[6] Shaw then sent a message to Faku which assured the king that his northeast border would be secure and promised British military assistance if the Trekkers attacked his people.[7] By exaggerating and twisting the governor's words, Shaw hoped to enhance Faku's allegiance to the missionaries while also convincing him to stop raiding the Thembu. Both these objectives were successful. However, it is also likely that the Mpondo monarch had acquired plenty of cattle from his 1836 and 1838 campaigns, which would ensure the loyalty of subordinate rulers to whom they were distributed, and simply wanted to allow his warriors to concentrate on the productive functions of their homesteads.

On the fourth of December 1838, Major Charters landed at Port Natal with one hundred British soldiers. After holding discussions with some of the Trekkers and British traders, Charters concluded that Faku's country extended only to the Mzimvubu River, "which is all Faku claims," and supported the Boer claims over the area between that river and the Thukela River. Furthermore, Charters confirmed his and Governor Napier's belief that "there was no foundation for the complaint respecting their having menaced Faku's territory."[8] Seven days after the occupation, Charters send a message to Faku via Jenkins, the Buntingville missionary, which officially informed the Mpondo paramount of the British presence at Port Natal. Charters also wrote that "His Excellency also hopes that Faku will abstain from all unjust aggression in his own neighbourhood . . . that he will give ear to the Missionaries who live at Buntingville, for they will give him good councils and point out to him the right path." Additionally, the message stated that "Let Faku have no fears that his boundary is to be violated by the English. It will not take place."[9] What Charters did not write to Faku was that he had already informed the governor that the Mzimvubu River formed the northeastern border of the Mpondo Kingdom. A few days later, on the sixteenth of December, the Trekkers inflicted a crushing defeat against Dingane's Zulu at the Battle of Blood River. Faku must have now realized that the Trekkers had replaced the Zulu as the major power to his northeast.

In late February 1839, Major Charters, escorted by a small group of junior officers and the interpreter Theophilus Shepstone (son of the Wesleyan missionary William Shepstone), left the British detachment at Port Natal and travelled overland through Faku's kingdom on their way back to the Cape Colony. The aim of Charter's journey was twofold. He wanted to personally explain the British occupation of Port Natal to Faku and also gain information on Pondoland.[10] However, Charters was extremely embarrassed when he visited the Buntingville mission and learned that Shaw, the Wesleyan director, had informed Faku that the British recognized the Mzimkhulu River as his northeastern boundary. In turn, Charters informed the governor that Shaw's message to Faku was "very like a wilful misrepresentation of Your Excellency's meaning." Furthermore, Charters reported that "It will be extremely difficult to remedy this error . . . as Faku's power is not to be trifled with, and these people are made to comprehend with much difficulty that such errors can be committed in the transmission of important communications."[11] It is not clear if Faku ever learned of the disagreement between Shaw and Charters over the northeastern border of Pondoland. Nevertheless, it is obvious that throughout this period Faku regarded his boundary as the Mzimkhulu River and after 1839 the Cape government, because of Shaw's promise, was obliged to support this claim.

When the British garrison at Port Natal withdrew in November 1839 on orders from London, the Trekkers declared their independence as the Republic of Natalia. By February 1840 the Boers had incited a civil war within the Zulu Kingdom, which led to the death of Dingane and the coronation of Mpande, whose power was dependent on an alliance with the Trekkers. While the Natalia Boers claimed all the land between the Mzimvubu River to the southwest and Black Mfolozi River to the northeast, in reality they controlled a much smaller area between the Mzimkhulu River and the Thukela River.[12] For Faku, these developments removed the Zulu threat that had hovered over his northeastern border for twenty years, but replaced it with a potentially more dangerous enemy that used firearms and horses to permanently conquer land and drive off African communities. Faku was now caught between two expanding colonial entities, the British Cape Colony which was still far to his southwest, and the Boer Republic of Natalia which was immediately to his northeast. Since white missionaries from the Cape had been operating in the Mpondo Kingdom for just over a decade, it was logical for Faku to attempt to use the more remote British as a foil to the nearby Boers who claimed half his country.

Sometime around 1840 Faku moved his great place from the Mngazi rivers northeast across the Mzimvubu River to re-establish his father's old capital at Qawukeni, about twenty miles from the coast on the small Mzimhlava River. Although the Mpondo had never really abandoned their territory east of the Mzimvubu, the movement of the great place also meant the shifting of large subordinate groups in the same direction. For security, Faku positioned his most dependable sub-chiefdoms, which had been part of the Mpondo Kingdom for many generations, in a close ring around Qawukeni. As Bienart points out, members of the royal family were assigned to supervise these settlements. Just fifteen miles north of the great place, Cingo, a younger son of Faku's mother, was given control over numerous Mpondo communities. Sitata, a half-brother and ally of the monarch, was stationed forty miles to the northwest of Qawukeni where the wagon road from the Cape to Natal entered Mpondo territory from the northeast. Furthermore, the large tributary chiefdoms that had gravitated to Faku in the 1820s, such as the ImiZizi, Cele, Nci and Cwera, were settled further away from the great place in a half circle facing the north and northeast borders.[13] This was obviously to guard against incursions by the Boers and/or Port Natal traders. While Victor Poto Ndamase, paramount chief of Western Pondoland who wrote in the 1920s, states that Faku did not move back to Qawukeni until 1844, missionaries visited the Mpondo king on the Mzimhlava River in early 1841.[14] This confusion might stem from the strong possibility that this northeast move was a gradual process that began around 1840 because of the Boer threat but was not complete until 1844.

In January 1840 the Natalia Volksraad directed two Trekkers, Servas van Breda and Dirk van Rooyan, to travel to Pondoland and conclude a treaty with Faku. As the Volksraad records for January to March 1840 are missing, and Wesleyan documents are silent on this issue, it is impossible to determine if the mission was successful. The two Boers may have visited Faku, but they certainly did not obtain an official treaty as it would certainly have been produced to justify subsequent Trekker actions southwest of the Mzimkhulu River.[15]

In April 1840 a Trekker commando led by Cobus Uys crossed southwest of the Mzimkhulu to attack a group of San hunter-gatherers who had allegedly stolen livestock from Natalia settlers. Given future operations by the Boers, it is likely that this raid was aimed at capturing San children who would become forced labour, referred to by the Boers as "apprentices," on their farms. Another and more certain objective of this patrol seems to have been a general reconnaissance of Faku's territory for future settlement. The commando reported having "discovered towards the S.West, far beyond the Rivers Omcomaas and Omsimculu [sic], a fine country, fertile beyond all description, and abounding in game, where a new village will be established."[16] If the Uys patrol had indeed gone as far as the Mzimvubu River, it must have been seen by Faku as a particularly serious threat to his security and sovereignty. However, Faku, whose warriors had never faced firearms, probably deemed it too dangerous to confront a sizable group of armed horsemen and the Trekkers returned home without encountering any resistance.

Around the same time that the Uys commando intruded into the Mpondo Kingdom, Faku's longstanding alliance with Ncaphayi, the Bhaca chief, seems to have broken down. While a quarrel between the two rulers over bride-wealth resulted in the violent death of a Bhaca man, this seems more like a symptom rather than a root cause of tension.[17] The Trekkers would later claim that Ncaphayi's Bhaca had assisted the San in raiding livestock from settler farms northeast of the Mzimkhulu River. As Faku wanted to avoid violent conflict with the Boers, he may have disapproved of Ncaphayi's involvement in such activities. The Natalia government would eventually claim that Faku had sought their assistance against Ncaphayi's Bhaca as early as 1839.[18] However, it is also possible that the Trekkers may have been exaggerating or even inventing Ncaphayi's role in these alleged thefts in order to justify a large raid against the Bhaca that took place later in 1840. In this case, Faku may have simply thought it prudent to abandon his alliance with the Bhaca, who had become a target for Trekker aggression.

In late November 1840, Commandant Pretorius led a large party of Boer horsemen and African warriors under the chief Fodo from Pietermaritzburg, the new capital of Natalia, southwest into Mpondo territory. Resting his commando somewhere near the Mzimvubu River, Pretorius sent three of his horsemen to visit Faku's great place. According to the these Trekkers, Faku told them that his army had fought the Bhaca just five days before and captured seven cattle that had been stolen from the Boers. Furthermore, it was claimed that Faku and his councillors stated that the reason for Ncaphayi's recent attacks on the Mpondo was their refusal to assist the Bhaca in their raids against the Boers. While the Trekker emissaries proposed that Faku accompany them to Pretorius's main camp to enter into a "permanent treaty of peace," the Mpondo king supposedly sanctioned an attack on the Bhaca but "declined to come on the ground of age and ill health, adding that he deemed it unnecessary to make peace with us, as we had always been friends and never enemies."[19] However, Faku later told his Wesleyan missionaries that the three Trekkers who entered his great place behaved in an unfriendly manner and demanded a cow that the Reverend Boyce had previously given to the Mpondo King.[20]

Upon the return of his three messengers from Faku, Pretorius and his lieutenants decided to attack Ncaphayi's Bhaca. On the morning of 19 December 1840, Pretorius led 190 of his men in a surprise attack upon the kraal of one of Ncaphayi's councillors. The Boers then split into groups and extended the assault to sixty-two neighbouring Bhaca kraals. After killing twenty-six men, ten women and four children, the commando withdrew with three thousand cattle and two thousand sheep and goats, along with many Bhaca women and children who were subsequently sold as "apprentices" to Boer farmers.[21] Prior to leaving for Natalia, Pretorius sent another delegation to Faku's great place, with a further invitation for him to visit the Trekker camp. Once again, the Mpondo paramount "excused himself as before, sending, however, one of his captains to act for him, who was received with much friendship by the commandant, and dismissed with assurances of a friendly disposition on our part."[22] However, Pretorius sent Faku a notice that he had been greatly offended by the king's unwillingness to visit the camp and warned that the Mpondo should return the Boer cattle they had taken from the Bhaca. Additionally, Fodo, leader of Pretorius's African auxiliaries, sent a confidential message to Faku, warning that the Boers intended to pay him another visit. A few days later, Faku became even more alarmed when it was reported to him that the Trekkers had made Fodo a prisoner as punishment for his slaughtering a few of the lame sheep and goats that had been taken from Ncaphayi's Bhaca.[23]

On Christmas Day 1840, Mpondo messengers reached Buntingville and informed the missionaries about Faku's fears of a Boer attack on his people. On 1 January 1841, the Reverends Palmer, Garner and Jenkins crossed east of the flooded Mzimvubu and arrived at Qawukeni on the Mzimhlava River. At once Faku told the Wesleyans that "he could not remain east of the Mzimvubu, and wished our advice." After a long conversation with the three missionaries, Faku concluded that he would move his great place to the area of the Buntingville mission, and he requested that the Wesleyans write a letter on his behalf which would inform the governor of his westward movement, confirm his ownership of the land up to the Mzimkhulu River and request "the colonial government to protect him from the fire that he feared was coming from Natal as he was a friend of the English."[24] Although the missionaries apprised Faku that his recent attacks on the Thembu, who were also allied with the Cape, would make it difficult to convince the colonial government to protect the Mpondo, a few days later they drafted the following letter, which was marked by Faku and his sons Ndamase and Bangazita:

> I, Faku, King of the Amapondo, being in great fear of the Boers at Port Natal, in consequence of several reports that have reached me, together with a late attack upon the Amabaca tribe in my immediate neighbourhood, also a peremptory summons for me to appear at the Boers' Camp that had been established in my country, am under the necessity of removing from the land of my Fathers east of the Umzimvooboo [sic]; but I hereby declare that I have not abandoned the said country, having only left it for the present in consequence of the circumstances above referred to; and I hereby desire the missionaries now at my kraal to forward this my letter to the Governor of the Colony, to remain with him as my witness that the land from the Umzimvooboo to the Umzimcooloo [sic] belongs to me Faku, king of the Amapondo, and the various tribes tributary to me.[25]

The same three missionaries went on to visit Ncaphayi, the recently attacked Bhaca chief, who convinced them that he had nothing to do with stock theft from the Boers. Subsequently, the Wesleyans sent another letter to Governor Napier, who was now in Grahamstown, asking that the Bhaca be protected from further raids by the Trekkers, who were still technically British subjects. The governor responded by sending a letter to the Natalia Volksraad, warning that further attacks on African groups to their southwest would force the British government to "take decisive measures."[26] Since Napier had been instructed by London to avoid more expensive border conflicts with the Xhosa, he certainly did not want Trekker aggression to force the Mpondo and Bhaca closer to the Cape Colony where they might come into conflict with the Gcaleka or Rharhabe Xhosa.

In mid-January 1841 William Shaw, the Wesleyan director, advised Governor Napier that the only way of stopping Boer attacks on the African groups of Pondoland was to either reoccupy Port Natal or establish "a strong military post on the Zimvooboo [sic] River."[27] Although Napier had been ordered by London to abandon Port Natal, he could easily comply with Shaw's second suggestion. Therefore, in late January the governor despatched Captain Thomas Smith, a Waterloo veteran, and 237 British soldiers of the Twenty-seventh Regiment and the Royal Artillery to march overland from the Cape Colony to the Mzimvubu River. Riding a few days ahead of the soldiers, Shaw crossed east of the Kei and Mtata rivers at the end of the same month, and held a hastily arranged meeting with Faku to inform him about the military expedition. Under orders to protect Faku's Mpondo from Trekker raids, Captain Smith's detachment reached the Mngazi River later in February and constructed a post from wagons and temporary earthworks.[28] After the arrival of this British expedition, the Natalia Volksraad informed Napier that:

> From this it is difficult to understand how Faku could have reason to request protection from us, unless it was furnished him by the missionary or some other person. We are, however, very glad that your Excellency has stationed a detachment of troops at the Umzimvooboo [sic], as we trust the troops will have sufficient influence to protect Faku against Capaai [sic];and that they will also assure the latter that their protection is no licence to him to enable him now to plunder us more securely.[29]

The Trekkers would later accuse the Wesleyan missionaries of having been bribed by Ncaphayi, the Bhaca ruler, who gave them a team of oxen for pulling a wagon. In responding to criticism by the Trekkers of missionary involvement in this affair, Shaw, director of the Wesleyan society, betrayed his ultimate hopes for the British detachment on the Mngazi River:

> it has placed the shield of British Protection over a large and powerful tribe [Faku's] who are the allies of the Colony, and it was, perhaps, intended as a necessary step towards the accomplishment of an event greatly to be desired, being alike beneficial to the Emigrant Farmers, the inhabitants of our own Colony, and to the native tribes at large, I mean the peaceful establishment of British Rule in Port Natal . . . and indeed in this instance we can have no ground for complaint since the cost is charged to the Military Chest, and our Colonists have nothing more to do with it but to receive it into their pockets in the shape of wagon hire, etc.[30]

Despite his humanitarian pretension about protecting the Mpondo from Boer aggression, Shaw was most interested in using the Trekker attack on the Bhaca of 1840 to justify a step towards eventual British political and commercial expansion into Natal.

Since Captain Smith's post had thwarted Trekker ambitions to settle the land up to the east bank of the Mzimvubu River, in August 1841 the Volksraad announced that it would expel all the Africans in its area to the territory between the Mtamvuna and Mzimvubu rivers. This was a direct threat to the northeastern half of Faku's country. As early as the end of September, the Reverend Shaw predicted that Smith's soldiers would be used to occupy Port Natal, and speculated that a small post might be left in Pondoland "to keep Ncaphayi and Faku quiet." However, it was not until early December that Napier, the Cape governor, declared that Boer designs on

> the territory lying between the mouth of the Umtafuna [*sic*] and that of the Umzimvubu, which territory forms part of the country belonging to Faku, a chief at peace with Her Majesty, without having obtained the consent of the said Faku, from which . . . there is reason to apprehend that warfare and bloodshed will be occasioned.

As a result, the governor announced his determination to take military possession of Natalia. By the first of April 1842, Captain Smith had led his soldiers northeast of the Mzimvubu River on their way to seize Port Natal, but contrary to Shaw's wishes the British did not leave a small military detachment in Pondoland.[31] Ultimately, in December of the same year, London agreed to the permanent annexation of Natal, which would become a British colony. After some fighting between the Boers and Smith's troops, who were eventually reinforced by sea, the former surrendered and the Republic of Natalia ceased to exist as an independent state. Many of the Boers began to cross northwest of the Drakensberg Mountains to rejoin their colleagues on the inland Highveld. In turn, Faku's Mpondo became an immediate neighbour of another British possession, the colony of Natal. While the Boer threat was removed, it would now be difficult for Faku to play one British colonial entity off against another.

After the occupation of Natal, Jenkins, the Buntingville missionary, became concerned that Qawukeni, the Mpondo capital, was too far away from his mission for him to have enough influence on Faku. Furthermore, Jenkins may have wanted to establish another mission closer to the British in Natal in order to improve communication and commerce with the expanding colonial world. At this time Shaw, the Wesleyan director, and Jenkins were already discussing the possible opportunities of attracting trading ships to the mouth of the Mzimvubu River, which was beginning to be called Port St. John's. In early 1844, Jenkins wrote to Shaw, asking permission to establish a new mission with Faku near Qawukeni. Responding positively about this "important mission with Faku," Shaw then pointed out that it would be difficult unless they received more missionaries and money from England. In another letter, Shaw promised Jenkins that "You may rely upon my doing all in my power to secure your appointment to Faku's new mission at the next District meeting."[32]

Appointed as governor of the Cape in early 1844, Peregrine Maitland, an aging Waterloo veteran and former authoritarian governor of several colonies in British North America, became sympathetic to the settlers' complaints about the treaties between the Cape Colony and the western Xhosa. Consequently, in early October 1844, Maitland summoned all the Xhosa chiefs between the Fish and Kei rivers to the colonial border town of Fort Beaufort, where he unilaterally cancelled the treaties. Once again, colonial patrols would be permitted to enter Xhosa territory in search of allegedly stolen livestock. Furthermore, Xhosa people living at missions outside colonial territory would be considered outside the jurisdiction of their chiefs. At the same time, Maitland and his assistants formulated a treaty to be signed between the British and Faku's Mpondo. The motivation for this was to formalize the friendship between Faku and the Cape, which had existed for some time, in order to enlist the Mpondo as allies in future campaigns against the Rharhabe and Gcaleka Xhosa. Theophilus Shepstone and William M.D. Fynn, diplomatic agents to the Ndlambe and Gcaleka respectively, were sent to the Mpondo Kingdom to get Faku to sign this document. On the twenty-third of November, the Reverend Jenkins brought Shepstone and Fynn to Qawukeni, Faku's great place. Jenkins must have given Faku advanced notice of this important meeting as many important members of the royal family were present, including Ndamase and Bangazita, the king's sons, Cingo, his brother, and Mgcwengi, his uncle. Although there is no detailed record of the meeting, Jenkins explained the terms of the treaty to Faku who marked it with an X along with the above-mentioned individuals.[33]

The treaty that Faku signed consisted of over a dozen separate articles. It began on an optimistic note by stating that "there shall be peace and amity forever between Her Britannic Majesty and her subjects and Faku, the Paramount Chief of the Amapondo nation, and his subjects and Faku promises to be the faithful friend of the Colony." Faku was not to allow his subjects to "harass or annoy" any British subjects to whom he had given permission to visit his territory or who lived on the borders of his kingdom. The Mpondo monarch was bound to surrender to the British anyone, including both his own subjects and members of other groups, who had allegedly committed or witnessed a crime while in the Cape Colony. Faku was committed to returning all livestock that had been stolen within the colony and taken to his territory. If the specific stock could not be found, the Mpondo King had to provide full compensation. All British subjects, including African servants and messengers, travelling between the Cape Colony and Port Natal were to be given safe passage through Pondoland. While Faku was expected to protect colonial traders operating in his area, Governor Maitland's document insisted that "he will not suffer the masters or mariners of any ships or vessels to land merchandise, or to traffic with his people in any part of his country, unless such vessel shall be furnished with a licence from the Colonial Government, authorizing them to land goods there." This was an indirect reference to the mouth of the Mzimvubu River, otherwise known as Port St. John's.

With reference to missionaries working within the Mpondo Kingdom, Faku was not only obliged to protect them but also to allow any of his subjects to live at the mission stations with all their property. Mpondo people living at missions were not to be "disturbed or injured in person, family or property, for refusing to comply with the customs touching witchcraft, rainmaking, polygamy, circumcision and forcible abduction and violation of females." Furthermore, Faku promised that he would "encourage" his followers to attend mission schools and be "gradually trained to become a civilised community."

Several articles of the treaty strictly limited Faku's relations with other states. The Mpondo paramount agreed to refrain from "making war on any of the tribes by whom he is surrounded" and that disputes with neighbouring groups would be settled by the mediation of the colonial government. However, Faku was to "be ready at all times, when called upon by that Government, to aid and assist the Colony with all his captains and warriors in any enterprise which may be necessary for the protection of the Colony, or the promotion of the general welfare and security." In short, the colonial governor restricted Faku's ability to deal with enemies, but compelled him to provide military support to the colony on demand.

In return for all these concessions to the British, the treaty recognized Faku as the ruler of a huge block of territory. The treaty states that:

> as a proof of friendship, the Governor, admitting the rightful claim long since made by Faku, hereby acknowledges that he is the paramount Chief of the whole territory lying betwixt the Umtata River from its mouth to the Waterfall Wagonford, thence along the ancient line of boundary between the Amapondo and Tambookie [Thembu] nations to the Kahlamba [Drakensberg] Mountain on the west; and the Umzimkhulu, from its mouth along the principal western branch to its source in the Kahlamba Mountains on the east; and from the coast inland to a line to be drawn along the base of the Kahlamba range of mountains, between the sources of the said rivers.

Governor Maitland, in the document, also promised Faku that he would protect this territory from claims by any British subjects but warned that all African groups living in this area, even those not previously under the

Mpondo state, were to remain within these borders. The treaty also stated that the colonial government would generally protect the Mpondo Kingdom and assist it to fulfil the previously mentioned terms. In addition, Maitland pledged that anyone who committed a crime in Pondoland and fled to the Cape Colony would be arrested and tried by colonial authorities. Finally, the colonial government was to pay Faku "an annual present of useful articles, or money, to the amount of seventy-five pounds sterling . . . so long as he continues to observe the terms of this treaty.and to remain the faithful friend of the Colony."[34]

It is fairly clear from his future communications with the colony that Faku, who was now in his early sixties, understood the terms of this treaty. As Cragg points out, it was a profoundly flawed document that left the Mpondo wondering what colonial official would handle issues such as negotiations with neighbouring groups and accepting stolen cattle found in Pondoland. However, Faku may have been glad about the vague nature of some articles of the treaty, as it gave him considerable freedom of interpretation. In exchange for a few virtually unenforceable restrictions, Faku secured a military alliance with the powerful Cape Colony, which also recognized his paramountcy over a huge region. While Faku had previously controlled the coastal territory between the Mzimkhulu and Mtata rivers, he now gained additional land further north to the base of the Drakensberg Mountains. This brought Faku's territory much closer to that of Moshoeshoe, the great Sotho king, with whom he would cultivate friendly relations. Cragg sees the expansion of Pondoland as a failure of the treaty, but from Faku's perspective, it was probably one of the main reasons why he agreed to it.[35] Also, the promise of a large annual present of valuable trade goods was certainly a strong inducement. Arguably, Faku's state was now the largest and most powerful African polity along South Africa's Indian Ocean coast.

4

The Expansion of the Cape Colony and Natal
(1845-52)

Shortly after the re-establishment of Qawukeni, the Mpondo capital east of the Mzimvubu River, and the treaty of 1844, tension began to develop between Ndamase, Faku's eldest and right-hand son, and supporters of the young Mqikela, his great son and heir. By 1845 Ndamase was in his mid-forties and had led Mpondo armies in many campaigns over the previous two decades. Over the years he had built up his own private herds and a substantial number of personal followers. At the same time, Mqikela had just turned fourteen and might – according to some oral traditions – have been somewhat sickly. However, as the legitimate heir with a high-ranking mother, Mqikela certainly must have had his supporters within the paramount's council. As Faku himself had come to power by usurping a younger yet higher ranked half-brother, the king must have sympathized with Ndamase yet realized the danger of a potential civil war between the rival brothers. Faku knew of the disastrous results of the Zulu civil war between Dingane and Mpande, who were also half-brothers. In turn, Faku sent Ndamase and his personal subjects across the Mzimvubu River to govern the district chiefs of the southwestern half of the kingdom, which was known as Nyandeni. According to Victor Poto Ndamase, a twentieth-century paramount chief of Western Pondoland and historian, soon after Ndamase crossed the Mzimvubu River he killed a leopard and followed custom by sending the skin, a royal symbol, to Faku, as a sign of his continued loyalty. The king then returned the skin with a message saying, "Let the tail be given to Ndamase, that he may apprehend with it. Let the tails of all leopards which are slain in Nyandeni (Western Pondoland) be given to Ndamase, and not sent across to Qaukeni (Eastern Pondoland)."[1] Since a king's messenger carried a leopard tail as a badge of office, this privilege meant that Ndamase had been given the status of a semi-autonomous ruler within the Mpondo state.

Notes to chapter 4 are on pp. 180–82.

Mpondo oral traditions, from both east and west Pondoland, provide a somewhat different version of these events. One of Ndamase's top fighting men, Dlanjwa, went into a lion's den and singlehandedly killed the beast. Upon receiving the carcass, Ndamase sent the skin to Faku's council, but kept the mane for himself. This was seen as a direct challenge to the supremacy of Mqikela's great house. Consequently, Bekameva, a son of Faku who was nearly as old as Ndamase and belonged to the ritual supporting house of the great house, took his men and drove Ndamase and his followers west of the Mzimvubu River. In a variation of this account, after Ndamase had insulted the great house, Faku, who wanted to save his eldest son, warned him to move across the Mzimvubu River at a place where the water was calm. However, the river was overflowing and could not be crossed. Then, on Faku's advice, Ndamase directed his people to cut down trees and make bundles of logs on which to float across the water. With Ndamase's top men leading, all his followers paddled across the Mzimvubu in this manner. Subsequently, Ndamase established himself as ruler of the Mpondo groups that were already west of the river, such as the Gingqi and Konjwayo. At the same time, he led campaigns that drove the Mpondomise, who had refused to accept Mpondo dominance, west across the Mtata River and north towards the present-day town of Tsolo. Ndamase then posted his full brothers, Mbangata, Bangani and Dikiso, along his western and northwestern frontiers to guard against attacks from the neighbouring Bomvana, Mpondomise and Thembu.[2]

Although these versions of the division of Pondoland into east and west are somewhat different, they agree that Faku's eldest son, Ndamase, essentially became ruler of his own territory. From that point on, Ndamase could and often did declare war against neighbouring groups without involving his father. Upon the paramount's death it would be easy for Ndamase to become completely independent from Eastern Pondoland, which would then be under Mqikela, Faku's heir. By the mid-1860s, about one third of the entire Mpondo population lived under Ndamase's authority west of the Mzimvubu River.[3]

Sometime after the 1844 treaty, Faku and Moshoeshoe, the founding ruler of the mountain state of Lesotho, entered into an alliance. Faku declared that there would be no boundary between their two kingdoms and invited Moshoeshoe to send some of his people to occupy the land at the foot of the Drakensberg Mountains. Since the 1844 treaty had given Faku a claim over all the territory to his north up to these mountains, this was one way of controlling the area without diverting Mpondo groups from the kingdom's heartland closer to the coast. However, it would be over ten years before Moshoeshoe was able to take up Faku's offer.[4]

In January 1845, the Xesibe and Bhaca allied in an attack upon Mpondo sub-chiefdoms and killed fifteen men and a few women and children before withdrawing with several large herds of cattle. Immediately, Faku enlisted the Reverend Jenkins, who was still at the Buntingville mission, to write a letter to the colonial government demanding protection as stipulated in the 1844 treaty.[5] As a result, Captain Smith, the British commander in Natal, was "instructed to interfere between the two parties, and to use my influence to restrain Ncapai from attacking Faku's people." Smith then wrote to Jenkins to inform Faku of British intentions. Within a month, Captain Kyle, another British officer, was dispatched from Pietermaritzburg to visit Ncaphayi, the Bhaca leader, to arrange a treaty with his people that would prevent further conflict. However, Smith thought that this would be a difficult assignment because it was unlikely that Ncaphayi would return the cattle that his people had allegedly taken from the Boers of Natal and even more unlikely that the Bhaca would cease hostilities against Faku.[6]

However, while the Bhaca were negotiating their own treaty with the British around August 1845, Ncaphayi personally led an attack upon some Mpondo kraals. In subsequent fighting, the Bhacas were driven off and Ncaphayi fell over a cliff and was badly injured. When a group of Mpondo warriors found the Bhaca leader, he begged them to put him out of his misery. They complied.[7] Within a year, most of the Bhaca escaped Mpondo dominance by moving into Natal under Mdushane, Ncaphayi's nephew. On the other hand, a small group of Bhaca remained in Pondoland under Ncaphayi's widow and eventually his son, Makaula, but distanced themselves from Faku by moving thirty miles north. They engaged in periodic skirmishes with the Mpondo for the next two decades.[8]

According to Mqikela, Faku's heir who was interviewed in 1880, the Mpondo ruler refused calls from his people for an army to be sent against the rebellious Xesibe. This was despite the fact that the Xesibe had taken cattle belonging not only to Faku but also to his brother Cingo and his son Bekameva. Sometime later in 1845 elements from three of Faku's vassal chiefdoms, Mbulu, ImiZizi and Ndela "went out on the sly against the AmaXesibe and took thirty head of cattle." Faku then temporarily left Qawukeni, his capital, and went to the Mtsila, a river in the north of his country, for a few months, to keep an eye on both the troublesome Bhaca and Xesibe.[9]

In early June 1845, the Reverend Jenkins visited Faku and officially proposed the establishment of a new station near Qawukeni. According to the missionary, Faku "fully consented to everything that could be desired from me."[10] This was not surprising, since a mission would ensure colonial protection from the Bhaca raids that were happening at this time. Around the same time that Faku's warriors killed Ncaphayi, the Bhaca chief, Jenkins established a new mission northeast of the Mzimvubu River near Faku's great place. Eventually, it was named Palmerton in honour of the Reverend Palmer, a Wesleyan missionary who fell off his horse and died in 1846 while leading refugees from Clarkebury mission to the Mtata River. Jenkins was instructed by Shaw, the Wesleyan director, to familiarize himself with Faku's people near the Mzimkhulu River and to "get those people called Fynn's people under your pastoral care."[11] These latter people must have been the remnants of H.F. Fynn's private African army, which had been based around the Mzimkhulu and was probably still engaged in various forms of trade.

In February 1846, San hunter-gatherers allegedly stole a large herd of cattle from white settlers in the colony of Natal. As the San lived within the borders of the Mpondo state as defined by the treaty of 1844, the British administration in Natal sent a message to Faku demanding that he return the stolen animals. Initially, Faku ignored the message because he had never recognized the scattered San as part of the Mpondo Kingdom. After the Natal officials made further complaints to Faku, he disclaimed responsibility for the San and requested colonial assistance in driving them out of his territory. Since similar incidents of stock theft from Natal had been blamed on the San, in September the Natal Executive Council resolved to send a commando southwest of the Mzimkhulu River to ask for the support of Faku and Mdushane, the local Bhaca leader. However, the Natal officials were unable to organize this expedition.[12]

In April 1846, the Cape colonial army once again invaded Rharhabe Xhosa territory east of the Keiskamma River. In the subsequent Cape-Xhosa conflict, Governor Maitland was indecisive about enlisting the active assistance of the Mpondo. As well, Shaw was worried that the Rharhabe and Gcaleka would cross east of the Mbashe River to escape from the colonial forces and use their recently acquired firearms to slaughter Faku's people. However, Henry Francis Fynn, colonial resident with the Thembu, became determined to mobilize the Mpondo against Sarhili's Gcaleka. In May, William Fynn, Henry's brother who had been at the signing of the 1844 treaty and had been the colonial resident with the Gcaleka, withdrew to Pondoland and urged Faku to attack Sarhili's people. Faku was eager to assist the colonial government in order to capture cattle from the Gcaleka, but was hesitant about embarking on a military expedition to the southwest while the Xesibe and Bhaca, both to the northeast, were still rebellious. The Mpondo king was also aware that as the Gcaleka had firearms, he would have to concentrate the bulk of his forces against them and not worry about attacks from other quarters.

William Fynn allayed Faku's fears by visiting the Xesibe and Bhaca to convince them to launch their own raids against the Gcaleka to the southwest. In July, Mdushane, the Bhaca leader, advanced west with his warriors to the abandoned Clarkebury mission to prepare for the coming offensive. Simultaneously, Faku led a large army southwest to attack the Gcaleka, but was met near the Mbashe River by the Reverend F.P. Gladwin, one of Shaw's Wesleyans, who persuaded the Mpondo king to turn back. For Faku, missionary protection was more valuable than the Gcaleka herds. The Wesleyans closer to the colony believed that Theophilus Shepstone, a government interpreter who was the son of one their missionaries, had accompanied Faku's army. Lacking enough support to proceed against the Gcaleka, Mdushane's Bhaca seized cattle from the pro-colonial Thembu around the Clarkebury mission and returned home. The missionaries and William Fynn blamed each other for this fiasco.[13] Shaw's Wesleyans may not have wanted the Mpondo to invade Gcaleka territory because they were using the opportunity created by the war to move five thousand "Fingos," mostly Gcaleka collaborators gathered around the Butterworth mission, into the colony as a reliable source of labour.[14] This would have been nearly impossible had Faku launched a large-scale invasion of the Gcaleka kingdom. W.R.D. Fynn, William Fynn's son who was twelve years old at the time, was interviewed in 1913 by the historian George Cory. He claimed that sometime in 1846 his father, on instructions from the governor, was able to convince Ndamase, Faku's eldest son who was west of the Mzimvubu River, to lead a raid on the Gcaleka, but that "it had no effect on the war. The Pondos were too afraid of the Gcaleka to do much."[15]

Although the colonial government continued to wage war against the Rharhabe and Gcaleka for most of 1847, it did not solicit Faku's assistance. In early February, a group of Mpondo conducted a night attack on the Bhaca who were living around the Shawbury mission. The Mpondo warriors "succeeded in taking off all the cattle, five persons killed, 10 wounded, 15 houses burned, and other property taken." To make matters worse, many of the cattle that were captured belonged to the local Wesleyan missionary, the Reverend Garner. Upon hearing the news of this incident, Jenkins rode to Qawukeni, the Mpondo great place, to see Faku, who claimed that the raid had been "done without his knowledge" and that he "would have the cattle restored." Five days later, Faku sent twenty-seven of Garner's cattle to Jenkins, but the latter missionary returned them as upwards of several hundred had been seized. Three days later, the Mpondo paramount sent fifty cattle to Jenkins, who once again refused to accept "them on the ground that not all were here." Faku then sent a message to Jenkins to say "that the AmaCwangula [the Mpondo sub-group that had conducted the raid] refused giving them [the cattle] up on the ground of an attack made on them by the Bacas." Jenkins responded by telling the king's messenger that "there is a captain in the land, he must know what to do if his word is despised." This statement came very close to demanding that Faku use force to recover the Shawbury cattle. The next day Mbeki, the leader of the Mpondo sub-group in question, sent about 170 cattle to Jenkins, who would not accept them, but allowed the small herd to remain in a kraal at the station as several were going lame from constantly travelling between Qawukeni and Palmerton. According to Jenkins, "Faku sent to tell his people that he must die as they hesitated about the cattle taken from Shawbury." Near the end of February another fifty head were sent to Jenkins by Mbeki, whose men said that they were busy looking for the rest of Garner's herd. When Mbeki sent only four cattle to Qawukeni, an enraged Faku ordered the animals to be slaughtered and the herders narrowly escaped with their lives. The Mpondo king then announced that he would make war unless the stolen stock was returned to the missionaries. On the fifth of March, Jenkins visited Faku and told him that the Wesleyans were only demanding the "school cattle" that had been taken from Garner, but that he would have to decide whether or not to also restore the Bhaca herds. Eager to retain missionary support, Faku told Jenkins that "I will see and make the whole place right." That evening Mbeki sent another twenty-eight head to Palmerton where there was now roughly 250 cattle meant for Shawbury. Nearly two weeks later, in mid-March, Faku visited Palmerton to renew his promise to Jenkins regarding Garner's cattle. Within another two weeks, Mbeki had produced an additional forty-four head and Ndamase, the king's son who ruled west of the Mzimvubu River, sent Jenkins "100 head of Garner's cattle."[16]

Despite the fact that Jenkins admitted that he had received nearly all of the Shawbury cattle, the missionary kept urging Faku to recover the rest. Around the eleventh of April 1847, Faku led a large army southwest across the Mzimvubu River to seize some of the Reverend Garner's stolen cattle from people under Ndamase. However, the Reverend Gladwin, the Buntingville missionary, intercepted Faku's army and convinced the king to take his forces back to Qawukeni. Gladwin seems to have feared that this expedition would result in an Mpondo civil war between Faku and Ndamase. A few days later, on the eighteenth of April, Jenkins visited Faku, who showed his displeasure by having the missionary wait for two hours before granting him an audience. Frustrated by the fact that the Wesleyans were demanding cattle but preventing him from using force to seize them, Faku told Jenkins that "I have done, the case is taken out of my hands, make it right yourselves." After telling the missionary to recover the Shawbury cattle himself, the Mpondo king declared "let no more complaints come from that side. Gladwin and Damas [sic] must take that side; I know them not." Jenkins then thanked the Mpondo king for his cooperation in obeying Gladwin's instructions. Faku would not permit Jenkins to speak about Gladwin, and the former missionary left Qawukeni after giving the Mpondo king one of Garner's Shawbury cattle as a reward for his efforts to restore the stolen stock. With all the frustrations of this case, such a small gift was probably seen by Faku as an insult. A few days later, Faku came to Palmerton to request that Jenkins write a letter to the British Government in Natal explaining "what he had done, and how he was prevented by missionaries to punish evil doers in his own land." While Jenkins refused to compose the letter, Faku insisted that he would send some men to pick it up. Within a few months, Jenkins had written a letter on Faku's behalf to Henry Pottinger, governor of the Cape, the exact contents of which remain unknown.[17]

At the end of 1847 William Fynn, the unofficial colonial resident with Faku, returned to war-ravaged Gcalekaland to resume his original duties with Sarhili, the Gcaleka king. Harry Smith, the new governor of the Cape Colony who had just established British rule up to the Kei River, decided to post a permanent resident with Faku to supervise the articles of the 1844 treaty with a view to more effectively secure Mpondo military support in future operations against the other Xhosa groups. Having commanded the British army in the Eastern Cape during the War of 1835, Smith knew that Henry Francis Fynn was well acquainted with Pondoland and Faku. After riding overland from the Cape Colony, Fynn arrived at the Mzimvubu River in late July 1848, where he was met by Faku. The new resident read a letter from Governor Smith to the Mpondo king which stated that "I send back your older friend Fynn, in order that you may communicate with me direct, and that he may assist you and your people and the missionaries."[18] Fynn also gave Faku a large quantity of valuable trade items as presents from the governor, including fifty blankets, fourteen dozen Malay handkerchiefs, six dozen spades, six dozen hoes and six dozen hand axes.[19] Faku's reply was overly subservient:

> I am now no longer an orphan my Father [the governor] has not forgotten his child. The Abalungu [whites] who to this country during the War said they came to see me for protection. I have no country it belongs to the Government they are my refuge in all difficulties. I shall appeal to my father and his mouth shall direct me. My whole country will be happy now my Father has seen me in sending you to reside here. I will again thank him.[20]

The Mpondo ruler presented Fynn with an ox and invited him to take up residence near the great place of Qawukeni.[21] Remembering Fynn's role in the Zulu raid on the Mpondo Kingdom in 1828 and his threatening visit in 1835, Faku must have felt it wise to placate his new British Resident while at the same time keeping a close eye on him. In the first week of August, shortly after Fynn established his headquarters, the Reverend Jenkins, who was certainly aware of the new resident's reputation for violence, presented him with an elephant's tusk, which Faku had given him at the start of the 1846 War "as a token of friendly alliance to the British Government." Around the same time Faku reported to Fynn that the Reverend Gladwin had sent him ten cattle as a symbol of gratitude for "the Chief's kindness to him during the late war."[22] As Gladwin had been directly involved in foiling William Fynn's attempts to mobilize the Mpondo against the Gcaleka in 1846, this gift seems to have been a reminder to Faku that the missionaries were still available for council and that he should be wary of the new resident.

Under directions from Governor Smith, H.F. Fynn's first major assignment was to secure Faku's permission to settle colonial Zulus from Natal west of the Mzimkhulu River, the eastern boundary of the Mpondo state. After liaising with colonial officials in Natal, Fynn approached the Mpondo king sometime in September 1848 and presented the governor's proposal.[23] Despite Faku's previous welcome of the new resident, this was too much. The king's reply "was in direct opposition to any body of Zuloes [sic] being located in that country referring to the Treaty in which he said that both Messeurs Shepstone and W. Fynn had particularly stated that the country to the Umsumkulu [sic] was given to him by the then Governor Sir P. Maitland."[24] Fynn tried to assure Faku that the Zulu would be prevented from attacking the Mpondo by the colonial administration of Natal, but the king remained unconvinced. However, the resident informed his superiors that all they had to do was select an area to settle the Zulu and simply inform the Mpondo chiefs of the decision.[25] Citing ill health as an excuse, Faku delayed for about a week before consenting to another meeting with Fynn on this issue. In early October, Faku told Fynn that he would withhold approval of the proposal until he was satisfied that the governor's intention in appointing a resident was not to secure his country. While once again referring to the land rights granted to him in the 1844 treaty, the king did send several of his men with Fynn to see the location that had been earmarked for the colonial Zulu. Faku organized another meeting on the tenth of October where the Mpondo chiefs and Jenkins met with Fynn, who read a message from Governor Smith requesting that the Zulu in question be allowed to settle west of the Mzimkhulu River and explaining that the role of the British

Resident was to maintain peace. An intense silence hung over the gathering until Fynn presented Faku with a scarlet cloak from the governor. Although seemingly pleased with this gift, the Mpondo king told Fynn that he would give his answer in a few days. As promised, Faku visited Fynn's residence several days later to offer his thanks for the cloak and give consent to the movement of colonial Zulus into his territory. In return, Fynn honoured Faku's desire for a European-style dwelling by arranging for the construction of a square brick house at Qawukeni. After a few months of delay on the part of the Natal administration, Fynn eventually settled "Government People" on the west bank of the Mzimkhulu River.[26]

Fynn's next task was to investigate the theft of stock belonging to the Natal settlers that had been supposedly committed by San hunters who were living in Mpondo territory. Beginning in December 1848, Fynn claimed that the San thieves were secretly in league with a Bhaca sub-chief named Cetwa, the chief Mandela who lived beyond the Mtata River and Hans Lochenberg of Buntingville, chief of a number of Fingoes. Interestingly, Hans Lochenberg was the mixed-race son of the frontiersman Nicholas Lochenberg, who had been killed by the Qwabe in 1829. In April 1849, Fynn reported to the Natal administration that he intended to gain Faku's cooperation against the Bhaca and he summoned Cetwa and Lochenberg to answer the charge against them. When Cetwa arrived to claim that he was innocent, Fynn arrested him and called upon Faku to attack the Bhaca. Upon hearing that Faku was planning to attack the Bhaca on Fynn's request, Jenkins pleaded with the resident to find another way to solve the case. However, the next day, the second of May, Fynn sent a note to Jenkins informing him that:

> Faku will proceed to-morrow morning early to punish the
> AmaBaca. Be pleased to see that none of the people of your
> Institution interfere in the matter, and that they all remain at
> the Station. And you may assure them if any proceed to join in
> the way . . . I will certainly punish them.[27]

Before sending his army against the Bhaca, Faku asked Fynn if Jenkins knew about the operation. Fynn answered in the affirmative, as if to say that the missionary did not object. That evening, Jenkins, unaware of Fynn's misrepresentation, observed the Mpondo army passing Palmerton at a distance. On the third of May, Faku's warriors, accompanied by four of Fynn's men, attacked Cetwa's people, seizing a large quantity of sheep and goats along with 140 cattle. In the subsequent fighting there were casualties on both sides, but no one was killed. However, the Mpondo destroyed the Bhaca's crops, which meant that the latter would go hungry in the coming year. After his army withdrew, Faku gave Fynn ninety of the captured cattle, which were then sent to the Natal settlers. Since Hans Lochenberg, the Fingo chief accused of stock theft, had not responded to Fynn's summons, the same Mpondo army went to the Buntingville mission and took 111 of the Fingo leader's cattle, which were then brought to Faku's great place. When Lochenberg appeared before Fynn on the seventh of May, the former was told that his cattle would be detained until he could prove that he had nothing to do with the alleged stock theft. Pleading with Fynn that he was innocent, Lochenberg also claimed that it was not the San hunters who had taken cattle from Natal but other people further up the Mzimkhulu River. Fynn kept Lochenberg's cattle, but did release Cetwa.[28]

By the first of January 1849, William Shaw, the Wesleyan missionary leader, was aware of a rumour in the Cape that the colonial government wanted to enlarge Natal through acquiring a strip of Faku's territory southwest of the Mzimkhulu River. Since Shaw did not think that the scheme was serious, he advised Jenkins to keep it a secret from the Mpondo king.[29] In late April, just before Faku's attack on the Bhaca, H.F. Fynn informed Jenkins that in order to make room for additional British settlers in Natal, Governor Smith wanted to move Africans from Natal southwest of the Mzimkhulu into Faku's territory. Additionally, powerful interests in Britain wanted to acquire up to one million acres in either southern Natal or Faku's country to establish a Roman Catholic or convict settlement. In turn, Smith had directed "Fynn to use his influence with Faku for him to make a *voluntary offer of all his country to the British Government*." However, Jenkins was concerned that:

> Fynn does not propose to ask Faku to make a voluntary surren-
> der of his country to the Government - I think he is too well
> aware he would meet with little success. But I plainly see he
> aims at convincing Faku and the Government that *he* [Faku] *is
> incapable of governing his own people* and specifically those clans
> at some distance. These clans already wish to be recognized as
> Government people, especially those between here and the
> Mzimkhulu; and if they succeed, no doubt many more will
> follow, should they be encouraged. Fynn will recommend to
> the Government to take possession of the Zimvubu, and
> thence to the Umtata as that part contains more inlets and
> bays and fine rivers than on any part of the coast from Natal.[30]

Jenkins's fears were well founded and Fynn, in his report to Governor Smith in Cape Town, recommended that the colonial administration acquire the land between the Mzimkhulu and the Msikaba rivers and added that the people of this area already considered themselves under colonial authority. Of course, it had been Fynn himself who had brought Africans aligned to the colonial government, some of whom had worked with him as mercenary raiders in the 1820s, into this part of the Mpondo Kingdom. Jenkins's reply to Fynn's report made four clear points. First, in the 1844 treaty the colonial government had recognized Faku's ownership of the territory in question and it would be unjust to unilaterally deprive him of it. Second, Faku would have to be paid a fair price for the territory and part of the money should be given to the missionaries to advance "Christian instruction and civilization" among the Mpondo. Third, Fynn's report had deliberately understated the number of Africans living in the area. Fourth, the African groups in the area, contrary to Fynn's report, were not at "the disposal of the [colonial] Government" but were subjects of Faku, whose kingdom had been granted British protection by the 1844 treaty. As a result, Fynn altered his final report to state that Faku's consent had to be obtained and a payment made in exchange for the land.[31]

The Wesleyan missionaries were hostile to Fynn's scheme for several reasons. In early May they had fallen out with Fynn over his accusation of stock theft against Lochenberg, an important mission resident, and Faku's attack on Cetwa's Bhaca. Furthermore, the Wesleyan Methodists were horrified at the prospect of a settlement of Irish Roman Catholics and/or convicts in their sphere of influence. Therefore, Shaw directed Jenkins to "keep yourself entirely free from advising Faku, either to put himself under the Government or granting any land in his territory. They will take it, but do not let it be said you assisted them to get it."[32]

Sometime in early June, Faku became aware, perhaps through Jenkins, of the colonial plan to annex his land between the Mzimkhulu and Msikaba rivers. On the eleventh of June, Jenkins visited Qawukeni, the Mpondo capital, and was told by Faku that "he had never been asked to give his country to the Government, neither had he." Throughout the next few weeks many of Faku's people visited Jenkins's Palmerton mission. On the third of July, Jenkins sent a message to the Mpondo ruler that made a veiled reference to the negative influence of Fynn. "Is it because a man of war has come into your country that I now never hear news. Do you look upon me as a woman because I do not carry a shield to war. Do I not give you all the news from Natal and from the Colony. Then how is it I have no news from you." A few days later, Faku and many of his "chief men," eager to salvage their decade-long relationship with Jenkins, attended a Sunday service at Palmerton. Flattering Jenkins, "Faku said that the preaching today must break the ears of the Pondos."[33]

Around the same time, Faku personally took over a murder case involving people at the Buntingville mission from Fynn, as the British Resident had no right to interfere in the internal affairs of the Mpondo state. Additionally, when Faku had to send some cattle to Natal, he ignored Fynn, the official intermediary for such matters, and sent the animals through Jenkins. At this time it was vital for Faku to gain the favour of the missionaries as allies against Fynn's land acquisition scheme. This worked well, and in August, William Shaw, the seasoned Wesleyan lobbyist who had complained to Governor Smith about Fynn's actions, told Jenkins:

> to say to Faku and to the widow of Ncapayi, to pay no attention whatever to Fynn when he attempts to interfere with any of their people or affairs. Tell them plainly our Government have not sent Fynn to be a *ruler* in the land, but only as the eyes and ears of the Government. And if any of *his* dependents presume to attack them, to report the matter immediately.[34]

Furthermore, Jenkins advised Faku that if he did want to give up any Mpondo land, it should be done in the presence of witnesses, including missionaries, and that "the price and boundaries should be properly fixed. But if he allows Fynn to go on settling natives as *Government people* in his country, he will lose his land before long."[35]

The Wesleyans' complaints about Fynn's treatment of Cetwa and Lochenberg, the accused stock thieves, prompted the colonial government, in early March 1850, to send Walter Harding, a member of the Natal Legislative Council, to Pondoland to conduct an official inquiry into the affair. However, Harding had another objective, which was potentially more significant. While travelling from Pietermaritzburg to Mpondo territory, Harding sent a letter to Jenkins outlining the real reasons for his visit. Besides investigating the dispute over cattle supposedly stolen from Natal, Harding was "also to negotiate with Faku an extension of the Natal Boundaries towards that Chief's Territory, so as to include within the Natal District a tract of country at present lying wasted, and to which Faku never, I am told, had, or laid, any claim." Harding continued to ask Jenkins to see whether "Faku is inclined to alter the Treaty as proposed, i.e. by extending the Native Boundary to some river between the Umzimkulu and Umzimvubu."[36] It is difficult to see how Harding could have believed this territory did not belong to Faku, as the king's great place and many of his large subordinate chiefdoms were located within it.

Establishing a camp at Qawukeni, the Mpondo capital, towards the end of March, Harding had several meetings with Faku, but refrained from discussing his primary goal until the Reverend Jenkins was present.[37] The missionary, who had been summoned by Harding, arrived on the first of April, and a conference was organized with the Mpondo king and his councillors. Harding explained that he had come

> to obtain Faku's consent to the enlargement of the Natal boundary into Faku's territory. This, he said, the Government did on the ground that thousands of cattle and hundreds of horses had been stolen from the Natal country and traced into Faku's; and, by treaty, he, Faku, was bound to restore those cattle and horses, or make compensation for them. But inasmuch as the Government knew Faku was not himself or his people implicated in those thefts, and that he had always been on the most friendly terms with Government, they had not imposed this burden on him. But now he (Mr. H.) was sent to propose a new boundary in order to relieve Faku of this burden.[38]

Faku then withdrew from the discussion for a short time to confer confidentially with his "chief men" as well as Jenkins. After the Mpondo king reviewed the proposal with his brothers Cingo and Sitata and his sons Bekameva and Nonkobe, he concluded that "I will agree that the English shall have the country to the Umtamvuna, as all on that side are not my people, neither will they listen to me. And I will not have the upper country as that is the path of the rogues." Objecting to the rashness of this decision, Jenkins urged Faku to "give no answer till you first consult with all your great men. Call them here, and also those who were beyond the river." The Mpondo king accepted this advice, but then went to Harding to inform him of the delay. However, Faku then told the Natal official that "I see no objections to what you say, for the people on the other side are not my people, nor will they hear me."[39] Since Faku had been so determined to claim all the land up to the Mzimkhulu River in the late 1830s and early 1840s, it is strange that he was now willing to cede such a large section of the same territory to Natal. While Jenkins's diary is the only account of Faku's exact statements during this meeting, it is unlikely that the missionary fabricated these words as he was strongly opposed to Harding's proposal. Faku probably inferred from Harding's statement that the colonial government would demand thousands of cattle and horses from the Mpondo kingdom if the land in question was not ceded to Natal. A subsequent statement by Faku indicated that he wanted to free himself from the responsibility of apprehending San cattle rustlers, who operated along the Mzimkhulu. It is also likely that Faku's tributary chiefdoms on the borders of Natal were becoming rebellious and were involved in stock-related conflicts with the European settlers in Natal. Finally, Fynn had moved mysterious "Government people" from Natal into that part of Mpondo territory, and Faku may have seen the cession as a way to get rid of them.

The Wesleyans objected to Harding's scheme. Mathew B. Shaw, the son of the Wesleyan director William Shaw and a resident of the Morley mission, wrote to Jenkins that he should advise "Faku to be extremely cautious before he gives any answer to the Natal Government respecting the alteration of his treaty. Advise him to take time to consider, so that you can get my father's opinion on the subject." Continuing, M.B. Shaw stated that Jenkins should also tell the Mpondo king "to *deny* that it is impossible for him to 'punish and give satisfaction' by any people 'residing in the limits of his territory.'" The San who were allegedly stealing stock from the colonists, according to M.B. Shaw, did not even live within the Mpondo borders. Also the young Shaw reported that the Mpondo monarch's supposed inability to prevent stock theft from Natal "is only a pretext to get the country from Faku for emigration." Jenkins was advised to inform Faku that even if he gave up the territory the settlers of Natal would advance southwest and they would once again claim that the Mpondo were stealing their stock. Lastly, M.B. Shaw instructed Jenkins to press hard for the restitution of Hans Lochenberg's cattle, which had been confiscated by Fynn for alleged stock theft, and to "Ask Harding *point blank*, what are Fynn's duties? I advise you to take notes of any conversation you have with Harding."[40]

On the eleventh of April, Jenkins, accompanied by his missionary colleague Garner, arrived at Qawukeni on Faku's invitation. The Mpondo king and his "principal men" asked Jenkins to advise them on Harding's proposal. However, the missionaries insisted that the Mpondo men speak first. According to Jenkins, all Faku's councillors, with one exception, "objected to cede to the Government that part of the country." Jenkins then advised them to tell Harding that they were rejecting his scheme. Faku then repeated three times that "this is our determination."

Jenkins then approached Harding and told him privately that the Mpondo did not want to surrender any of their land. Shortly thereafter, Faku and about 450 of his men came to Harding's camp. The Natal official then asked the Mpondo paramount what they had decided, but Faku responded cautiously by saying "tell us the news." Subsequently, Harding informed Faku "that in future he must hold himself responsible for all the cattle so taken from Natal if he would not consent." Immediately, Faku held a short consultation with his councillors and then announced, "I agree as far as the Umtamvuna." Jenkins was astonished at this sudden change of heart and "cried out to caution them, but Faku said, we know what we are doing." The missionary, in an attempt to preserve more land for the Mpondo, suggested that the new boundary be the eastern branch of the Mtamvuna River, but Faku said, "No, the western side." Pleading with the Mpondo king, Jenkins asked, "do you not see that the responsibility still rests on you as the treaty is not altered?" Faku said, "No; the English will take care of the Bushmen, and besides, I shall go and live in that part myself." The Mpondo ruler thought that by moving his great place closer to the new border he would prevent the stock theft that had jeopardized his relations with Natal.

Although Faku attempted to "obtain something annually for the country," Harding refused and the Mpondo king accepted only one hundred cattle as payment for the ceded territory.[41] Harding produced and signed a document that finalized the alteration of the territorial agreements in the 1844 treaty. It surrendered the country lying east of the western branch of the Mtamvuna River and a line "from the western branch of the said Umtamvuna River where it rises in the Tugela . . . in a straight line to the base of the Qathlamba [Drakensberg] Mountains." Harding estimated that the size of the ceded territory was roughly between one and a half million and five million acres.[42] After Faku put his mark on the paper, the Reverends Jenkins and Garner signed as witnesses to "protest against both the manner in which the Government obtained that country, and against the Pondos for themselves consenting." In fact, Jenkins believed that the Mpondo had been "overwhelmed with fear," and that "Faku had no right to that part but by an act of the Government. Hence he did not cede his own original country, for they never resided there in the memory of any man."[43] While this missionary's first statement was probably an accurate assessment, the second was contradicted in numerous claims by Jenkins's Wesleyan predecessors in the 1830s who had supported Mpondo authority up to the Mzimkhulu River. Desperately, Jenkins was searching for any excuse to prevent Faku from ceding land to Natal. After all, if this strip of territory came under the administration of Natal, then the missionaries would not enjoy such a free hand in operating among its people. Criticizing the Mpondo ruler for giving in to Harding and Fynn, William Shaw, head of the Wesleyan Society in South Africa, wrote that "Faku acts too childishly to be much regarded by Government. . . . He acted most foolishly."[44]

In early May, Harding held a three-day commission of inquiry, which found that there had been no evidence to link the Bhaca chief Cetwa and the Fingo leader Lochenberg with stock theft from Natal. As a result, H.F. Fynn, the British Resident in Pondoland, was instructed to return the cattle which he had used Faku's warriors to confiscate. However, after

Harding returned to Natal, Fynn made no effort to restore Cetwa's and Lochenberg's stock.[45]

Just before the inquiry, Harding informed Jenkins, Garner and a few residents of Palmerton that Faku, now about seventy years old, was soon to abdicate and let Ndamase, his eldest son and a semi-autonomous ruler west of the Mzimvubu River, move back to the Qawukeni Great Place to become the new Mpondo king. This rumour seems to have been started by Fynn, who then passed it on as fact to his superiors in the Cape Colony. While Jenkins told Fynn that it would be useful for Ndamase to assist Faku in governing the entire kingdom, he "feared it would never be done" and claimed that "it is dangerous for anyone to attempt anything of the kind." Towards the end of May, Jenkins spoke to the king's great wife, Nomandi (also known as Mamanci), who seemed "evidently concerned from what she said about Faku's endeavour to get Damas [sic] to come over to his father to share in the government of the country. She said it was contrary to the customs of the AmaMpondo." Nomandi's nineteen-year-old son, Mqikela, was the recognized heir to the monarchy, and his position would certainly be jeopardized by the return of Ndamase to the east side of the Mzimvubu River. According to William Shaw, "It is true that Fynn mentioned to me his proceedings respecting Faku and Damas, but I told him it was a very difficult and delicate business. No doubt if he does not mind what he is about he will bring on war between the two portions of the tribe." William Lochenberg, a resident of Palmerton and another son of the late frontiersman Nicholas Lochenberg, told Jenkins that Ndamase's status could not be changed "without the consent of all the nation; and consequently Fynn's endeavour to do so will be a cause of war and bloodshed. He said Fynn called Damas for this subject, and told him that it was the wish of the English that he was to return [east of the Mzimvubu] and soon he would hear more of it." On the second of July, Jenkins went to Qawukeni and asked the Mpondo king and his councillors about these rumours. Faku "said this news has come from no black man." When the missionary stated that it was the king himself who had supposedly called for the return of Ndamase, Faku "denied it most positively and said, if there was much talk about a matter of that kind it would lead to war."[46] After all, Faku had sent Ndamase to administer Western Pondoland in order to avoid a conflict between him and Mqikela's supporters. There was no reason why he would change this policy. This seems to have been a crude and unsuccessful ploy by Fynn to destabilize the Mpondo Kingdom in order to justify further land expropriation by Natal.

The new lieutenant-governor of Natal, Benjamin Pine, became determined to enlarge his territory at the expense of Faku's kingdom. The continuation of alleged stock theft from Natal settlers would once again serve as an excuse for colonial aggression against the Mpondo and the attempted cancellation of the 1844 treaty. Pine would later write to Governor Smith:

> it seemed to me that measures should be adopted to convince Faku of the necessity of ceding the entire sovereignty of a country the inhabitants of which he could not prevent from committing depredations on Her Majesty's subjects, and thus relieving himself of the obligations of a treaty which he could not observe.[47]

This would be accomplished by demanding that Faku strictly enforce the 1844 treaty, which stipulated that he would return all stock supposedly stolen from the settlers and brought into his territory. Sometime in mid-September 1850, H.F. Fynn, the colonial resident with the Mpondo, following Pine's policy, held a meeting with Faku and his councillors where he demanded that they surrender roughly one thousand cattle to an armed party that was coming from Natal. Although it was later contested by Fynn, it seems he did not explain the reason why this was happening. Surprised by this sudden call, the king and his advisors refused to give their response that day. A few days later, at a second meeting, Faku assured Fynn that the full amount of stock would be collected. On the suggestion of Fynn, Faku sent messengers to all of his separate chiefdoms ordering that cattle tribute be ready in ten days.[48]

While this caused great surprise and agitation among the Mpondo people, Faku attempted to appease Fynn by quickly giving him "upwards of a hundred" head from the royal herd. Later in the same month, Walter Harding, who just three months before had negotiated the expansion of the Natal border into Mpondo territory in exchange for freeing Faku from the responsibility of stock theft, led a group of armed and mounted settlers southwest into the Mpondo Kingdom and made camp three hours ride from the Palmerton mission. Using Fynn as a messenger, Harding insisted that Faku surrender 1,024 cattle, which was the total number the Natal authorities had reported as stolen. At his capital of Qawukeni, Faku and his councillors asked Fynn why the Natal settlers were demanding these cattle. In a threatening manner, Fynn asked "are no people often killed without telling them why? If you do not give the cattle I will go home and you must stand to all that is coming." Fearing that Harding's commando would attack, the Mpondo king quickly produced a portion of the herd and Fynn himself collected the remainder from surrounding kraals. Before leaving, Fynn coerced Faku into signing a "letter of thanks" to the colonial government. However, the Mpondo king had no way of knowing what it really stated. First Ndamase and then Faku, with a large group of his followers, rushed to Palmerton to seek the advice and protection of the Wesleyans. When Jenkins inquired why the Mpondo had submitted to the Natalian demands, Faku asked "How could we help giving our cattle? We are afraid of the English. You must know all about it, the letters go from you to Fynn."[49]

Harding was well aware that Jenkins, throughout June and July, had been employing a San group to seize cattle and horses, supposedly rustled from Natal, from another San group called the Amatola. In addition, Jenkins's San mercenaries had also captured an uncertain number of people from the Amatola who, like the stock, were being held at Palmerton. In mid-June, Jenkins recorded that "the Bushmen sent to inform me they had returned with 10 cattle, some branded, and eleven horses. They fought with the Amatola and killed five men, and brought eight children." At the same time Harding was extorting one thousand cattle from Faku, the former also instructed Jenkins "to be good enough to send to my camp all the cattle and horses recently captured by the Bushmen from the Amatola, as also to cause all the men, women and children captured on the same occasion to be sent on tonight."[50] Several questions arise over this matter. Why had Jenkins employed San raiders to capture stock and people from the Amatola Bushmen? If Harding was only interested in acquiring cattle and horses that had been taken from Natal, why did he demand that Jenkins hand over these prisoners? Would they be sold as "apprentices" to Natal settlers?

Harding and his settler gunmen, together with the Mpondo cattle, began their return to Natal in early October 1850. However, they were quickly overtaken by a messenger with the "letter of thanks" that had been marked by Faku and two of his councillors and witnessed by Fynn. It contained the following statement:

> Admitting the justice of the present claim upon me of 1024 cattle which I am now paying, I request the Government will perform their promise by giving me at once efficient aid and assistance to drive out and dislodge the people who may have committed these thefts, and brought the stolen property to a part of the country comprehended in the treaty, a country I never desired to possess, and was secured to me by treaty to prevent such troublesome people entering it.
> I cannot continue to be responsible for the acts of wolves. My people cannot pass out of the country we occupy, surrounded as we are by 4 tribes, who are ever our enemies, we cannot even hunt, fearing collision with the tribes around us.
> I beg the Government will take the country under their

management. I never desired to be chief over countries I cannot occupy or tribes I cannot govern.[51]

Interpreting this as an offer for the colonial government to annex all of Pondoland, Harding returned six hundred cattle to Faku and had Fynn tell the Mpondo king that the remainder would be restored when the cession was complete. Subsequently, Harding, who believed that his mission to Faku had been a fabulous success, wrote to Governor Smith requesting the immediate annexation of the Mpondo Kingdom. For Harding, the acquisition of Pondoland would provide additional land for the white settlers who were "pouring into the colony," and serve to further subdue the Rharhabe and Gcaleka Xhosa by putting "a European population in rear of the Kaffirs."[52] Around the same time, it was rumoured that Faku, in revenge for Harding's cattle fine, had directed his men to attack the local San [Bushmen] hunters, and a large number of the latter were killed.[53]

In late October, the Reverend Jenkins visited Pietermaritzburg and spoke to Governor Smith and Lieutenant-Governor Pine about the confiscation of Faku's cattle. The missionary stated that Faku had ceded the strip of territory between the Mtamvuna and Mzimkhulu rivers to Natal so that the colonial government would "relieve him of the responsibility of the cattle stolen by the Bushmen." Referring to the Harding commando of a few weeks earlier, Jenkins continued to claim that "Faku and his people were not apprised why the demand [for cattle] was made." It was here that Jenkins learned of Faku's "letter of thanks" and its alleged invitation to place his entire kingdom under colonial administration.

A few days later, in early November, Faku went to the Palmerton mission to ask Jenkins, who had just returned from Natal, if he had any news about why Harding had seized his cattle. The Mpondo paramount "denies that Fynn told him why the demand for cattle was made." When Jenkins asked the king why he had agreed to cede all his country to the British, a surprised "Faku also denied that he signed a letter or document giving any part of the country to the Government. He said, I do not know it. No, No, I do not know it." Mbulawa, a councillor of the king, added that "although Faku is the captain he cannot do such a thing as that; the nation must be called and agree to it in the first place."[54] Cragg, a historian who wrote in the 1950s, claims that fear might have caused Faku to act rashly by telling Fynn that he could have the country but that upon reconsidering he denied ever making the agreement. However, this is somewhat unrealistic considering subsequent statements by Faku and all his councillors as well as the fact that the Harding commando only demanded cattle and not land.[55] Given Fynn's previous duplicities, such

as when he falsely accused Cetwa and Hans Lochenberg of stealing livestock from Natal, it seems almost certain that he exploited Faku's inability to read in order to trick him into signing the document in question.
This became a common practice of colonial empire builders during the
"Scramble for Africa" in the late nineteenth century. Faku had never
agreed to place all his kingdom under colonial rule.

Faku requested Jenkins to write a letter on his behalf to the lieutenant-
governor of Natal, Benjamin Pine. Initially, the missionary was reluctant
to become involved in the dispute, but Faku became "annoyed" and
convinced him to satisfy the request. In the middle of November, Jenkins
went to the Qawukeni Great Place and held a meeting with the Mpondo
king and a large group who were generally displeased about Fynn's and
Harding's cattle seizure. Faku dictated to the missionary, who "wrote the
substance of what he requested."[56] It stated:

> I, Faku, Chief of the Amapondo Nation write these words to
> say that I have heard with surprise a letter which had come
> from me to you to say I had given my country or a great part of
> it to the Government.
> My word to the Governor is this. It is not my letter. I never
> made such a letter. I saw Mr. Fynn came to me to say I was to
> write a letter of thanks to the Government that Mr. Harding
> was returning home and had received the cattle Mr. Fynn
> telling me I should know why the cattle were demanded when
> he returned from Pietermaritzburg and I signed it. Also Ucingo
> and Umbulana but no words were spoken about giving away
> my country to the Government. Such a letter I do not know. I
> hope therefore the Governor will enquire who made that
> letter. I request also to acquaint the Governor that when it was
> demanded of me to turn out a thousand head of cattle I was not
> informed that this was made because of Bushmen aggression on
> Natal. Neither can the Government expect this from me since
> I was relieved from this responsibility by Mr. Harding a few
> months ago when I agreed to cede the country to the
> Umtavuna River.
> I request the Governor to send me a copy of the letter said to
> be my letter.[57]

Toward the end of the first week of December, Faku received a letter from
Lieutenant-Governor Pine which stated that the cession of all Pondoland
to the British had released the Mpondo king from his responsibility for
stock stolen from Natal. Although an original is not available, this
message was probably sent before Pine received the letter that Jenkins
had drafted for Faku. Enraged by Pine's letter, Faku and many of his
people went to the Palmerton mission to tell Jenkins that:

They protest against what is said in the Governor's letter, and state they gave the cattle as they were threatened with war. Faku never sent after Harding; he never gave away his country. Faku resolved to send to Mr. Fynn to inform him that as he had heard these things he had sent a letter to the Governor, an answer to which he daily expected, and when he received it would come to him with the people and myself also.[58]

All this was repeated again when Faku, along with his councillors and many followers, visited Palmerton on Christmas Eve. Upon instructions from William Shaw, Jenkins told Faku "that the Governor, Sir H. Smith, knew nothing about this, and is angry that any such demand was made upon him."[59]

Once Lieutenant-Governor Pine received the letter which Jenkins had drafted for Faku, he dispatched Captain Gordon, a British officer, and John Shepstone, another son of the Wesleyan missionary William Shepstone, to Pondoland to conduct a commission of inquiry into the entire affair. The two commissioners arrived at Palmerton in the first week of January 1851. Among those present at the inquiry were Faku, his councillors, Fynn, William Lochenberg, Jenkins and M.B. Shaw. Four basic facts were established. First, it was "proved that Harding got the country to the Umtamvuna river with the distinct understanding that Faku should be released from former responsibility for Bushmen aggressions in Natal." Second, the Mpondos denied that Fynn had ever informed them that the 1,024 cattle he demanded were in payment for theft from Natal. When they had asked Fynn why the cattle were being taken he responded by saying, "Did you ask Tshaka that question when he invaded the country? Turn them out, and let me go and stop the army." Third, all the Mpondo witnesses denied that Fynn had been authorized to write a letter on Faku's behalf that gave away their land to the colonial government. Confronting the British Resident in front of the commission, Faku insisted that "Those are not my words, but your words Fynn. . . . You come from Harding, and said to me I must write a letter to thank the Government that the cattle had been received. That is all I know. The others are your words." Fourth, when the Mpondo king was shown the letter he had dictated to Jenkins, the former said, "Those are the words I know; those of Fynn I do not know; that is my letter." In conclusion, although Captain Gordon declared that Fynn was not to blame for the dispute, he announced that all the Mpondo cattle would be returned. Furthermore, the commission maintained that "the country remains in Faku's possession as heretofore, and shall not be touched; and he is considered to be responsible for all the territory as settled by the new boundary from the Umtamvuna upwards to the Ingeli and thence to the

Kathlamba mountains."[60] Undoubtedly, this decision was influenced by the rebellion of the Rharhabe in British Kaffraria, the newly conquered colonial territory between the Keiskamma and Kei rivers, which had begun on Christmas Day 1850. The British were not in a position to alienate the Mpondo, whom they saw as potential military allies in yet another Cape-Xhosa war.

Just one day after the start of the Rharhabe uprising, Governor Smith, who was based in the Cape, wrote to Lieutenant-Governor Pine in Natal requesting that a force of three thousand Zulus be organized to attack the rebels from the northeast. Since Pine knew that he could never accomplish such a task, he instructed Fynn to gather three thousand Mpondo and/or their neighbours and advance towards British Kaffraria. This was an absurd order, as Pine knew very well that Fynn had lost Faku's confidence, if indeed he ever had it. Therefore, Fynn, although he reported in January 1851 that "Faku has ordered his tribe to prepare for war," concentrated on raising a levy of African mercenaries from groups who were living in Natal south of the Mkomanzi River and his own followers around the Mzimkhulu River. However, this force was so badly managed that it was eventually disbanded at the end of May before it even left the Natal region.[61]

Throughout the first months of 1851, the Mpondo people were nervous about the war to their southwest and the force of Natal Africans that Fynn was assembling on the Mtamvuna River. Memories of Fynn's 1828 raid were still strong, and the cattle seizure by Harding had caused popular discontent with colonial interference in Mpondo affairs. Nevertheless, in mid-January, Jenkins reported that "I do not think there is any fear that this tribe is likely to join with the kaffirs although Faku has certainly been irritated in no small degree by the above proceedings of the Government." By early March, the Mpondo were complaining to the Wesleyan missionaries that the Natal officials were returning their cattle in small and sporadic instalments. Late in the same month, Jenkins recorded that "All the country [is] in great alarm about Mr. Fynn." The next day, Faku called the missionary to his Qawukeni capital to draft a letter to Fynn demanding "the *remainder of the cattle*."[62]

On the fourth of April 1851, Fynn visited Qawukeni to enlist the military support of the Mpondo against the Gcaleka of King Sarhili. According to the British Resident, the Mpondo ruler "expressed his desire to make a simultaneous attack on the enemies of the Colony." However, some days later, while touring the Transkeian region to rally support against Sarhili, Fynn heard a rumour that "Faku has sent to the Chiefs of several tribes secretly informing them each that the Natal Force was intended for their destruction and if they would unite with him their weapons should be pointed in the direction of Natal."[63] As early as the end of 1850, when the Harding crisis was heating up, Faku had sent an envoy to Sarhili offering his daughter to him in marriage. The Mpondo messenger later said that "Faku's message to Rili [*sic*] was this: 'Rili I have sent you my daughter. I wish to form an alliance with some one. I am alone, exposed to the wolves.'" However, Sarhili refused the offer and his men assaulted the Mpondo envoys, driving them out of the Gcaleka great place.[64] In early 1851, Faku even sent an offer of alliance to the Thembu, whom he had attacked in the late 1830s. Fynn's force was such a threat that it caused Faku to put aside old hostilities in a rare attempt to rally African states.

Responding to a rumour that Fynn's Natal force had attacked an Mpondo sub-group, the Jali, Faku quickly assembled a large army at Qawukeni in mid-April. Upon observing Mpondo warriors leaving their villages ready for battle, Jenkins sent messengers to Faku to assure him that the rumour was not true and beg him to disperse his army. When the Mpondo king heard the missionary's plea, he said "We can trust Jenkins," and sent his men to their homes. Faku then sent a message to John Shepstone and Fynn stating that:

> My country is in confusion and alarm; the Zulus must not pass too near. I must not be asked to go against the kaffirs. I cannot fight them, but in my own country I can fight them. The AmaXesibe and AmaJali are to sit still, and not go out with Mr. Fynn. If they are touched, I am touched.[65]

Within two weeks Shepstone sent a response to Faku via the Palmerton mission. While the exact details are not known, it caused the Mpondo monarch to ask his councillors, "Why is this we are eaten up by that man? How is it that when it was said the cattle should be returned that they are not? Who stops them?" Faku then asked Jenkins to send another letter to Natal demanding the remainder of the cattle that had been taken by Harding. At this point only about 280 cattle had been received from Natal, and most of those had been distributed by Fynn to low-ranking sub-chiefs in an attempt to divert their loyalty from Faku to himself. Jenkins told Shepstone that the immediate return of the cattle to the Qawukeni great place was vital "to save the fidelity of Faku to the Government." Around the same time that Fynn's force was being disbanded, Faku, through Jenkins, sent a message to Shepstone, stating that "he is perfectly satisfied as to the destination of the force, and wishes to assure him of his desire to live in peace and amity with the Government."[66]

Around 1850 or 1851, Faku's mother, Mamgcambe, died of old age. However, she had given strict instructions that no one was to be "smelled out" for witchcraft because of her death, and she was obeyed. Jenkins attributed this to her partial conversion to Christianity, which had occurred two decades before in the early days of the Buntingville mission. Sometime later, Faku's great wife and the mother of Mqikela, Mamanci, converted on her deathbed and also forbade any witchhunting because of her demise.[67]

Earlier in 1851 Faku had given M.B. Shaw, son of the Wesleyan director, permission to graze his stock on the banks of the Mdumbi River, which was located in Western Pondoland, in exchange for some blankets. However, when messengers of the Mpondo king travelled to the Morley mission to collect the blankets, M.B. Shaw informed them that he would like to lease the area in question for ten cattle a year. Shaw asked Jenkins if he would accompany him to Qawukeni, but the missionary knew that Shaw wanted more than grazing rights and refused to participate in the negotiations. According to Jenkins, Shaw then gave John Burton, an African servant from the Palmerton mission, a cow as payment to escort him to the Mpondo great place and act as intermediary in his dealings with Faku. However, Shaw had told Jenkins that he was simply taking Burton as a guide on a hunting trip. In the middle of September, Shaw and Burton visited Qawukeni and obtained a written lease for the territory between the Mtakatyi and Mtata rivers, generally known as the Mdumbi River country, for two hundred years for the price of two thousand cattle, which was to be paid in annual instalments of ten. When Jenkins heard about this he was angry and wrote to Shaw requesting that he burn the document.[68] This issue would later cause intense problems in the area.

In September 1851 a rumour circulated among colonial officials and missionaries in the Eastern Cape that Faku had sent envoys to visit Sandile and the prophet Mlanjeni, who were leading the Rharhabe rebellion in British Kaffraria. After a short time, the Mpondo ambassadors returned to their ruler with several representatives from Sandile and charmed sticks from the prophet. Allegedly, Faku agreed to send a "a large body of his men to the assistance of Sandili." While this might have been an exaggeration, Faku would later confirm that the rumours were true, but that he had no "wrong intentions in sending men to Umlanjana" [sic].[69] H.F. Fynn, who was soon to admit to his superiors that he had lost Faku's trust over the Harding commando, visited Qawukeni to inquire about these rumours. The Mpondo king told Fynn that he "did send ten men to Mlanjeni requesting he would visit this country to point out those guilty of Witchcraft" and that "they did not see Mlanjeni but they saw only Sandilli" [sic]. Fynn then reported that "the Chief Faku with my recent knowledge of him is in my judgement the most dishonest in principal" [sic], and that the Mpondo ruler secretly harboured "sympathy for the Kafirs success against the Colony."[70] Several weeks later Fynn wrote to Cape Town, alleging that part of Faku's message to Mlanjeni stated "The wild beasts who you are at war with I have also in my Country and such is their power over me that they take my cattle from me without our being able to throw our assegais [spears] in our defence." Furthermore, Fynn claimed that the ten Mpondo envoys had participated in a battle against the British, and that Faku had told a neighbouring chief that "I know the whites will kill me for my connection with Umlanjeni."[71] On the twentieth of October 1851, Faku and three hundred Mpondo men arrived at Fynn's residence to address these rumours. The Mpondo king declared that his only motivation for contacting Mlanjeni was to seek advice on the recent death of his mother and that "the enemies of the Colony shall be his enemies." When Faku asked Fynn if he was satisfied with this explanation, the British Resident replied in the negative and accused the Mpondo of sheltering fourteen Rharhabe refugees. Within a few days of this meeting, the Mpondo king sent a messenger to Fynn to say that the fourteen fugitives had been sent away.[72]

It is very likely that Faku, a well-known supporter of witch-hunting and rainmaking, simply wanted to enlist the skills of Mlanjeni, a famous witch-finder and prophet, in removing perceived malevolent spiritual forces from Pondoland. It is also possible that with the Rharhabe enjoying success in the Waterkloof campaign near the Cape colonial town of Fort Beaufort, the Mpondo ruler wanted to investigate Mlanjeni's prophecies which claimed that the Europeans' bullets would turn to water. Additionally, since Faku had experienced cattle seizure and land expropriation by the Natal British, he may have been seriously considering joining the rebellion if it seemed likely to succeed. However, Fynn's evidence should be treated with some scepticism, as he had previously lied about Faku's statements. Whatever the reason for this deputation to the rebel Rharhabe, it seriously angered Governor Smith and made him want to test the loyalty of the Mpondo King.

By the end of October, Smith was planning a large-scale raid for cattle and labour against Sarhili's Gcaleka who lived just east of British Kaffraria. As part of this operation, the governor hoped to revive the old idea of enlisting the Mpondo. In order to catch the Gcaleka in a pincer movement, Smith, in late November, wrote to Faku seeking Mpondo military assistance. Reminding the Mpondo King about how the British had destroyed the Ngwane at Mbolompo in 1828 and referring directly to the Mpondo envoys who had visited the Rharhabe, the governor informed Faku that:

You placed yourself in a false position towards the Great Queen, my Governor, whose bounty you yearly receive, or towards Sandili. Your conduct has been bad. Now I call upon you to collect your armies and to fall on Kreli. – My troops will, be in his country by the time this message reaches you – and spoil his cattle which keep and divide as you please. This Kreli beat your daughter sent to him in marriage, and drove her out of this country. Does the Chief Faku tamely submit to such indignity being put upon himself, his daughter and his tribe? Do this, I say – for I will have no half friends; if you do not, I will withdraw the British Resident and stop your yearly donation.[73]

The threat of withdrawing Fynn and the annual payment was tantamount to cancelling the 1844 treaty and implied that colonial forces would not hesitate to raid the Mpondo in the same way they were about to do with the Gcaleka. Faku received this letter in early December and he insisted that Jenkins, who had been summoned to the Qawukeni great place, read it three times in front of his sons and councillors – Bekameva, Ganatana, Mbulawa, Njameka and many others. According to the missionary, the king's councillors answered, "We consent to go; we understand being called in this way; we go. But we must send out spies in the first place, and wish men from Mr. M.B. Shaw to tell us who are friendly to the English, and who are not. Write and tell the Governor said Faku, 'We go.'"[74]

Almost immediately, preparations were made to mobilize the Mpondo army, and fast-moving scouts were sent southwest into Gcaleka territory. Simultaneously, messages were sent to Ndamase, Faku's eldest son and ruler of the Mpondo west of the Mzimvubu River, to join the campaign; he agreed to be ready by 10 December 1851. The Wesleyan missionaries of the Palmerton, Buntingville and Morley missions, who had opposed Mpondo involvement in the 1846-47 war but saw the current rebellion as a major threat to their work, sent some of their "school people" to serve as guides for Faku's army. Jenkins sent a messenger to Jojo, the rebellious Xesibe chief, to warn him to "to be quiet when the Pondos are out." On the fifteenth, Faku "sent to all the country for all to be ready at a moment's notice." However, the next day, when Ndamase and Faku were to meet at Palmerton to launch the offensive together, the Mzimvubu River was "too full to ford." This prevented Ndamase from coming to Faku and prevented the main Mpondo army from marching southwest. Waiting two days for Faku's force, which was still unable to cross the river, Ndamase then led his warriors southwest to the Morley mission, which was within striking distance of Gcalekaland. On the twenty-second, the Mpondo king sent two mounted messengers across the flooded Mzimvubu to tell Ndamase to wait for the main army. Without

Faku's men, Ndamase's Western Pondoland contingent would not have sufficient numbers to challenge Gcaleka firearms. However, it rained heavily for the next two days and Faku's subordinate rulers began to return to their homes, as it became obvious that the river would not become fordable in a short time.

On Christmas Eve 1851, M.B. Shaw, now at the Morley mission, insisted that Ndamase and Ludidi, a local Fingo chief, lead their combined force of three thousand men west of the Mbashe River to seize Gcaleka cattle which had been moved to that section of the coast. Lacking superior numbers and equipped only with spears, Ndamase's and Ludidi's warriors were shot to pieces by Gcaleka firearms. On New Year's Day 1852, Ndamase and the remnants of his force joined a British army column under Colonel George MacKinnon, which was raiding Gcaleka kraals around the Butterworth area. The rain continued, and over the next two days Faku, spurred on by Wesleyan reports that "the Gcalekas will be finished and the Pondos will get *thousands of cattle*," gathered part of his army around the Palmerton mission and seemed eager to advance southwest. For the Mpondo, this seemed like a good opportunity to replace stock lost to the Harding commando. Both Jenkins and Faku sent men to observe the Mzimvubu River, and they returned on the third to report that it was still "overflowing its banks." Faku then disbanded his force and instructed Jenkins to write to the governor "to say he will proceed again when the river is low, if required."

About two weeks later, in mid-January 1852, the river became fordable, and Faku once again summoned his warriors. However, rain came again and the campaign was postponed indefinitely. Around the same time, the British army withdrew west into British Kaffraria with thousands of cattle and Gcaleka collaborators. Ndamase then returned to his own great place of Nyandeni. It is worth noting that around this time H.F. Fynn became seriously ill and travelled to Natal to seek medical attention.[75]

In mid-March 1852, Faku went to the Palmerton mission to hear a message for him, sent by M.B. Shaw who had been in communication with the governor. Reading Shaw's letter, Jenkins told the Mpondo king that "the Governor thanks Faku for his readiness to go out against the Gcalekas" and "directs me to suspend hostilities against Kreli." Furthermore, Faku was informed that M.B. Shaw had replaced the Fynn brothers, H.F. and William, as "British Resident with all the tribes lying between the Kei and the District of Natal." Obviously, H.F. Fynn's failure to raise a force of Natal Africans for service against the Rharhabe and Gcaleka had caused Governor Smith to lose confidence in him. M.B. Shaw, who had used his close missionary connections to help organize Fingo and Mpondo raids on the Gcaleka in late December 1851, looked like a much better candidate. After apologizing for sending envoys to the rebel prophet Mlanjeni, Faku told Jenkins to write to the governor, thanking him for his message and stating that the Mpondo "will still be ready to move." In order to further ingratiate himself to the missionaries, Faku, in the presence of his councillors, signed a document "giving the lands of the Station [Palmerton] to the Wesleyan Missionary Society."[76]

On the twenty-first of April 1852, M.B. Shaw and Jenkins rode to Qawukeni, where the former presented himself to Faku as the new British Resident. Arrogantly, Shaw proclaimed that:

> I am appointed by the Governor to be the government of the country from Rili's country to the Umtamfuna [*sic*]. I am the mouth of the Governor, and I am to take care of you Pondos. When you have any complaint or case or anything to talk, Faku must sent direct to me at Morley, and I will send to Faku my news. I am to make all things right for you.[77]

The Mpondo monarch then observed that H.F. Fynn had come "with the same words." Continuing, Faku asked, "Where is my teacher, Mr. Jenkins? He has been many years with me. Write to Natal and Grahamstown and say he is not to go away out of my country. He is under your feet, and I am under Mr. Jenkins' feet." This seems to indicate that the Mpondo ruler considered Jenkins to be his unofficial British diplomatic agent who would report to M.B. Shaw. Subsequently, the missionaries and Faku discussed the case of an English trader who had shot an African servant to death the previous morning. M.B. Shaw and Jenkins praised Faku for referring this case to the Natal administration, as both the murderer and victim were from that colony.[78]

By July 1852, the new Cape governor, George Cathcart, was planning another colonial invasion of Sarhili's Gcaleka Kingdom. The objective was to capture cattle, which would be used to feed the colonial army that was fighting a protracted guerrilla war against the Rharhabe within colonial territory. Instructing M.B. Shaw to mobilize the African groups east of the Mbashe River, Cathcart suggested that "the Chief Faku would probably cooperate with most advantage on the seaward and southern districts," where the Gcaleka had driven many of their cattle for safekeeping. In late July, M.B. Shaw sent messengers to Faku, informing him of the governor's plan and instructing him to launch an assault on the Gcaleka at the same time as the British from the Cape. It is interesting that Jenkins refused to deliver this message as he did not want a missionary to be seen by the Mpondo as urging Faku into the war. On the other hand, M.B. Shaw, who lived at the Morley mission, was organizing a massive offensive against Sarhili's people, which would involve a large Thembu army gathered around the Clarkebury mission and a Bhaca force rallied around the Shawbury mission. The Buntingville mission, within Ndamase's territory, mobilized nearly 450 men. After consulting with his principal confidants, the Mpondo king sent back a message to M.B. Shaw that he would respond to the governor's call. At the end of the same month, Shaw sent more messengers to Faku; they were assured that the Mpondo would attack the Gcaleka. Ndamase took a force from Western Pondoland to the Morley mission, M.B. Shaw's residence, but remembering his losses seven months before, he would not proceed without Faku's army. By the sixth of August, the Mpondo army under Faku and his brother Sitata was assembled at the Qawukeni great place and was preparing to move southwest. However, Governor Cathcart's colonial force was already retiring from Gcalekaland with vast herds of cattle, and on the tenth, M.B. Shaw sent a message to Faku postponing what would have been a massive offensive.[79] Since the colonial army was already mobilized, it hit Gcalekaland before the Mpondo paramount was able to gather his fighting men from their various communities. Faku, like other rulers in the region, was willing to participate in the campaign, but he was not given enough time to prepare.

Assessing the effectiveness of the 1844 treaty, Cragg maintains that "the frontier wars of 1846-47 and 1850-53 showed that Faku was practically worthless as a military ally against the Xhosa."[80] While Faku never did engage the Gcaleka in any of these Cape-Xhosa conflicts, this was not entirely his fault. In 1846 Governor Maitland did not make any effort to mobilize the Mpondo, and when H.F. Fynn personally convinced Faku to join British raids upon the Gcaleka, a Wesleyan missionary stopped the Mpondo army just before it went into action. In late 1851 Governor Smith, with the active assistance of the Wesleyans, successfully enlisted Faku's military support, but a flooded river prevented the Mpondo army from raiding Gcalekaland. Over half a year later, Governor Cathcart and the Wesleyans tried to resuscitate Smith's plan, but failed to give Faku, who was still willing to participate, enough time to mobilize his forces. Despite H.F. Fynn's attempts to stimulate an Mpondo civil war and trick Faku into signing away his entire kingdom, the Mpondo ruler still believed that his continued security depended on cordial relations with the British. If Faku was useless as a military ally of the Cape Colony, it was mostly because of bungling by British officials and missionaries. However, through these failed attempts to assist the British, the Mpondo monarch did gain the goodwill of the colonial government, which could be exploited to ensure the continued independence of the kingdom. For example, Faku's potential as a military collaborator influenced colonial officials to redress Harding's cattle seizure and overturn Fynn's plot to place Pondoland under colonial administration. Having heard news of colonial conquest up to the Kei River and in Natal over the past thirty years, the Mpondo ruler was well aware that his kingdom would crumble if faced with concerted European firepower. To maintain peace between his people and the British, Faku was even willing to surrender a strip of territory along the Natal border which he had strove to keep during the 1830s. Although Faku explored alliances with other African states such as Moshoeshoe's Lesotho and even Sandile's Rharhabe, they were not powerful enough to guarantee the security of his kingdom. During the late 1840s and early 1850s, his overriding concern was to avoid the fate of the Rharhabe, Gcaleka and Zulu who had been ravaged and dispossessed by the expansion of the Cape and Natal.

5

Direct Colonial Intrusion in Faku's Final Years (1852-67)

*I*n late August 1852, just after a final abortive attempt to launch a raid on Gcalekaland, Faku, now about seventy-two years old, became extremely ill. Many people did not expect him to survive. The Reverend Jenkins of the Palmerton mission believed that Faku's illness would prompt a wave of witchcraft accusations and executions as various factions within the great place battled for political control. However, the missionary visited the nearby Mpondo capital of Qawukeni in early September where an ailing Faku promised "that no man should be put to death on his account." Within a week the paramount was convalescent and not one witchcraft accusation had taken place. William Shaw, the Wesleyan director based in the Cape Colony, was alarmed by a rumour that Faku had died, but upon hearing that this report was false he wrote, "I hope his [Faku's] life may be spared some time longer."[1]

Sometime in October 1852, as Faku was recovering from his illness, a group of Mpondo fighters attacked a Bhaca community. Although the exact objective of the raid is unknown, there had been hostility between the Bhaca and the Mpondo Kingdom for some time and most of these conflicts centred around accusations of stock theft. On this occasion, two Englishmen who were working at the Shawbury mission, one unidentified man and another named Hancock, led a group of "school people" to help defend the Bhaca, even though they were not living under the protection of the station. Encountering unexpected firepower from the Shawbury contingent, the Mpondo raiding party withdrew with heavy casualties. The two Englishmen later claimed "that they each shot 30 Pondos!" Subsequently, M.B. Shaw, the new British Resident in the area, complained to the Wesleyans, his father's subordinates, that he did not approve of their people interfering in "tribal disputes." However, he betrayed his real feelings by saying that "These wars between tribes are

---

Notes to chapter 5 are on pp. 183–85.

much to be regretted, but *politically* they have their advantage, as their tribal *disunion* will prevent the formation of a combined confederacy which might ultimately prove dangerous to British interests."[2]

When the British had finally suppressed the Rharhabe rebellion in British Kaffraria in February 1853, Faku, through Jenkins, sent a large elephant's tusk to Governor Cathcart "as a token of his continued peace and friendship with the Government." Furthermore, the Mpondo king asked why he had not received his annual subsidy, as stipulated in the 1844 treaty, for the previous two years. The confusion of war probably prevented the colonial government from honouring its commitment, usually paid in the form of trade goods. While Cathcart sent the Mpondo ruler a saddle and bridle as a gift, the subsidy payment continued to be delayed for another year because of bureaucratic confusion. Faku, who had always been heavily involved in local trade, became particularly annoyed about this issue.[3]

By the end of 1851, the Natal administration had decided to make space for more white settlers by expelling Africans in their area southwest into the strip of land between the Mzimkhulu and Mtamvuna rivers that had been ceded to them by Faku. This would create an overcrowded reservoir of migrant labour for nearby settler farms. However, Theophilus Shepstone, who eventually became Natal's Secretary for Native Affairs in 1853, believed that such a concentrated population of Africans had to be sandwiched between two white settlements in order to avoid stock theft and rebellion. Therefore, Shepstone planned to create a new settler colony with a chain of military posts between the Mtamvuna and Mtata rivers with the mouth of the Mzimvubu, Port St. John's, as its primary outlet for seagoing trade. This was the heartland of Faku's kingdom, but Shepstone foresaw no difficulty in convincing the Mpondo to move to the Mzimkhulu River, which would be within the new African labour reserve. Referring to the Mpondo ruler's land rights as outlined in the 1844 treaty, Shepstone, as early as 1851, had reported that:

> I apprehend that the political circumstances which rendered desirable the acknowledgement of his supremacy over so large a tract . . . have ceased to have any weight. His relinquishing it would in reality be surrendering a right acknowledged only by us, and never asserted by himself. There is, however, space sufficient to provide abundantly for Faku . . . as well as to carry out the plan I have recommended.[4]

While Faku was organizing an army to assist the British at the Cape, colonial officials in Natal were conspiring to deprive him of his territory. However, by early 1854 the imperial British Government had made it clear that it was unwilling to expand its territories in South Africa. As a result, Shepstone modified his plans to remove the idea of a new settler colony. He now proposed to acquire personal supremacy over all the chiefs between the Mzimkhulu and Mzimvubu rivers, with the exception of Faku who was to abandon the area in question and move west. The Natal Africans would then be moved into this territory, where they would live according to their own laws but under Shepstone's supervision. In fact, Shepstone, who had grown up in Pondoland while his father was a Wesleyan missionary at Morley, reported that he could accomplish this task without any coercion and that Faku had previously, and on several occasions, offered him as much land as he wanted within the Mpondo Kingdom.[5] Later events would prove that the Mpondo paramount was not so eager to give away his territory to the ambitious Shepstone.

With the support of a few white traders who operated in Pondoland, Shepstone left Pietermaritzburg in mid-May 1854 and travelled south-west across the Mzimkhulu and Mtamvuna rivers to implement his scheme. Shortly after setting out on this expedition, Shepstone wrote to one of his supporters that "I care very little what Faku may say, so long as I have the other chiefs on my side." By early June, ten African chiefs, including those of the Bhaca, Xesibe and Nci, had acknowledged Shepstone as their paramount. When Shepstone sent African messengers ahead to canvas Faku's opinion on the plan, a rumour swept through Pondoland that the Natal official was leading an expedition to destroy the Mpondo Kingdom. In turn, Jenkins calmed Faku and arranged a meeting between him and Shepstone in late July. According to Shepstone, "Faku hugged and caressed me like a baby and seemed to be quite willing to do anything I wanted." However, after hearing Shepstone's request for all the Mpondo land east of the Mzimvubu River, Faku "refused altogether giving or ceding territory to him." Realizing that part of the border of the territory acquired by Harding in 1850 remained rather vague, Jenkins tried to defuse the situation by suggesting to the Mpondo ruler that he could give Shepstone "a kloof or two" along the upper Mtamvuna River to create a distinct border between his kingdom and Natal in that area. Faku agreed to this, but Shepstone interpreted it to mean he had been given control of all the tributaries of that river, a fairly large area.

Angry at Shepstone for attempting to manipulate Faku's words, Jenkins refused to accompany him to the Qawukeni great place for a second meeting with the Mpondo king. On this occasion, Faku "ceded no coun-try but gave free access to the Zimvubu for trade, the navigation of the river, and Mr. Shepstone to have the control of the English (4 families) going there for that purpose." Nevertheless, Shepstone, who promised to return all the remaining cattle taken by the Harding commando, convinced Faku to sign a document ceding "all the waters running into the Umtamvuna river" and commercial control of the Mzimvubu mouth (Port St. John's), "a mile on each side of the river as far as the tide went over which Mr. Shepstone was not to allow traders to go." Although Shepstone had not acquired any additional land from the Mpondo except for the Mzimvubu River mouth, he returned to Natal satisfied that his influence with the local chiefs could be used to extend his territory southwest of the Mtamvuna River. A few weeks later, M.B. Shaw, who seemed to have very little knowledge of Shepstone's intentions, visited the Mpondo great place to investigate the agreements. After explaining his version of the Shepstone concessions, Faku stated that he was "quite satisfied as to the country ceded previously" to Natal in 1850.[6]

In February 1855, Shepstone fulfilled his promise to Faku by sending 170 cattle, compensation for the Harding seizures, to Qawukeni. However, in late May, M.B. Shaw, suspicious of Shepstone's plan, visited the Mpondo capital and was surprised that neither Faku nor his subjects were very concerned about the impending removal of Natal Africans to the land between the Mzimkhulu and Mtamvuna rivers. M.B. Shaw believed that this was because Faku planned to use this migration as an excuse to move the core of his kingdom north to the foothills of the Drakensberg Mountains so he could develop closer ties with Moshoeshoe's Lesotho. According to Shaw, this would cause warfare between the petty chiefs who already inhabited the area. Reading this report, George Grey, the new governor of the Cape Colony who favoured assimilation of the African population over Shepstone's proposed segregation, wrote to London that the plan would "bring about much more complicated political events than Her Majesty's Government appear to have been led to believe." By the end of the year, it became obvious that Shepstone would not be permitted to establish his own African kingdom on the periphery of Natal.[7]

As early as September 1851, M.B. Shaw had obtained a two hundred year lease from Faku for the area between the Mtakatyi and Mtata rivers, known as the Mdumbi River country. By early 1855, up to four thousand Africans had settled in this area. "School people" had left the Morley mission because of limited grazing opportunities and moved to this area. Two small Mpondomise sub-groups under chiefs Mlata and Gezani moved back into the Mdumbi area which they had inhabited before the Qwabe invasion of 1829. Furthermore, Ludidi, Shaw's old Fingo ally from the previous war, had become involved in a conflict with Ndamase, the Mpondo ruler west of the Mzimvubu River, and moved his followers from the Morley mission to Mdumbi country. Since all these people gave Shaw cattle in order to stay in this area, they began to recognize him as their ruler and considered themselves under British protection.[8]

The Mdumbi settlement was becoming a local alternative to the Mpondo Kingdom, particularly the western section under Ndamase. Throughout 1854, M.B. Shaw had alienated Ndamase by expelling some of the latter's subjects from the lease area because they did not recognize his authority. Additionally, Shaw accused Nogemani, a subordinate ruler of Ndamase, of receiving cattle stolen from the Mdumbi people. When Ndamase complained to his father, Faku, about the situation, he was told to drive Shaw out if he claimed to have acquired anything beyond simple grazing rights. Attempting to conceal his personal empire building, Shaw reported that Ndamase's sudden hostility towards him had been caused by "the vicious influence of an embassy from Moshesh," the Sotho king who had recently defeated an invading British army, and recommended that a military post be established at the mouth of the Mtata River. In Faku's eyes, Shaw was blatantly abusing the lease he had obtained in 1851. In March 1855, Shaw instructed his people "that they were not to allow the Mpondo army to come through" what he considered "the Government land."[9]

Sometime in late May or early June 1855, William Shaw visited the Palmerton mission as part of a general tour of the Eastern Cape missions. Praising Jenkins for his hard work at this station, William Shaw observed that the people of Palmerton "have already erected a considerable number of neat and commodious cottages and upwards of twenty more were in process of erection." During this visit, the Wesleyan director conducted interviews with Faku, whom he described as "old, and apparently in a state of dotage," and many other subordinate chiefs and councillors. According to Shaw, "Everywhere they received me kindly and all seem well affected towards the missions and missionaries. Their conversion to God would be a great event . . . but they do not yet see the desire of their hearts in this respect."[10] Ironically, Faku and his subjects gave William Shaw a warm welcome at the same time that his son, M.B. Shaw, was establishing a rival chiefdom in the Mdumbi country.

In retaliation for two years of continued stock theft upon his subjects, Ndamase, in June 1855, launched a three-pronged offensive against the Mpondomise, some of whom lived in and near the Mdumbi settlement. Many of these people had recently lived within the boundary of the Mpondo Kingdom and had been tributary subjects of Ndamase and Faku. Before taking three divisions of warriors to the field, Ndamase sent messengers to M.B. Shaw informing him of the purpose of this operation. Advancing north, Ndamase's division "swept off vast numbers of cattle, goats, sheep and horses and some guns," which had been captured from the handful of young men and boys who had been protecting the stock.

The second Mpondo division under Mtiki attacked the great place of the Mpondomise chief Gqirhana. This was where most of the Mpondomise warriors were located, and Mtiki's force was driven off after sustaining twenty-four fatalities, among whom was the Mpondo commander himself. The third Mpondo division, led by Nogemani, crossed northwest of the upper Mtata River and fought their way down its west bank, seizing cattle from both Mpondomise and Thembu herders. Since this last Mpondo division had passed through a part of the Mdumbi country, and Nogemani, its leader, had been involved in a dispute with the Mdumbi people, M.B. Shaw came from the Morley mission to mobilize his subjects. While still west of the Mtata River, Nogemani's men were attacked by a force from the Mdumbi settlement, commanded by M.B. Shaw and an African teacher named James. Tired and hungry from two days of raiding, the Mpondo fought briefly, but were easily driven off. The Mdumbi people then pursued Nogemani's warriors, killing up to eighteen of them and capturing 180 cattle that had been seized from the Mpondomise and Thembu. According to some Mpondo witnesses, M.B. Shaw shot three Mpondo men himself.[11]

Shortly after this incident, Ndamase sent a message to the Reverend Charles White of the neighbouring Buntingville mission, requesting him to send a letter to M.B. Shaw "to ask him why he killed the children of the Amampondoland." Responding, Shaw claimed that the Mdumbi people had taken up arms when they heard that the Mpondo commander Nogemani was about to attack Mlata, one of the Mpondomise chiefs. Supposedly, the British Resident had ridden along with the Mdumbi commando until they met Nogemani's force, but a fight broke out before he could do anything to stop it. Shaw maintained that he did not participate in the combat and that "he is sorry about the accident." Upon hearing this message, Ndamase told White that "Shaw must move with his cattle" and that he was planning to get revenge by sending Mpondo fighters "to attack the Umdumbi people." When White visited Mdumbi country to warn Shaw's people about the impending Mpondo offensive, they said that they were not afraid, as Shaw had sent for military assistance from the Cape Colony. At the same time, Ndamase sent messengers to King William's Town to complain to Colonel George Maclean, the Chief Commissioner of British Kaffraria and M.B. Shaw's immediate superior, and Faku "resolved to have no more communications with M.B. (Shaw) as Government Agent."[12]

In mid-July 1855, Faku called for Jenkins to visit his Qawukeni great place to discuss the Mdumbi crisis. Putting this off for three weeks in the hope that Faku "would cool down," the missionary went to the Mpondo capital during the first week of August. Initially, Jenkins heard accounts of the skirmish at Mdumbi from some of Ndamase's and Nogemani's men who had personally witnessed M.B. Shaw shooting two Mpondo warriors. Faku then requested that the missionary write a letter to the governor informing him about the conduct of M.B. Shaw and his people. According to Jenkins, this document was composed "in as mild a strain as I possibly could." Faku asked if the British government intended to make war on his kingdom and demanded the return of all the cattle that had been captured from Nogemani's force. Continuing, the Mpondo ruler then told Jenkins that M.B. Shaw and any other Europeans must immediately remove all their property from the Mdumbi country and warned that he would not be responsible for the property of any European who lived around the Morley mission, M.B. Shaw's residence. The missionary believed this indicated that Faku was preparing to wage war against the people of that area. Before leaving, Jenkins advised Faku to delay taking any military action until he heard from the colonial authorities. However, as the missionary rode away from Qawukeni, he observed men from Ndamase arriving for an audience with the paramount. Later the same day, Jenkins was "privately informed" that the objective of Ndamase's messengers was to ask for Faku's permission to send out an army against the Mdumbi people. The missionary quickly sent a message to M.B. Shaw warning him of a possible attack.[13]

In late August, Colonel Maclean, the Chief Commissioner of British Kaffraria, sent a note to Jenkins asking him to tell Faku that his letter was being forwarded to Governor Grey, who was travelling through the Eastern Cape on his way to Natal, and that the governor might visit the Mpondo great place to address the crisis. Attempting to both dissuade Faku from attacking the Mdumbi settlement and allay his fears of a retaliatory British raid on the Mpondo, Maclean's message stated that M.B. Shaw's actions had been "inconsistent with his position as an Agent of the Government." In order to pacify the Mpondo ruler, Maclean arranged for Jenkins to pay Faku the annual subsidy, including substantial arrears, stipulated by the 1844 treaty but unforthcoming for about five years.[14]

While Governor Grey did not visit Pondoland, Maclean dispatched Major Thomas Addison, another British officer, to investigate the Mdumbi affair. Arriving at the Buntingville mission in Western Pondoland in late October 1855, Addison requested that Faku give orders for all relevant witnesses to be sent to the mission to give evidence. The Mpondo king complied. On the day of the inquiry, the Reverend Jenkins took the stand and stated that he understood that the Mdumbi country had been leased by M.B. Shaw as grazing land, but that the people who had moved there considered themselves under British protection. Additionally, the missionary stated that it was common practice for

Mpondo armies to move through mission land without giving any prior notice. This implied that the movement of Nogemani's raiding party through Mdumbi should not have caused Shaw to raise an alarm. Shaw, who "appeared very cool and distant," cross-examined Jenkins, but achieved very little. Addison concluded that Shaw had been responsible for the crisis as he had used the Mdumbi country to build up an African group that was in competition with the Mpondo Kingdom. Subsequently, Maclean recommended to the governor that Shaw be dismissed as British Resident in the area and that he should compensate Faku for the loss of eighteen men. Governor Grey acted upon the first recommendation and directed Maclean to personally visit Faku to explore the second.[15]

In January 1856, Major Addison left Buntingville and travelled east to the Palmerton mission. In the company of Jenkins, Addison visited Faku and informed him of the findings of the inquiry. The king was generally pleased and informed the major that had it not been for Jenkins's advice "not a soul would have been left at the Umdumbi." Following the governor's instructions, Colonel Maclean visited Qawukeni sometime in April and held discussions with Faku and his son Ndamase on the Mdumbi incident. While Maclean does not seem to have promised any reparations for the loss of Mpondo cattle and men, he assured the Mpondo ruler that Shaw would leave the Mdumbi. Furthermore, the chief commissioner reminded Faku of his obligation to protect the missionaries and advised him to listen to "the great truths of God's word." During the conference, Ndamase warned Maclean that the matter of James, the African teacher who had assisted Shaw during the Mdumbi skirmish, had not been addressed. In turn, Maclean forced James to return two horses that belonged to Ndamase. A few days after the chief commissioner left Pondoland, Faku sent a message to Jenkins that "he and his people are highly satisfied with the just and honourable arrangement." Reporting to Governor Grey, Maclean expressed his appreciation of "Mr. Jenkins who afforded me much necessary information, and every assistance in his power, and who having deservedly much influence with Faku, has . . . acted in the Christian character of a peace maker between that Chief and the Government."[16] While Faku and the colonial officials seemed happy to settle the conflict, the lack of compensation caused anxiety and resentment in Western Pondoland.

Around the same time that Addison and then Maclean held their respective conferences with Faku, the Wesleyans enacted a previous decision to move their Clarkebury station. The Reverend James S. Thomas, a Wesleyan missionary, negotiated with the Mpondomise chief Gqirhana for a new site. However, both the Mpondo and Thembu also claimed the area that was chosen. Additionally, Thomas made a serious mistake by letting James, the African teacher from Morley who had fought against Ndamase's men at Mdumbi, move to the new mission with the cattle he had captured from Nogemani's Mpondo. In April, just after Maclean left Qawukeni, some of Ndamase's subjects raided stock from James's kraal. When Jenkins heard about this, he rushed to Qawukeni to complain to the Mpondo king. According to the missionary, "Faku *seems* indignant; says he knows nothing of it, and will enquire into it." On the other hand, Jenkins overheard people protest that "the Amakumsha (school people) of Shawbury, Morley, and Umdumbi can kill the Pondos and nothing is said about it." Jenkins left Qawukeni fearing that Ndamase (who had not yet officially informed his father about the raid) and his followers "will yet be at their retaliating work."[17]

Thomas arrived at the new mission, now named Beecham Wood, in early June 1856 and because of the raid mentioned above he allowed James and other former Morley residents to put their cattle in his private kraal. In the early morning darkness of the fourteenth of June, a group of Ndamase's followers attacked the mission to take back their cattle from James, and when the Reverend Thomas went outside to investigate he was stabbed to death. Jenkins heard about this roughly a week later and immediately rode to Qawukeni to tell Faku, who appeared "to be deeply grieved and annoyed at the conduct of his son." Promising to travel to Palmerton within the next day or two with his councillors to decide on the best reaction to this incident, the Mpondo ruler said "I had already called Damas [*sic*] to account for the first attack, and before my messengers got there, he repeated it." Not waiting for Faku to report to Palmerton, Jenkins went to the Buntingville mission, which was located in Ndamase's area, to personally investigate the murder of the Reverend Thomas. On the twenty-fifth of the same month, Ndamase, along with his brothers Bangani and Dikiso, two councillors and "Umqetengo," a representative of Faku, visited Buntingville. Ndamase told Jenkins that he was "deeply grieved" about the death of Thomas, "which was occasioned by a commando which went out without his knowledge." Jenkins, who had known Ndamase for nearly nineteen years, believed this testimony. Ndamase went on to state that he had already restored the cattle taken from Beecham Wood, that he would willingly surrender the sub-chief Mbola, a nephew of Faku who had led the attack, together with the actual murderers, and that he would comply with any other demands made upon him such as the payment of a cattle fine. Jenkins then made Ndamase and his councillors mark a written agreement that outlined these three points. Before returning to Palmerton, Jenkins sent a recommendation to Maclean that the matter be dealt with swiftly, but that James's cattle should not be returned to him as they had been originally taken from Ndamase's Mpondo.[18]

The violent death of a missionary in Pondoland was unprecedented. During the first week of July, Faku and five hundred of his subjects visited the Palmerton mission for three days. Among this entourage "a large body also of the principal women of the tribe came to console with Mrs. Jenkins on the sad event." On the seventh of July, the Mpondo king told Jenkins that "they have come to sympathise (to cry) with me about the lamented death of Mr. Thomas." Faku then requested the missionary to write a letter on his behalf to the governor to apologize for the incident and explain that neither he nor his son Ndamase had been aware of the attack on Beecham Wood. Confirming Ndamase's previous declaration, the Mpondo ruler stated that all the livestock taken from the mission had been restored, that the sub-chief Mbola and the murderer would be executed and that the group who conducted the raid would pay a fine of two hundred cattle. In conclusion, Faku proclaimed "I desire to do the thing that is right, and to show I have no hostile feelings to the Missionaries nor to the Government." This letter was marked by Faku, his sons Mankebe and Mqikela, his brothers Cingo and Sitata and his councillors Gastana and Mqetengo as well as initialled by Jenkins, who noted that it was "written by me and in my presence."[19] Clearly, Faku and the other Mpondo royals of the great place viewed the killing of the Reverend Thomas as an extremely serious incident which jeopardized their alliance with the Cape Colony and congenial relationship with the Wesleyans.

Just three days later, Colonel Maclean, the Chief Commissioner of British Kaffraria who had not yet received Faku's letter to the governor, sent a note to Jenkins asking him to pass on a message to the Mpondo king. Maclean demanded that Faku execute the murderers and provide some cattle as compensation to Thomas's widow and children. Furthermore, Maclean stated that if this was not done, he would withhold the Mpondo king's annual subsidy. However, by early September 1856, this ultimatum had not been carried out. Ignoring repeated calls from his father, Ndamase refused to visit Qawukeni to discuss the Thomas murder. Finally, he sent his brothers and councillors. It should be noted that at this time Ndamase was busy defending Western Pondoland from periodic raids by a coalition of Mpondomise, Mdumbi people and Khoikhoi fugitives from the Cape.

On 4 September 1856, a large assembly was held at Qawukeni where an unidentified brother of Faku, father of the sub-chief Mbola who had led the raid on the Beecham Wood mission, pleaded for the life of his son as Mbola had planned the attack to recover Mpondo cattle and not to kill the missionary. Also, Mbola's father promised to pay between four hundred and six hundred cattle to the colonial government if his son was spared. While the Mpondo ruler had invited Jenkins to this meeting, the missionary declined to attend, as he feared it would seem "contrary to the Gospel I am preaching amongst them." Although Faku did not decide immediately, the appeal must have been successful: Mbola was not executed. Around the same time, Governor Grey, who gave a positive reply to the Mpondo king's letter of early July, refused to accept two hundred cattle from Faku as compensation for the murder and stated that he was now only interested in hearing that the murderer was dead. Faku then gave these cattle to the Buntingville station as a sign of goodwill. A few weeks later, Ndamase sent the man who had stabbed the Reverend Thomas to the Buntingville mission with a request that he be sent to King William's Town for execution. The Reverend Charles White, who was in charge of the mission, refused to have anything to do with the case, as he did not want to be seen as a colonial agent. Ndamase then sent the murderer to Faku's great place where he was detained for three weeks. Eventually, the Mpondo king and his councillors sentenced the man to be strangled to death; this was done in the presence of witnesses from Palmerton who confirmed that it was the correct individual. Within a short period, Faku's subsidy was paid in the form of various articles he had ordered from the Cape Colony.[20]

Little is known about Faku and events in Pondoland from 1857 to 1859. As the Rharhabe and Gcaleka kingdoms were being destroyed by the infamous Cattle-Killing movement of 1856-57, Mhlakaza, a councillor at the Gcaleka great place whose niece Nongqawuse had supposedly prophesied that the whites would be driven into the sea if the Xhosa killed all their cattle and refrained from planting, sent messengers to Faku demanding that the Mpondo destroy their herds "or become a nation of moths." After listening to these statements, Faku replied "In all great matters of this kind I have been accustomed to listen to my missionary. I will send for him and hear what he has to say, and be guided by his council." After the Gcaleka messengers failed to dissuade Faku from calling Jenkins, they quickly left the great place and there was no cattle killing within the Mpondo Kingdom.[21] There is no evidence that the lung sickness outbreak, which had decimated Rharhabe and Gcaleka herds just before the Cattle-Killing and is generally seen as one cause of the movement, ever spread to Pondoland.

Following the Cattle-Killing and the arrival of German settlers in British Kaffraria in 1858, the Frontier Armed and Mounted Police (FAMP), led by Walter Currie, crossed east of the Kei River and drove Sarhili's Gcaleka over the Mbashe River into Bomvanaland. Subsequently, the colonial government moved some Rharhabe collaborators to Idutywa, a colonial outpost in the former Gcaleka territory, and

Fingoes to the Wesleyan mission at Butterworth. This meant that the Cape colonial border had unofficially advanced to the Mbashe River, which was uncomfortably close to the Mpondo Kingdom. It also meant that Sarhili, the Gcaleka ruler who had rejected a proposed marriage to Faku's daughter in 1850, and many of his subjects were now living between the Mbashe and Mtata rivers which put an old enemy on the Mpondo Kingdom's southwestern border. Approaching eighty years of age, but still functioning as the Mpondo ruler, Faku must have been greatly concerned about these developments.

As the colonial government had not appointed another British Resident in Pondoland after the dismissal of M.B. Shaw in 1856, Jenkins acted as the governor's representative with Faku and arranged for the payment of the king's annual subsidy through the Natal administration. However, communication on this matter was uncertain and sporadic. For example, in May 1858, after much delay, Colonel Maclean, based in British Kaffraria, arranged for a colonial trader to purchase eight red blankets in Natal and send them to Faku as part of his overdue subsidy. Around April 1859, Faku sent a message to the governor along with an "elephant's tusk as an offering of peace and friendship." With Sarhili between the Mbashe and Mtata rivers, Faku wanted to remind Grey that the Mpondo were still loyal allies of the British. In response, Maclean told Jenkins that "We must support old Faku if there is any chance of his coming into trouble," and sent twenty-five pounds for the Mpondo king whose subsidy, as usual, was in arrears.[22]

Sometime around 1858 or 1859, Jojo's Xesibe attacked the ImiZizi, a tributary state of the Mpondo Kingdom, killing two influential men and making off with three hundred cattle. Subsequently, an ImiZizi army attacked the Xesibe but was shocked to discover that Jojo had enlisted support from the Jali and Ntshangasi, two neighbouring groups who were also vassals of the Mpondo state. Overwhelmed by superior numbers, the ImiZizi warriors were defeated. The Xesibe and their allies were then able to once again raid the unprotected ImiZizi villages, where they seized an additional five herds of cattle and killed the ImiZi chief "Vang'indaba" in his own kraal.

Upon hearing the news of this conflict, Faku was greatly surprised, and Mqikela, the king's heir, urged his father to "Let us go with an army against Jojo." However, when Mqikela had organized a force at the great place, Faku returned from another kraal and forbade his great son to attack the Xesibe. The Mpondo army was disbanded. Two months later, messengers from the ImiZi pleaded with Faku to avenge the death of their chief. Nevertheless, the Mpondo ruler stated that "You must not go out to fight against Jojo. I am crying as well as you for Vang'indaba." At the same time, Faku followed the articles of the 1844 treaty by reporting the matter to Theophilus Shepstone, Natal's Secretary of Native Affairs, who did not respond. Without Faku's consent, the frustrated ImiZizi, who had by now convinced the Jali to switch allegiance to the Mpondo state, attacked the Xesibe. In the subsequent violence, a great many ImiZizi were slain and Jojo was able to seize more of their stock. Notably, during this battle Bekameva, one of Faku's older sons and an important figure in Mpondo politics, was taken prisoner by the Xesibe. When ImiZizi messengers came to the Mpondo great place with news of their defeat and Bekameva's capture, an angry Faku declared that "I told you not to go out: you acted contrary to my advice." On instructions from the Mpondo king, Jenkins went to Jojo, the Xesibe chief who was also a nephew of Faku, offering one hundred cattle as ransom for Bekameva. Although the Xesibe agreed to release Faku's son, Bekameva escaped before all the cattle were paid. In turn, Faku abandoned the hope of getting help from his colonial neighbours and launched a retaliatory assault on the Xesibe with violent stock raiding continuing for the next few years.[23]

In early March 1860, Faku sent a group of warriors to the west bank of the Mtamvuna River to attack the Nci, a small tributary state of the Mpondo kingdom, for "various insults to him." The Mpondo ruler then sent Mqikela, his great son, to the Palmerton mission in order to have Jenkins send a message to Theophilus Shepstone, the Secretary of Native Affairs in Natal. Mqikela stated that if the Nci repeated these mysterious insults, the Mpondo army would pursue them to the Mzimkhulu River. When Jenkins reminded Mqikela that the Mpondo must respect the Mtamvuna River as the border with Natal, the heir asked "is it not the Umzimkhulu?" The missionary then stated that Faku and his councillors "must know themselves what they signed for the boundary and that ought ever to be respected."[24] Obviously, Mqikela objected to the Harding agreement of 1850, in which Faku had ceded the land between the Mzimkhulu and Mtamvuna rivers to Natal. It is also likely that Mqikela thought that since Shepstone had not utilized the territory in question as he had intended to do in 1854, it had reverted to Mpondo control. Aware that the octogenarian Faku would not live much longer and that Ndamase enjoyed a firm grasp on Western Pondoland, Mqikela may have wanted to enlarge the eastern half of the kingdom, which he would soon inherit. He did not realize that the colonial government was formulating plans to deprive him of this opportunity.

In November 1860, Governor Grey sent Jenkins a memorandum for Faku, stating that Adam Kok's Griqua, a mixed-race group who were living north of the Drakensberg Mountains and were in conflict with the republican Boers of the Free State, would be resettled by the colonial government in the northern portion of the Mpondo Kingdom. Jenkins reported that the Mpondo ruler "was not a little startled when I read it to him. He and the Chief Men had much to say on the subject." Furthermore, the missionary was alarmed that Faku had recently been sent a "splendid horse" by Moshoeshoe, the Sotho king who was also in conflict with the Boers of the interior. Moshoeshoe had been a distant friend of the Mpondo king for many years, but now seemed to want to create an alliance against both the Boers and British. Subsequently, Faku enlisted Jenkins to write a letter to the governor asking how his land could be taken for the Griqua as the Mpondo borders had been guaranteed in 1844. In response, the governor contradicted himself by declaring that "Faku is mistaken, and that no land has been given to Adam Kok, nor has the Government any intention of interfering or intruding on Faku's just rights."[25] This was an outright lie. It is not certain if Jenkins ever read this message to Faku; before it arrived at Palmerton, Walter Currie, commander of the Frontier Armed and Mounted Police, was already in Pondoland to negotiate a new border.

Governor Grey intended to visit Faku himself in order to arrange for the settlement of Sarhili's Gcaleka in the Mdumbi country in Western Pondoland and Kok's Griqua in the northern section of Eastern Pondoland just south of the Drakensberg Mountains. However, Grey became ill in King William's Town and sent Walter Currie, the policeman who had driven the Gcaleka off their land a few years before, to conclude the agreements. Currie, accompanied by a mounted police escort, arrived at the Qawukeni great place in mid-March 1861 and convinced Jenkins to introduce him to the Mpondo ruler. Faku absolutely refused to discuss the Mdumbi area; Ndamase was not at the meeting and it fell within his jurisdiction of Western Pondoland. However, Faku allegedly proposed to give the British control over all the territory within Eastern Pondoland that was not actually inhabited by Mpondo groups. The Mpondo ruler suggested that the border of the eastern section of the kingdom should follow "the sources of the Umtamvuna to the top of the Ingeli Mountains to the top of the Insizwe Mountain to the Umzimvubu to its source." Faku could not discuss the land west of the Mzimvubu River as Ndamase, the semi-autonomous ruler of that area, was absent. However, Currie insisted that the Mpondo king continue the imaginary line which would constitute the new border west across the Mzimvubu. Initially, Faku argued with Currie over this issue, but the former became intimidated by the colonial police and made a vague statement that the new border could be extended west from the Mzimvubu River to the wagon crossing on the Mtata River. Believing this to be a final agreement, Currie then asked Jenkins to draw up a written contract before abruptly riding off to establish the exact location of the new border. The missionary did not produce this document. Currie did not return to Qawukeni to ratify the agreement, but rather went back to the Cape Colony and reported that he had acquired the northern, inland half of both Western and Eastern Pondoland, which was suitable for not only the Griquas but European settlers as well.[26]

In July 1861, the governor sent a message to Faku thanking him for ceding the northern section of Pondoland. However, the Mpondo ruler arranged for Jenkins to write a response which hinted that Currie had misunderstood the agreement. For Faku, the discussions had been preliminary to a formal written treaty which had yet to be signed. In turn, Phillip Wodehouse, new governor of the Cape Colony, ordered Currie to return to the Mpondo Kingdom in order to secure Faku's continued friendship with the colonial government. In late January 1862, Currie, who was in the Eastern Cape town of Grahamstown preparing for this expedition, wrote to Jenkins asking that he invite Faku and his councillors to meet him on the Mzimhlava River near the great place of Jojo, the Xesibe chief, on the first of March. Currie intended to discuss the borders between the Mpondo, Natal and Adam Kok's Griqua, who had not yet arrived in the area. Because Faku's age meant that he could not travel to the meeting place, he sent a message to Currie inviting him to Qawukeni. Currie agreed to this request and arrived at Palmerton in late February. However, Faku sent another message asking the police commander to wait at the mission until Ndamase, his eldest son, arrived from west of the Mzimvubu River. After Currie told the messenger that he would leave within two days to meet with colonial officials from Natal, Mqikela, Faku's son and heir, and a councillor rushed to Palmerton. Unfortunately, Currie refused to wait any longer and he left the mission before seeing Faku. On Jenkins's advice, the Mpondo ruler sent a message to Governor Wodehouse, expressing regret at the misunderstanding and asking for another conference on the boundary issue. Four weeks later, Currie wrote to Jenkins that "There was no misunderstanding on the first occasion of my visit at the Great Place." Additionally, Currie believed that Moshoeshoe's son, Nehemiah Moshoeshoe, was behind this trouble, as he was trying to claim the land at the foot of the Drakensberg Mountains which Faku had offered to the ruler of the Sotho Kingdom in the 1840s.[27] Distracted by other matters such as the conflicting land claims of Adam Kok's Griquas and Natal, Wodehouse put off dealing with the Pondoland border. Waiting in vain for a reply to his last letter to the governor, Faku must have felt abandoned by his colonial allies.

Sometime in 1862 Jenkins, who was now fifty-six years old, decided to establish a new mission thirty miles north of Palmerton on the fringe of

Xesibe territory. Although the evidence is somewhat vague, Faku seems to have promised Jenkins that he would relocate his great place to somewhere near the new mission, named Mfundisweni. However, the Mpondo king did not do this, and Jenkins's new station remained obscure. Faku's change of heart may have been influenced by several movements into the territory just north of the new mission. Towards the end of 1862, Sotho people under chiefs Nehemiah Moshoeshoe and Poshuli occupied parts of the northern reaches that had formerly belonged to Faku. In January 1863, Adam Kok and three thousand Griquas moved into the same territory just north of the Mpondo Kingdom between the Mtamvuna and Mzimvubu rivers. Nearly twenty years later, in 1880, Jojo, the Xesibe chief, claimed that the establishment of the Mfundisweni mission had been a plot by the Mpondo "to take possession of my country, with a thing which is begotten by Government that I could not attack, and they have used in attacking me."[28]

Another reason why Faku did not move north to the new Mfundisweni mission was that around the early 1860s there seems to have been internal conflict at his Qawukeni great place. When Faku became dangerously ill, a number of witch-hunters declared that Cingo, the king's brother and close confidant over many years, had bewitched him. This meant that Cingo was sentenced to a slow, horrible death. This case was so serious that even Jenkins, who had intervened successfully in similar situations, considered it too dangerous to interfere. However, Mary Jenkins, the missionary's wife, convinced him to go to Qawukeni and appeal to Faku to save his brother. Although the witch-hunters initially prevented Jenkins from seeing the ailing king, he eventually had an audience with Faku in the same hut where Cingo had been confined. Referring to his belief that someone had bewitched him, Faku asked Jenkins, "Teacher, do you see how some of my own people hate me, in sending the wild cats to kill me?" The missionary replied by stating, "Faku, to my certain knowledge there is not a man in the tribe who would do such a thing against his chief and father. They love you too well to think of doing such a thing." A surprised Faku then asked, "Do you think so?" Jenkins answered, "I am sure of it," and said that Mrs. Jenkins, whom, he described as Faku's "best friend," had begged him to intervene on Cingo's behalf. While Cingo sat silently, the missionary said, "Faku, I plead for the life of your brother Cingo, because I know he is not guilty, and I know you are not the man to stain your hands with the innocent blood of your own brother." After a few moments of deep thought, Faku proclaimed, "My Umfundisi (teacher), you have saved Cingo! He will not be killed!" Suddenly, a look of great relief came over Cingo, who, once set free, invited missionaries to conduct religious services in his village.[29] While it is difficult to determine, a witchcraft accusation against such a high-ranking member of the royal family must have had some political or material motivation. As it became obvious that Faku, who was now in his eighties, would not live much longer, various factions within the great place may have begun to jockey for power. Cingo, as a long-time ally and full brother of king, was probably seen as a potential rival by Mqikela, Faku's heir, and his supporters.

In the early 1860s the colonial government decided it wanted control of the mouth of the Mzimvubu River, otherwise known as Port St. John's. There were several reasons for this ambition. First, a small group of white traders, who were visited several times a year by ships from Natal and the Cape, had settled at the Port. The Natal Legislative Council began to recognize that they were losing revenue, as Natal merchants were avoiding customs duties by shifting their operations from Durban to Port St. John's. Second, British officials at the Cape feared that if the Free State Boers conquered Moshoeshoe's Sotho, which seemed like a real possibility at this time, then the Boers could easily expand south to the coast and take over the Mzimvubu mouth. If the Boers were to enter into an alliance with another imperial power, it would represent a serious threat to British ships on route to and from India. Third, a more immediate threat was that unidentified merchant vessels were periodically landing firearms at Port St. John's; the firearms were then traded to the Mpondo. While both colonial officials and Wesleyan missionaries were concerned about Faku's people acquiring guns, Jenkins was more worried about the importation of Western-style liquor, which he thought would corrupt potential converts to Christianity.[30]

In early 1865, rumours of an impending war between the republican Free State Boers and Moshoeshoe's Sotho Kingdom led Governor Wodehouse to plan for a pre-emptive British occupation of Port St. John's. However, around the same time it was proposed to Faku, through Jenkins, that a telegraph line pass through his territory, establishing rapid communication between the Cape Colony and Natal. Remembering the still-unresolved border issue initiated by Currie, Faku was worried that the telegraph was yet another attempt to take away Mpondo land, and he rejected the proposal. Therefore, Jenkins, whom the governor had asked for advice on his plan to acquire Port St. John's, reported that it was not an appropriate time to approach the Mpondo king about this subject. In turn, Wodehouse informed the missionary that he was prepared to show his goodwill to Faku by increasing his annual allowance to one hundred pounds, while at the same time providing his son Ndamase, ruler of Western Pondoland, with a yearly stipend of fifty pounds. Furthermore, the governor wrote, "The matter of St. Jon's [sic] river is of much importance, that is, *as to its not falling into other hands*, but I must trust to your discretion for the selection of *the time and mode of buying, about an arrangement.*"[31]

Sometime in the middle of 1864, the Sotho ruler Moshoeshoe, a distant but long-established ally of the Mpondo king, had sent a message to Faku saying that he regarded himself as a child of the British Queen and advising Faku to live in peace with her.[32] By the middle of August 1865, Jenkins thought Faku had cooled down about the border issue and arranged a conference at the Qawukeni great place. When the missionary arrived at the Mpondo capital, Faku had gathered a large number of his councillors and subordinate rulers. Although Ndamase was unable to attend, he was represented by several of his sons and brothers. Jenkins presented the Mpondo paramount with a horse and some blankets that had been sent to him by the governor. The missionary then announced that "the Governor being so satisfied with the friendly alliance maintained on the part of Faku's people to the Colonial Government, is now pleased to increase his annual subsidy to 100 pounds, and Damas [sic] also in future to receive 50 pounds." The assembly seemed pleased with this statement and the elderly Faku asked Jenkins to relay to the governor "his grateful acknowledgment of the confidence placed in him and his son Damas." After some discussion, the Mpondo officials resolved that since "*the House is one*, and must remain so," Ndamase would receive his subsidy at Qawukeni at the same time as his father. After the meeting, Jenkins approached Faku in private to advise him that the governor was concerned that another colonial power would get control of Port St. John's. According to the missionary, Faku promised that "he will entertain no negotiations about that Port but with the Government of the Colony."[33]

Waiting for three months so as not to arouse Faku's suspicion, Jenkins arranged another conference at Qawukeni in the first days of December 1865. The missionary told the Mpondo ruler and his councillors about the governor's proposal to purchase the Mzimvubu mouth, Port St. John's. However, Faku expressed great concern; messengers from the Natal administration had arrived a few days before to inform the Mpondo that the border with that colony was to be advanced southwest to the Mtamvuna River, with the exception of the Griqua area in the north. While the territory between the Mzimkhulu and Mtamvuna rivers had been ceded to Natal by Faku in 1850, after many years the colony had not yet established its authority over that strip of country. As a result, many of Faku's subordinate rulers had moved back across the Mtamvuna River where they had built kraals and planted fields, and were now pleading with their king to reverse the cession. Also inhabiting the area in question were "Fynn's People," colonial-oriented Africans from Natal who had been moved west of the Mzimkhulu River by H.F. Fynn in the 1840s. Faku sent messengers to Natal to explain that his people had moved back into the area and to request that the Mzimkhulu/Mtamvuna strip be officially given back to the Mpondo. In the context of Natal's anticipated expansion to the Mtamvuna River, the Mpondo king and his councillors were extremely sceptical of what Jenkins had said about Port St. John's. The missionary, who maintained that "other parties" were eager to take over the port, was hounded by numerous questions, such as the object of the cession of the port, the quantity of land required, the number of Europeans to reside there and the compensation offered. Unable to answer any of the Mpondo queries, Jenkins forwarded the following response to the governor:

> Faku hopes to be able to accede to the wishes of your Excellency in reference to the Port of St. John's, but before he can give a final answer, he hopes that your Excellency will send an accredited person who will be able to give such information as required. The principal men of the tribe must assemble at the Great Place to consult, and also an agent or a person from your Excellency be present who can give all necessary information. That as soon as Faku can assemble the various chiefs he will inform the Governor as to the time for the above agent to be in the country.[34]

The missionary claimed that Faku "was very cautious in any reply he made, and equally inquisitive upon every point. The fact is he and his people *fear least the territory and subjugation be the object*, at the same time wishful to keep on amicable terms with the Government."[35]

Although Natal's renewed interest in the land between the Mtamvuna and Mzimkhulu rivers caused Faku to be cautious about ceding Port St. John's, other developments made him not want to alienate the British. Ndamase had been unable to attend the December meeting with Jenkins as his people had been raided by the Mpondomise of Mhlontlo. Several weeks previous, a Bhaca group had attacked an Mpondo community and killed six people before withdrawing with a large herd of cattle. In addition, Adam Kok's Griqua were accusing the Mpondo of stealing over one hundred horses from them. Finally, Kok's Griqua, Ludidi's Fingo and some Bhaca had recently worked together to seize many cattle, sheep and horses from Moshoeshoe's Sotho subjects to the north.[36] Faku did not become involved in this last issue, but he was well aware that he might be the next target of such aggression and would need British protection.

Natal's response to Faku's request that the land between the Mzimkhulu and Mtamvuna rivers be officially given back to the Mpondo state was to send a military expedition under Colonel J. Bisset to the latter river. In late December 1865, Bisset invited Jenkins to the firing of a twenty-one gun salute on New Year's Day to mark Natal's annexation of this territory. The colonel informed Jenkins that "I do not expect that Faku will meet me, but I am sure, with your influence, you will be able to impress upon him the necessity of respecting the territory on this side of the *Umtamvuna* for the future." Additionally, Theophilus Shepstone, Natal's Secretary of Native Affairs who had accompanied Bisset's force, requested that Jenkins apprise Faku of the ceremony to mark the annexation of what he called "No Man's Land," and that from then on the laws of Natal would rule in that area.[37] While it is unclear if Jenkins actually informed the Mpondo ruler about this expedition, Faku certainly knew about it, as some of his subordinate rulers and their communities inhabited what Shepstone described as "No Man's Land."

On the first of January 1866, the Natal officials on the Mtamvuna River publicly announced that the land between that river and the Mzimkhulu River was annexed to Natal and would be henceforth known as the "Alfred Country." In attendance were procolonial factions such as Adam Kok, with two hundred mounted and armed Griquas with an artillery piece as well as some of the mysterious "Fynn's people," who could field up to 2,600 fighting men. However, Kani, a subordinate of Faku and the senior ImiZizi ruler east of the Mtamvuna, and many of his sub-chiefs along the coast refused Shepstone's orders that they were to attend the ceremony. In fact, prior to the ceremony, Kani's subjects had seized some cattle from "Fynn's people" as punishment for them welcoming annexation and twice abused government messengers who had been sent to invite them to hear the annexation order. During the ceremony some of Kani's messengers hinted that their chief "had become accustomed to look upon Faku as his paramount chief, and that his course would more or less depend upon Faku's decision." A week after the ceremony, Shepstone believed that Kani was directing his subjects to gather ammunition and had sent messengers to Qawukeni to ask for Faku's advice. Colonel Bisset reported a rumour that "Faku intends sending an army into this country directly we leave, and 'eating up' those who have shown allegiance to the Queen's Government." Shepstone wrote to Jenkins asking him to warn the Mpondo king that if Kani continued to be troublesome he would be expelled southwest of the Mtamvuna River and "that Faku will not think of compromising the amicable relations which he has so long maintained with the British Government by countenancing any such scheme as is attributed to Kani and to the Amapondo chief." Colonel Bisset told Jenkins that "I am sure I need not point out to you how unwise it would be for Faku to become hostile to the British Government; surrounded as he is on all sides by tribes in alliance with our Government, he would, in case of war, be destroyed as a nation."[38]

By the end of the first week of January, Kani met Bisset and Shepstone and informed them that he would not submit to the rule of Natal. The two British officials then insisted that Kani move into Faku's territory southwest of the Mtamvuna River, but allowed most of his ImiZizi follow-ers to remain as they were harvesting crops. It seemed that the Natal authorities wanted to get rid of Kani as he would not accept their rule, but at the same time wanted to keep his people in the Alfred Country, possibly as a source of labour for the Natal settlers. Once Kani had left the Alfred Country, the Natalian force moved slowly back to Pietermaritzburg. Contrary to Bisset's predictions, Faku did not send an army across the Mtamvuna River, but merely asked Jenkins to find out which tributary of that river was considered the exact boundary with Natal. Since Faku was not prepared to support him and most of the ImiZizi wished to remain on their land even under the rule of Natal, Kani eventually returned to the Alfred Country in June 1866, after providing the resident magistrate, H.A. Wilson, with forty-seven cattle as a sign of submission.[39]

By April 1866 Governor Wodehouse had become even more deter-mined to acquire Port St. John's, as it seemed inevitable that the Free State Boers would soon overrun Moshoeshoe's Sotho state and sweep south to the coast. As a result, the governor delegated Alfred White, a trader in Pondoland and the Reverend Jenkins's brother-in-law, to nego-tiate with Faku for the British purchase of this harbour along with the navigable portion of the Mzimvubu River. To avoid a repeat of the Currie fiasco of a few years before, Wodehouse authorized White to present the Mpondo king with up to five hundred pounds in order to acquire his writ-ten consent.[40] Arriving at Mfundisweni mission in late June 1866, White and Jenkins lost no time in arranging a conference with the Mpondo king and his councillors.

On the second of July, White and Jenkins arrived at the Mpondo great place and were well received by Faku, whom an earlier visitor had described as "bent, decrepit and senile."[41] The meeting was delayed until the king's messengers could fetch Mqikela, Faku's heir and now the effec-tive ruler of Eastern Pondoland, and Mqeketa, Ndamase's principal coun-cillor from Western Pondoland. Once these two had arrived, Faku explained to White and Jenkins that he wanted to hear their proposal before calling a general meeting of all chiefs to discuss it. In turn, White revealed that the governor's fears about Boer expansion from the interior caused him to desire "without any delay, a cession of the navigable part of the St. John's River, with a certain portion of land adjoining, to the British Government." Continuing, White warned Faku "of the want of respect for native rights on the part of the Boers," and reminded him how the British had protected the Mpondo Kingdom from Boer attacks from Natal in 1840. However, the trader then stated that the British could not afford the expense of sending an army to protect the Mpondo, and suggested that a permanent British presence at Port St. John's would serve as a deterrent to future Boer aggression. Finally, White advised Faku that since the landlocked Boers were eager to secure a port for commerce with the outside world, they would eventually try to take Port St. John's, but would not dare if it were already in British hands.

After White had finished his presentation, Mqikela stated that "they were loth [sic] under any circumstances to part with country, but that if any misfortune compelled them to part with their country it should not be to the Boers or Basutos [sic] or any other nation than the English who had always been their friends." Faku's heir explained that it would take some time to make a decision on this important matter, as Ndamase and all the other chiefs and councillors would have to be called together for consultation. Mqikela then asked, "as the Boers were white people like the English, why could not the English Government prohibit them taking any steps for the possession of Port St. John's?" White told the Mpondo great son that the Boers had once been British subjects but were now independent, just as the Xesibe and Mpondomise had once been Mpondo subjects but were now autonomous. Therefore, according to White, "Faku should at once cede the St. John's and thus save himself any future trouble and annoyance." As a rejoinder, Mqikela stated that Walter Currie, as a representative from the Cape Colony, had acquired Mpondo land on which to settle the Griquas, who were said to be British subjects but soon came into conflict with Faku's people. After a long discussion on this issue, White claimed that Currie had never said the Griquas were British subjects and that since they were not British subjects, the British Government was not responsible for their actions. However, Mqikela and the other Mpondos at the meeting were not convinced and seemed afraid that if they ceded more land to the British, the same thing would happen. Throughout the entire conversation, Faku remained silent, but at the end he asked White to convey to the governor "their cordial greetings and earnest desire that the most friendly relations may always exist between the British Government and themselves." After the meeting, White lamented that Jenkins had previously told the Mpondo king that the governor would be satisfied with only the land up to the top of the heights on both sides of the Mzimvubu mouth. The trader had hoped for a much larger cession, but this now seemed impossible.[42]

Although White expected Faku and his advisors to organize a large conference within a fairly short period, there were several delays. Problems west of the Mzimvubu River prevented Ndamase, who had just financed the erection of a new mission house and church at Buntingville through the sale of royal cattle, from travelling east to his father's Qawukeni great place. Since a drought the previous year meant that most of his people's food reserves had been consumed, Ndamase sent many of his followers to cultivate the more fertile banks of the Mzimvubu River. This weakened the defensive ring of kraals that Ndamase usually maintained around the frontiers of his territory. Seizing this opportunity, Mhlontlo of the Mpondomise, around July 1866, launched an attack against the kraal of one of Ndamase's sons, located on the Tsitsa River, and captured a large number of cattle and horses. Although Ndamase maintained that the Tsitsa formed the northern border of Western Pondoland, the river was also claimed by Mhlontlo. In retaliation for the raid, Ndamase, in early August, mobilized his army and invaded Mpondomise territory to recapture livestock and weaken Mhlontlo's power. While Ndamase had given notice to the missionaries at Shawbury, a station within Mpondomise country, that they should not get involved in the conflict, armed Fingoes from that mission intercepted part of the Mpondo army and seized some cattle. The missionaries fled Shawbury in fear that Ndamase would take revenge against them, but it was later revealed that Mhlontlo, the Mpondomise leader, had forced the Shawbury Fingoes to intervene against the Mpondo.[43]

East of the Mzimvubu River, in early August 1866, between five thousand and eight thousand Mpondo warriors under the command of Mqikela invaded the territory of the Bhaca chief Makaula. Although the Mpondo and Bhaca had been raiding each other for stock since the early 1840s, Bhaca oral tradition attributes this particular campaign to Mpondo claims that the Bhaca were settled on Mpondo land but did not recognize their authority. Initially, the Bhaca fled and the Mpondo fighters advanced, seizing livestock along the way, until they reached Makaula's great place. Surprisingly, the Bhaca leader rallied his men and engaged the Mpondo in vicious hand-to-hand combat, which resulted in the latter's withdrawal toward the Mzimvubu River. An interesting Bhaca oral tradition maintains that the Bhaca spread magical "medicine" on a calf which was then driven into the Mpondo army. As the Mpondo warriors attempted to stab the calf, they actually stabbed one another and their war doctor cried out, "It is the ghost of Ncaphayi, whom we slew in battle." Pursued by the Bhaca for ten miles, Mqikela and his men came upon the Osborn mission, where the inhabitants assembled and mowed down the Mpondo with repeated volleys of musket fire. The Bhaca then arrived and slaughtered many Mpondo around and even inside the mission buildings. Other Mpondo who had run past Osborn were also pursued by the Bhaca, who killed some of them in the water of the Mzimvubu. Although the Mpondo had several hundred firearms, they had not made effective use of them, and suffered up to five hundred fatalities. This was a major setback for Faku's kingdom and a personal humiliation for Mqikela, the future king. Mpondo oral history claims that when Mqikela had asked Faku for permission to attack the Bhaca, the latter refused, saying that a king was supposed to maintain peace. However, Mqikela secretly organized an army to raid the Bhaca and was subsequently defeated. After his heir returned home in disgrace, Faku angrily told him, "I would be glad if they killed you, I told you you were a king."[44]

Faku and his advisors did not discuss these campaigns with White, who was still waiting for the promised conference on the proposed purchase of Port St. John's. Instead, the trader was told that Mqikela had been extremely ill and only recovered in late September. Additionally, White was informed that Ndamase had been delayed, as two of his nephews had died of illness. On 26 September, White visited Faku and Mqikela at the great place and read them a letter from Governor Wodehouse asking why the cession was taking so long. Typically, Faku requested that White thank the governor for his "expressions of friendship and respect, and further to convey to Your Excellency his unaltered fidelity to and respect for your Excellency and the British Government." Directly addressing White's concerns, Mqikela expressed hope that the delays with negotiations had not caused offense and that since the period of mourning for Ndamase's nephews was now over, business would proceed as promised.[45] It is curious that Jenkins, who most likely knew about the conflicts with the Mpondomise and Bhaca since both involved missions, does not seem to have mentioned these events to White or written about them to other colonial officials.

Through White, Governor Wodehouse assured Faku that the British Government had nothing to do with Griqua raids on the Mpondo, and that this situation would not be replicated at Port St. John's as it would be kept under British authority. However, the conference on the Mzimvubu mouth does not seem to have been held, and by the end of 1866 it had become clear that Faku and Mqikela had no intention of making another cession to the British. Perhaps their disastrous campaign against the Bhaca made them nervous about surrendering more land to a foreign power. Fortunately for Wodehouse, his fear of the Free State Boers expanding to the coast was eventually allayed when Moshoeshoe, the Sotho ruler, agreed to come under British protection in 1868.[46]

While Mpondo oral history claims that Faku had given Adam Kok's

Griqua land in exchange for their becoming part of the Mpondo Kingdom, these mixed-race frontiersmen certainly acted like an independent force. Relations between the Griqua and Faku's Mpondo continued to deteriorate throughout the mid-1860s, with both sides accusing one another of stock theft. In late March 1866, Kok had returned five horses to Faku, claiming that they had been stolen by San [Bushmen] who had moved into his country. In written correspondence to the Mpondo ruler, Kok declared that "I hope not to have disturbed the friendship which exists between us by any words in this letter – I do, however, hope that you will also send back all stolen horses which are in your country and which belong to me and my people." In reality, by the end of 1866, Kok was conspiring to organize an alliance of various groups against Faku's Mpondo. However, these plans were abandoned when a British official, J.C. Warner, warned the Griqua leader that "it would be good for his health to drop the idea, and cultivate Faku's friendship." In the first months of 1867, Kok and Faku exchanged friendly communication through Jenkins and the Griqua leader proposed a visit to the Mpondo great place, but it is not known if this took place. Despite these gestures, both the Griquas and Mpondo continued to steal stock from one another, and in July 1867 a group of Griquas even rustled a few of Jenkins's horses from the Mfundisweni mission.[47]

In the final months of his life, Faku continued to maintain cordial relations with the missionaries and became more personally receptive to Christianity. In early September 1866, the chief Mhlangazi, a grandson of Faku, along with his family and followers, visited Qawukeni. Mhlangazi informed the venerable king that he and his people had all converted to Christianity, and requested permission to leave their place and move to Jenkins's Mfundisweni mission. After expressing great surprise, Faku paused for a moment and then said, "My children, you have done right! Go and sit down in peace! We want to remove to that part and be converted also as you have been!" Despite the jeers of the traditionalists, Mhlangazi and his people moved to Jenkins's mission. Around the same time, according to Jenkins, an Mpondo man who had heard the missionaries preaching asked Faku if he had any hope of going to heaven. The old king replied "Is Jenkins going to heaven?" The man stated that "Undoubtedly, he is." Faku, perhaps slightly in jest, then maintained that "I'll go where ever Jenkins goes. When Jenkins gets to heaven he won't stay there without me! I'm sure he'll come out and take me in with him!"[48] However, Faku did not formally convert to Christianity.

The last known communication between Faku – who could no longer eat solid food – and Jenkins concerned rumours of copper deposits in Pondoland. In late April 1867 Jenkins, whose own health had been deteriorating for several years, advised the fading Mpondo king that if copper mines were established in his area, he should place them under colonial control in exchange for an another annual allowance.[49] This became a moot point as the rumour ultimately proved to be false. Faku's last known official act was in August of the same year, when he sent the new lieutenant-governor of Natal, R.W. Keate, an elephant tusk as a sign of goodwill. After four days of illness, the roughly eighty-seven-year-old Mpondo king, who lived in what a missionary described as a "small, filthy hut," passed away on the twenty-ninth of October 1867 at his great place of Qawukeni. As dictated by custom, the late Mpondo king was buried at the entrance of his cattle kraal, which was then abandoned.

Jenkins heard about Faku's death fairly quickly and informed H.A. Wilson, Natal's administrator of the Alfred Country, who eagerly asked "Will the Pondo nation be divided between Damas [sic] and Umqikela?" In mid-November, two weeks after the king's death, Mqikela sent messengers to Palmerton to ask the Reverend John Allsop, a Wesleyan missionary, to write an official letter to the governor informing him of Faku's death. Later the same day, Mqikela, accompanied by the Mpondo royal councillors, arrived at the station and asked the missionary to write that "he desires to walk in the steps of his late father, and always show himself the ally of the British Sovereign." Additionally, the new king requested the governor's advice on what to do about the Griquas, who were allegedly preparing to attack the Mpondo in retaliation for stock theft by Sotho and Bushmen who were living in Mpondo territory.[50] Responding with what Shepstone described as a "patriarchal lecture," Keate informed Mqikela that:

> the Amampondo people have lost a safe guide and a judicious ruler, and the British Government a firm friend. Umqikela is old enough, however, to have observed his father's policy, and to have been convinced of its wisdom. If he will consider the past history of his tribe, he will find that its present importance and numbers have been the result of its peace. The traditionary policy of the Amapondos has been peace, and this policy has made them the people they are.
>
> The Lieutenant-Governor of Natal feels assured from the tone of Umqikela's message that he has determined to follow his father's example, and while expressing his deep regret for the loss which we all feel, His Excellency is encouraged to hope that the same good faith and friendship will subsist between the Government and the Amampondo people under Umqikela as under his father, Faku.[51]

After reminding Mqikela of his responsibility to protect the missionaries in his area, Keate's letter expressed doubt as to whether the Griquas were preparing to attack the Mpondo and warned the new Mpondo ruler to prevent his subjects from stealing from the Griqua.[52]

During the 1850s and 1860s, colonial officials from both Natal and the Cape put increasing pressure on Faku's Mpondo state for various land concessions. To the northeast, Theophilus Shepstone's attempt, in 1854, to establish his own personal African chiefdom/labour reservoir between the Mzimkhulu and Mtamvuna rivers was ultimately abandoned. However, ten years later, after Faku had reasserted his authority over this area, a new political climate enabled Natal to annex all the land up to the Mtamvuna, expelling those local leaders who would not accept colonial rule. To the southwest, in 1855, M.B. Shaw took advantage of his grazing rights in the Mdumbi area to set up a private chiefdom which became a rival to Ndamase's power in that area. As with Shepstone, Shaw became an embarrassment to his colonial superiors and was forced to retire from Mpondo territory. However, the most serious encroachment was in 1861, when Walter Currie, with the governor's support, bullied Faku into verbally giving away the northern half of his kingdom, a portion of which was then given to Adam Kok's Griqua. With horses and guns, the Griqua quickly became the most serious local threat to Faku's state. Given all these incidents, it is not surprising that Faku and Mqikela, in 1866, delayed negotiations over the British proposal to purchase the Mzimvubu mouth (Port St. John's) and eventually declined the offer. Although Faku's advanced age meant that Mqikela was effectively in control of the situation, the Mpondo royals had learned that their alliance with the colonial government was necessary for security, but that ceding land to the Europeans could only be disastrous.

Conclusion

*I*n examining Faku's career as king of the Mpondo, there are a number of recurring themes that merit further discussion. Most of these concern his reaction to the various forms of European contact that continued throughout his reign. Since Wesleyan missionaries featured prominently in many aspects of Faku's life after 1830, they will be mentioned in several of the following thematic sections. Additionally, in order to better understand Faku's place in history, it is necessary to compare him briefly with some other southern African leaders from the early to mid-nineteenth century.

Faku and Christianity

As Faku was nearly fifty when he first met European missionaries, his spirituality must have been already well developed. There is no doubt that he shared the same religious beliefs as his subjects, which involved the intervention of ancestors in worldly affairs and the malevolent supernatural power of witches. Of course, this conception of reality often clashed with the beliefs and doctrines of Christianity as interpreted by Victorian British missionaries, who were convinced that they were bringing "civilization" to a "savage" people. Many common practices within Mpondo society, such as polygamy and even dancing, were seen by the Wesleyans as sinful, if not satanic.

When Faku initially accepted the Wesleyans into his kingdom, it was not because he was interested in their spiritual message. Typical of many pre-colonial African rulers, the Mpondo king allowed missionaries to live and work in his territory in order to open a channel of diplomatic communication with the powerful Cape Colony, to encourage trade in luxury Western goods and to prevent raiding from other groups (including Europeans) who knew that missions enjoyed special colonial protection. Once a mission was established near his capital, Faku came to understand that there were some significant differences between the Wesleyans and other Europeans he had met, such as traders and hunters. Placing the missionaries within the context of his own worldview, Faku, at first, thought that they were powerful rainmakers who could enhance his people's agricultural activities. While he was soon disappointed in their supernatural abilities, the Mpondo king relied on the Wesleyans as diplomatic agents for the rest of his life.

As the missionaries mastered the Xhosa language and began to spread their spiritual message throughout the Mpondo Kingdom, some of Faku's family became interested in this new set of beliefs. The king's mother, Mamgcambe, seems to have been the first member of the royal household to publicly admit to being moved by the missionaries' words. Although she never formally converted, Mamgcambe participated in Christian services and education for the rest of her days and made a deathbed request that no witch-hunting was to take place because of her demise. At least one of Faku's wives, whose name is not recorded, had a similar experience. However, it must be remembered that these women showed interest in Christianity at the same time that the Mpondo Kingdom was trying to cultivate good relations with the Cape Colony, and their openness to these new beliefs may have been, at least partially, a diplomatic manoeuvre. It is interesting that female members of the royal family were the first ones to partially convert. In other parts of the Eastern Cape, such as among the Rharhabe who were closer to the Cape Colony, the mothers, wives and daughters of chiefs established intimate contacts with the local white missionaries and their families. Was this because women saw Christianity as a vehicle to escape some of the gender-based restrictions of Mpondo society? Or was it that they were actually less constrained by traditionalist structures of authority than male chiefs? This might be a fruitful topic for future research.

Despite a thirty-year association with the Reverend Thomas Jenkins, Faku himself never showed any ardent inclination towards conversion. Faku tried to placate the Wesleyans when they objected to the "smelling out" of supposed witches, but this practice continued throughout his rule. Towards the end of his life, Faku could joke that he knew Jenkins so well that he did not have to be a Christian to be allowed into heaven. Some writers have suggested that African rulers of this era could not openly become Christians because they did not want to jeopardize their authority by offending conservative elements within their societies. This may have been correct with regard to Moshoeshoe of the Sotho, who first encountered missionaries at the same point in his life as Faku. On the other hand, relatively junior members of a royal family, such as Kama of the Gqunukhwebe near the Cape Colony, could afford to convert and use their alliance with the Europeans in order to increase their personal power. However, Faku, who was in his sixties and seventies when dealing with the missionaries, was almost certainly a relatively conservative individual who saw that Christianity threatened to unravel the fabric of the very society in which he enjoyed the highest status. He had nothing to gain by converting and possibly everything to lose. It is also likely that he simply did not believe what the missionaries were preaching. To Faku, it must have sounded like utter nonsense.

While Faku was and is generally seen as a friend and protector of the missionaries, very few conversions were forthcoming in Pondoland during his long reign. As in other areas, the majority of mission people were outcasts from their own communities such as those accused of witchcraft or opportunists who wanted to gain power through association with Europeans. Faku's principle sons, Ndamase and Mqikela, both continued their father's policy of allowing the missionaries to operate freely in their respective areas, but did not convert themselves. It was only after colonial rule was established in the 1890s that Christianity became popular among the Mpondo. It could be said that one ironic legacy of Faku's reign, although he was always friendly to missionaries, was to delay the spread of Christianity among his people.

Faku and the Military

Throughout most of Faku's reign, the Mpondo Kingdom was continually embroiled in either defensive or offensive warfare. Therefore, military capability was an extremely important aspect of the state. Early in his career, Faku was responsible for a major military adaptation that gave his people an advantage over some of their neighbours. The ban on circumcision schools in the 1820s meant that all the young men of the kingdom would be healthy enough to fight and could be mobilized on short notice. This was a radical development and illustrates that Faku was not completely bound by the demands of his culture. On the battlefield, the Mpondo king was a skilled and decisive leader who employed terrain to get the best possible advantage and could easily identify and exploit an enemy's weakness. Faku was also wise enough to recognize and cultivate the special courage and resourcefulness of his eldest son, Ndamase, who led the Mpondo army on many occasions. However, the basic principle of Mpondo warfare under Faku was to overwhelm their enemy with superior numbers and this was not conducive to later confrontations with Europeans who used firearms.

Unfortunately, as Faku passed the age of fifty he became less innovative in military matters, and this corresponded exactly with an increase in colonial intrusion. Unlike Moshoeshoe, whose famous Sotho armed cavalry was feared by both the British and Boers, Faku and Ndamase did not even try to build up an arsenal of firearms and a cadre of trained musketeers. As a result, Faku, monarch of one of the largest states in southern Africa at the time, was often frequently intimidated by fairly small groups of European gunmen, such as those led by H.F. Fynn, Pretorius and Currie. Where Maqoma and Sandile of the Rharhabe used guerrilla warfare to reduce the effectiveness of colonial firepower, Faku chose to avoid hostilities with Europeans at all costs. In the final analysis, this was certainly better for his subjects, who never had to endure the scorched-earth campaigns employed by the British further to the west. Even with guns and guerrilla tactics, African societies could not survive colonial attacks on their productive capacity, in other words their crops and herds.

Faku and His Neighbours

From the earliest point in his career, Faku approached his African neighbours in a rather pragmatic manner. He entered into alliances and embarked upon raiding expeditions depending on his interests and objectives. Faced with a strong Zulu state and Port Natal gunmen to his northeast, the Mpondo king, in the 1820s and 1830s, frequently raided west at the expense of the Bomvana and Thembu. Once the power of the Cape Colony began to extend into the Transkei region from 1828, Faku attempted to use his association with the British to dominate other African states. The treaty of 1844 seemed to represent the ultimate success of this strategy as it gave the Mpondo ruler authority over a much-expanded territory, most of which was inland to the north. At this point he also began to foster an alliance with another major power in the region, Moshoeshoe, the Sotho ruler. However, the treaty eventually caused more problems than it was worth, as Faku found it difficult to control some of the new groups under his jurisdiction and he was often held responsible for their conflicts with neighbouring settlers in Natal. Both before and after the treaty, it was incredibly difficult for Faku to control stock theft in a large open area where domestic animals could be moved quickly and most of the population engaged in a pastoral economy.

A little-known fact about Faku is that throughout his life he was intimately involved in trade with both other Africans and Europeans. Ivory and cattle hides, and maybe captives in his early days, were exchanged for beads, blankets and iron implements. In this context, the 1844 treaty gave

Faku a continuous supply of luxury items that could be converted into livestock or other desired commodities. On the other hand, the conditions of the treaty forced the Mpondo ruler to eventually break ties with local San [Bushmen] hunters, who had been some of his most important suppliers of ivory, because they were accused of stealing livestock from Natal settlers. It is rather surprising that Faku did not use his trading network and connections to build up a supply of firearms, but he may have thought that this would jeopardize his relations with the British. Also, with the expansion of colonial settlements and the compression of African groups into smaller areas, elephants began to disappear, which meant that Faku's ivory trading probably declined in the last half of his life.

In dealing with the Europeans, Faku frequently tried to play one colonial power off against another. He did this effectively with the Cape British and the Natalia Boers in the early 1840s, but this became more difficult after the British annexed Natal. In fact, Faku played a major, yet often forgotten, role in convincing the British to formally occupy Natal in 1842 and 1843. Toward the end of Faku's life, in negotiations over Port St. John's, the British attempted, albeit unsuccessfully, to reverse this tactic against the Mpondo by warning that the Free State Boers might overrun the Sotho and advance on the Pondoland coast. It should not be forgotten that a dominant aim of Faku's alliance with the Cape was to prevent European firepower, including that of the Boers, from being used against his people.

After 1830, the Wesleyan missionaries quickly became a central part of Faku's plan to develop and maintain cordial relations with the Cape Colony. In return for access to Mpondo territory and protection, the missionaries functioned as unofficial, and sometimes official, diplomats for the Cape. For example, Jenkins's correspondence and journal, like those of other Wesleyans in the area, clearly shows that his thirty-year relationship with Faku and the Mpondo was mostly dominated by political concerns. At first glance, this might indicate that the Wesleyans in nineteenth-century Transkei were typical examples of missionaries who were primarily concerned with advancing colonial interests. However, unlike the well-known stereotypes of missionaries as either naive humanitarians or covert agents of colonial conquest, the Wesleyans in the Mpondo Kingdom played a variety of roles, many of which were often extremely ambiguous. Thomas Jenkins and his wife Mary showed obvious sympathy for the Mpondo in general and Faku in particular, and often stayed out of matters where they knew that the colonial authorities were likely to force an unfavourable agreement upon their hosts. Of course, Jenkins and other Wesleyans knew that they had to live far from colonial protection and did not want to seem responsible for anything that could provoke hostility with the Mpondo. On the other hand, some Wesleyans consistently sided with the Cape Colony, as during the War of 1835 when the Reverend W.J. Davis attempted to bully Faku into aiding the colony. Another possible reason for the overtly political concerns of Jenkins and his colleagues was that their Methodist denomination had developed as a splinter group of the Anglican church in late-eighteenth-century Britain because the latter was not involved enough in worldly concerns such as poverty relief. Therefore, Methodist ministers of the early to mid-nineteenth century would not generally have had an overly academic/theological background. In the same time and region, missionaries from other denominations, such as the Presbyterians of the Glasgow Missionary Society, wrote much more about their theological concerns and reflections than the Pondoland Methodists, who would record in their diaries that they conducted services but would not overly analyze them.

Faku's relationships with white colonial officials often varied a great deal from person to person. While Faku consistently placated the Cape, he would not let some colonial officials push him too far, especially when he knew they had little support from Cape Town or were not all that personally intimidating. M.B. Shaw, the son of the Wesleyan director, tried to use his position as British resident agent to build up his own chiefdom in Mpondo territory. Faku and Ndamase dealt decisively with the problem and mobilized their missionary associates to remove Shaw. Conversely, H.F. Fynn, who was involved in a combined Zulu/Port Natal raid against the Mpondo in 1828 and was sent to Pondoland on official business by several governors, always seems to have inspired Faku's fear and compliance. This may indicate that Fynn, at least through Faku's eyes, was a particularly terrifying visitor with an unrivalled reputation for violence. If the Mpondo king had a near lifelong nemesis, it was certainly Fynn. It was the Wesleyans, notably Jenkins, who opposed many of Fynn's abuses as British Resident and displayed an obvious personal dislike for him. Similarly, Walter Currie, although he had less experience in Pondoland than Fynn, also seems to have been able to bully the Mpondo ruler into accepting unfair agreements. Currie's history as a battle-hardened veteran of the colonial police who led an invasion of Gcalekaland in 1858 must have been well known to Faku. However, to be fair, when Faku met Currie the former was in his old age and perhaps more vulnerable to extortion.

Faku and Domestic Affairs

Because of the nature of the evidence, more is known about Faku's external relations than his internal governance of the Mpondo Kingdom.

Like Mzilikazi, whose Khumalo clan formed the nucleus of a number of unrelated groups that constituted the Ndebele Kingdom, Faku kept the original Mpondo people together, but also forged a powerful state from many diverse communities. As the historian Omer-Cooper noted in the 1960s, Faku was certainly a nation-builder.

One of his earliest accomplishments was to stimulate an agricultural revolution among his subjects in the 1820s. Because of this, famine was almost unheard of in Pondoland throughout the nineteenth century. The intertwining military and health reasons for the abolition of male initiation schools has already been discussed, but it should be recognized that this must have certainly caused a great deal of social upheaval as the customary transition to manhood was officially eliminated. To embark on such a radical adaptation must have required considerable courage and foresight. Of course, some people resisted this change and continued to perform the ceremony in secret.

During the first half of his reign, Faku was a relatively autocratic ruler who did not depend upon a large council for advice. Under his rule, the Mpondo Kingdom became the most centralized state among nineteenth-century Xhosa-speaking people. Eventually, as Faku became older, he grew more open to suggestions from his sons, sub-chiefs, councillors and missionaries. Alliance with the Cape Colony in 1844 also gave him additional security, and he could afford to take more time in making consultative decisions. In Mpondo oral tradition, he is remembered as a great and just ruler.

Faku was the last king of a united Mpondo state. His division of the kingdom into east and west remains a reality to this day. Providing both Mqikela and Ndamase, his main sons, with their own areas of jurisdiction probably prevented a bloody civil war, which would have sapped the kingdom's strength. However, this divided the power of the large Mpondo state, making it more susceptible to colonial manipulation and annexation toward the end of the century.

Was Faku a Successful Ruler?

As far as is known, Faku was the greatest of all pre-colonial Mpondo kings and arguably one of the most effective rulers of a Xhosa-speaking population. Ruling in a period of intruding alien beliefs and serious threats to his sovereignty, Faku's pragmatic approach ensured the continued survival of his state and royal family. Today, Qawukeni, still the great place of Eastern Pondoland, is in roughly the same place as Faku's capital. Faku was neither a heroic martyr of early resistance to colonial invasion nor an opportunistic traitor who supported foreign conquest in order to enhance his position. Faku's overall policy lay somewhere between these two extremes. However, it was not until 1894, twenty-seven years after his death, that the Mpondo Kingdom, despite its proximity to established settler colonies, became the last African state in the sub-continent to come under colonial rule. While some historians have suggested that this was because Pondoland was not a top priority for colonial acquisition, the natural harbour at the Mzimvubu mouth (Port St. John's) was obviously attractive, and many colonial officials had attempted, with varying degrees of success, to gain land concessions from the Mpondo. Therefore, Faku's personal influence and negotiating skill must have had something to do with the longevity of his state. Also, Faku established a tradition in which colonial officials tended to treat the Mpondo aristocracy with a degree of respect not afforded to other African rulers. This meant that even after colonial annexation, the hereditary kings and chiefs of Pondoland, at least until the Native Administration Act of 1927, exercised more real authority over the local population of Pondoland than their counterparts in other areas of the Transkei Territories, where state-appointed headmen became more important.

A Final Note

In spite of Faku's stature as the most outstanding Mpondo king, his grave, which is surrounded by a maize field in the hills not far from today's Qawukeni, has no marking save for a few old fence posts. During the 1970s and 1980s, the Mpondo royal family attempted to erect a monument on Faku's final resting place, but were prevented from doing so by the Transkei government of K.D. Matanzima, himself a Thembu chief. Supposedly, Matanzima feared that the monument would unite and mobilize the Mpondo people against his Bantustan regime. Therefore, out of respect for the memory of Faku, none of the graves of the subsequent kings of Eastern Pondoland, such as the late Botha Sigcau who was the father of the current paramount chief, are marked with a name.

Pondoland after Faku

The End of Independence

Faku died at a time when colonial dominance was closing in on the Mpondo state. Less than six months later, in early March 1868, the Reverend Jenkins, advisor to the late Mpondo king for nearly thirty years, also passed away. This left Mqikela, now thirty-seven, without the benefit of an experienced missionary with contacts in the colonial governments of both the Cape and Natal. Although Mqikela seems to have become the new Mpondo king without any opposition, in effect he was only the ruler east of the Mzimvubu River, as Ndamase, now in his sixties, had long established his power over Western Pondoland. Soon after inheriting power, Mqikela launched a major military offensive against the Bhaca, who had defeated him badly in 1866, possibly to bring them back into the orbit of the Mpondo state. This attack was repelled at the cost of many Mpondo warriors. Observing that the Mpondo could no longer depend upon their superior numbers to win battles, Mqikela began to transform his army by acquiring large numbers of firearms from European traders. This was also important considering the persistent conflict with the Griqua, who had extensive expertise with firearms, and the continued colonial interest in gaining more Mpondo land.

From 1873 to 1878, all the African groups in the Transkei, except the Mpondo, signed treaties with the Cape and accepted white magistrates. While Pondoland itself had become somewhat peripheral to colonial interests, which were now centred on diamond fields in the interior, the British became determined to control all the ports along the South

Notes to the Afterword are on pp. 185-86.

African coast, including the Mzimvubu mouth. Ndamase, Faku's eldest son, died in 1876 leaving his heir, Nqwiliso, as the ruler of Western Pondoland. In 1878 Sir Bartle Frere, the British High Commissioner for South Africa, offered to purchase Port St. John's from Mqikela, but as in 1867, he refused. Frere then officially "deposed " Mqikela, which only meant that his one-hundred-pound annual subsidy, inherited from Faku, was discontinued. In turn, Frere officially recognized Nqwiliso, ruler of the Mpondo west of the Mzimvubu River, as a completely independent king in exchange for the sale of the Mzimvubu mouth (Port St. John's) for one thousand pounds. This gave Nqwiliso formal independence as ruler of Western Pondoland and provided him with enough money to buy firearms. Despite Mqikela's objections, Port St. John's finally came under British control. During this crisis, Mary Jenkins, widow of the Reverend Jenkins, tried to champion Mpondo interests by writing letters to the colonial administration, but this was ineffective. Two years later, during the rebellion of the Mpondomise against colonial taxation in 1880, Nqwiliso endeared himself to the colonial government by sending an Mpondo army north to relieve the besieged colonial town of Tsolo. Obtaining colonial support was probably not Nqwiliso's only objective in siding against the Mpondomise rebels, as their main leader, Mhlontlo, had been involved in bitter struggles with the western Mpondo in the 1860s.

In the early 1880s, Mqikela began drinking heavily, and Mhlangaso, one of the king's councillors who had been educated at the Lovedale mission in the Cape and was determined to preserve Mpondo independence, became the dominant personality at the Qawukeni great place. Making an alliance with local European traders who did not want to pay duties to the British government, Mhlangaso, in 1884, imposed tariffs on goods entering Eastern Pondoland from Port St. John's, which made it a less desirable port of commerce. Mhlangaso and his trader allies planned to establish an independent Port Grosvenor on the Eastern Pondoland coastline and entered into negotiations with German agents for support against the British. With the possible involvement of a rival colonial power, the British, in 1886, annexed the entire Pondoland coast and forbade any ships to land at the new port. Mhlangaso mobilized an army of 15,000 which was quickly disbanded when it became obvious that the British were actually preparing to invade Pondoland. The chiefs of Eastern Pondoland accepted the annexation of Port St. John's as well as the territory of the Xesibe, formerly a rebellious vassal state, and sold the British the portion of the Cape/Natal road that passed through their land.

With Mqikela's death in 1887, Mhlangaso's dominance began to be questioned. Although Mqikela died without a recognized heir, Sigcau, an adult son from a much junior wife or possibly a concubine, was adopted by the late ruler's great wife, Masarhili. Therefore, Sigcau became the new king of Eastern Pondoland and was supported by many chiefs who resented the influence of the councillor Mhlangaso. By 1889 Sigcau had come to dominate the great place. In 1891 tensions peaked between Sigcau and Mhlangaso with the outbreak of a civil war. While the king had more followers, Mhlangaso enlisted the aide of the ImiZizi, an Mpondo sub-group near the Natal border who had acquired the advantage of breechloading rifles. Periodic warfare continued for several years, and after a major but indecisive battle between the opposing Mpondo factions in 1894, Cecil Rhodes, premier of the Cape, annexed both Eastern and Western Pondoland without any serious resistance. Mhlangaso was sent into exile and his followers dispersed throughout the territory. During the civil war, Sigcau had granted mineral, railway and land concessions to a colonial company for six thousand pounds in various instalments and 1,900 pounds annually. However, after annexation the colonial state took over these concessions and reduced Sigcau's annual payment to one thousand pounds. West of the Mzimvubu River, Nqwiliso was provided with seven hundred pounds per annum, which included his money for Port St. John's. This made the Mpondo rulers dependent upon the colonial government for their income, and in 1895 European magistrates began collecting hut tax from the Mpondo people. Pondoland was the last African state in Southern Africa to fall under colonial rule.[1]

Pondoland in the Early Twentieth Century

In 1910, in the Union of South Africa, the British colonies of the Cape and Natal, as well as the former Boer republics of the Transvaal and Orange Free State, were brought under one settler-dominated government. This led to the creation of laws, such as the Natives Land Act of 1913, which further pushed African people into small impoverished reserves in which the only way to survive was for men to enter into the migrant labour system in the mines. In response to these pressures, members of the educated African elite formed the African National Congress (ANC) in 1912 in order to peacefully change the system from within. It was within this general context that Pondoland became, at various times, a centre of rural protest against external government interference.

In the early twentieth century, the Mpondo paramounts and chiefs enjoyed more power over their local communities than their counterparts in other regions of the Transkei. This was because Pondoland had successfully rejected the Council system, which had reduced the role of hereditary paramount chiefs (the colonial term for African kings) in land allocation and other matters, and elevated state appointed, local headmen. This did not mean that the Mpondo paramounts remained traditionalist. In this period, the paramount chiefs of both Western and Eastern Pondoland advanced either Westernization or traditionalism when it suited their interests. Schools were built and a Western-style educated class began to emerge.

The first major crisis in Eastern Pondoland in the twentieth century was protest over government-sponsored cattle-dipping programs, which were designed to combat the East Coast fever spreading south through Natal. In order to build tanks for dipping, the government, in 1906, introduced a one-off levy of two shillings and sixpence from every person who paid hut tax. With the further spread of the disease, this became an annual levy in 1909. In addition to resenting this additional taxation, many Mpondo people believed that bringing cattle together at the tanks would spread the disease further, feared that the dipping was harmful to their animals and resented the new fence built along the Natal border. While Mhlanga, a son of the late Mqikela and the regent of Eastern Pondoland after the death of Sigcau in 1905, supported dipping, the Mpondo people organized meetings to express their disquiet over the issue. The popular anti-dipping campaign was backed by Masarhili, great wife of the late king Mqikela and adopted mother of the late Sigcau, and a few councillors who were displeased with Mhlanga's regency. When Mhlanga died in late 1909, the government gave Marelane, the royal heir who had been attending school at the Lovedale mission, quick instruction on the dangers of East Coast fever and rushed him back to Eastern Pondoland. After some vacillation, Marelane chastised the anti-dipping camp and used his guards to enforce dipping regulations. Tension over dipping continued in Pondoland until 1915, and the Mpondo people were implicated in an armed uprising against dipping in neighbouring East Griqualand from 1914 to 1917. The South African state used Marelane's power as paramount to suppress popular protest. Since East Coast fever seemed less threatening to Western Pondoland, dipping did not become as controversial there, but Mangala, a son of the late Nqwiliso and regent after the 1912 death of his brother, paramount chief Bokleni, enforced a government ban on the movement of cattle until 1915.[2]

The Industrial and Commercial Workers Union (ICU), the first national African-organized labour union in South Africa, had been formed in urban centres such as the port of East London, but eventually spread into the rural areas of Transkei. In 1927 the ICU became involved in a millenarian movement in Pondoland which advocated the killing of pigs and abstinence from lard as a form of protection from lightning. The ICU opened branches in Bizana (an Eastern Pondoland town) in 1928 and Ngqeleni (a location in Western Pondoland) in 1929, but these were not very successful. Partially because one of the main organizers of the Independent ICU (IICU) was Joel Magade from Tabankulu in Eastern Pondoland, this new union, formed in 1929, cultivated strong support in rural areas throughout the Transkei. The increasing radicalism of the IICU prompted members of the mission-educated elite in Bizana, who advocated more moderate means to address such grievances as low pay, to break up a union meeting attended mostly by women and a few traditionalist men. In rural areas the IICU adopted millenarian prophecies of impending apocalypse to encourage people to get magical protection through obtaining yellow union cards. However, financial mismanagement and police repression caused the decline of the IICU by the early 1930s.[3]

Frightened by growing working-class consciousness among Africans, the South African government passed the Native Administration Act of 1927. The aim of this law was to break down African working-class protest such as the ICU, which was emanating from growing urban areas, and to emphasize ethnic divisions based in rural areas. Part of this strategy involved reviving and coopting African "traditional leaders," chiefs and kings, into the system of administration in rural areas where it was hoped that they would become symbols and brokers of ethnic/tribal affiliation. Ironically, this new law led to the reduction of the real power of Pondoland paramount chiefs as it induced the state to unilaterally impose the Transkei Territories General Council system on Eastern Pondoland, which had no council, and Western Pondoland, which had accepted a separate council a few years before. In Western Pondoland, Victor Poto Ndamase, who had become paramount chief in 1918 and who wrote a book in the 1920s which emphasized the historic influence of the Mpondo monarchy, accepted the Transkei Council system.[4] In Eastern Pondoland, in 1939, the South African state intervened in the succession dispute that had arisen after the death of the paramount Marelane in 1921. Although Nelson Sigcau, Marelane's son, was widely recognized as the heir by virtue of Mpondo custom, some local chiefs and state agents manipulated the situation so that Botha Sigcau, Nelson's half-brother, became paramount chief of Eastern Pondoland.[5]

The Pondoland Revolt

After the election of the Afrikaner Nationalist Party in 1948, the official state policy became apartheid, or separate development of races and ethnic groups. As part of a series of segregationist legislation, the Bantu

Authorities Act of 1951 identified a number of African reserves that would be given self-government and eventually become independent states known as homelands, or Bantustans. This system was intended to further divide the African population along ethnic lines and show the international community that South Africa had given a type of self-determination to its African majority. As in 1927, chiefs were to play a central role in this policy, and the 1951 law gave them not only salaries but sweeping powers in the would-be homelands. Of course, any chief who displeased the government could be removed. In Transkei, a large area in the Eastern Cape earmarked for self-rule, the Bantu Authorities Act was implemented in 1956. This led to corrupt paramount chiefs and their subordinate chiefs extorting money from local people in the form of livestock taxes or as bribes for favourable decisions in court cases or land allocations. Supporters of a chief could even collect money from villagers in order to buy the chief a car. Recently, at a hearing of South Africa's Truth and Reconciliation Commission in Eastern Pondoland, Mr. Clement Gxabu, a veteran of the Pondoland Rebellion of 1959-60 which will be discussed below, described how the role of chiefs in African society had changed:

> there came a time when . . . as the chiefs were leading the people they were representing the people and the desires of the people. Then unfortunately there came a time when they were working together with the government of the day. Then there was a division between the people and the chiefs. They would be given decisions by the government to take to the people. The people rejected such decisions. Then the chiefs would go to the magistrate, the magistrate who led the chiefs. Then the magistrate would ask whether the chief was being led or was he leading, was he a ruler or was he being ruled over? Then he would come back to us and say that we are going to obey him, no matter what.[6]

Towards the end of 1959, violence broke out in the Eastern Pondoland town of Bizana when the local people asked Mr. Saul Mabude, an advocate of Bantu Authorities and Chairman of the District Authority, to explain Bantu Authorities at a public meeting. When Mr. Mabude, for fear of his life, did not attend the meeting, an angry crowd surrounded and burned his house. The security forces responded by terrorizing the rural people of Eastern Pondoland. In turn, the Mpondo people began to organize across many districts and made it clear to Paramount Chief Botha Sigcau that Bantu Authorities would operate over their dead bodies and that he was the "boot-licker of Verwoerd,"[7] the South African prime minister.

In March 1960, Mpondo people from various districts came together to form the "Hill Committee," to coordinate the activities of the movement that became known as iKongo, a Xhosaization of congress, which seemed to be a reference to the African National Congress (ANC) which was gaining popularity at the time. Initially, the Hill Committee invited government agents and magistrates to hear their grievances, but when they were ignored, the rebels began to attack policemen, chiefs and anyone who was known to favour Bantu Authorities. The most serious incident of the rebellion took place near Ngquza Hill, between the Eastern Pondoland towns of Bizana and Lusikisiki where police in vehicles and helicopters fired on a meeting of Mpondos that was displaying a white flag of truce. At least eleven Mpondos were killed, thirty were wounded and twenty-one were arrested. At the commission of inquiry held shortly after the massacre, Mpondo people demanded the withdrawal of Bantu Authorities, relief from taxes, removal of Paramount Chief Botha Sigcau and representation in the South African Parliament. These demands were ignored, and in response the rebels initiated a boycott of white-owned stores in Pondoland.

Leading to another incidence of violence, Vukayibambe Sigcau, a half-brother of Paramount Chief Botha Sigcau, guided police to a rebel meeting near Flagstaff, another Eastern Pondoland town, in November 1960. The police began firing tear gas and guns, resulting in one Mpondo being killed and four others wounded. In a revenge attack, Vukayibambe Sigcau and two of his headmen were killed. This caused a dramatic increase in the number of police sent to Eastern Pondoland. Home guards were organized and more security was provided to chiefs. In December 1960, as the Transkei homeland moved toward self-government, a state of emergency was declared in Eastern Pondoland which banned meetings, restricted people entering and leaving the area and gave banishment powers to chiefs. As a result, thousands of men and women were imprisoned in 1961 and twenty people from Eastern Pondoland were sentenced to death for their part in the revolt. Eventually, the Mpondo people were subdued by force, but the killing of unpopular councillors and chiefs continued until 1969.

The Pondoland rebels did not seem to be against the institution of chieftaincy, just the way in which it was being manipulated and used against them by the Bantu Authorities Act. Wanna Johnson, a member of the Mpondo royal family and of the ANC, and a leader of the iKongo movement, was killed at Ngquza Hill. Also at the Ngquza Hill meeting, the rebels were preparing to discuss the possibility of approaching Victor Poto Ndamase, the respected paramount chief of Western Pondoland, about their problems with Botha Sigcau, their paramount in Eastern

Pondoland. After the Ngquza massacre, the movement sent a message to Nelson Sigcau, former claimant to the Eastern Pondoland paramountcy, to ask him "what he thinks of what is happening to the Pondo people,"[8] but he did not reply.

The role of African nationalist organizations such as the ANC and the Pan Africanist Congress (PAC) is not clear. After Ngquza, iKongo representatives approached Chief Albert Luthuli, the president of the ANC who was being detained at the time, asking for guidance. Luthuli advised the rebels to stop fighting and work to change the system from within.[9] However, it is certain that ANC Youth League activists became involved in directing the course of the Pondoland Revolt. For example, Anderson Khumani Ganyile, an ANC Youth League member who had been expelled from the University of Fort Hare in 1960 after a student uprising, returned home to Bizana where he joined the rebels. It is important to understand that political organizations like the ANC, whose rural programs of action were almost non-existent at this time, did not plan the revolt, but that certain members became involved later.[10]

Homeland Politics and the Mpondo Elite

Transkei's constitution, which was written in Pretoria in the early 1960s, ensured that chiefs, with fifty-eight seats in the legislature, retained political dominance over commoners, who were allocated only forty-five seats, to be chosen by adult male suffrage. In 1963 an election was held in the Transkei for the homeland's first government. Two candidates contested the position of chief minister. Kaiser D. Matanzima, a minor Thembu chief with support in Pretoria, advocated complete autonomy for the homeland in keeping with the spirit of separate development. The other candidate was Paramount Chief Victor Poto Ndamase of Western Pondoland, an advocate of multi-racialism, who campaigned on the platform that Transkei should not get independence but that it should be represented in the South African parliament. Supporting Victor Poto was Sabata Dalindyebo, the respected paramount chief of the Thembu and as such a rival of the upstart Matanzima. In Eastern Pondoland, the South African government gave Paramount Chief Botha Sigcau a large farm in exchange for his endorsement of Matanzima. Although Victor Poto Ndamase was supported by thirty-eight elected commoners in the Transkei legislature, forty-seven chiefs threw in their lot with Matanzima, who then became first chief minister of the Transkei. In Eastern Pondoland, the election was held in the repressive atmosphere of a state of emergency, and eight candidates from the Pondoland Peoples Party, a group with ties to the rebels, were arrested. After the election, Matanzima formed the ruling Transkei National Independence Party (TNIP) and Victor Poto Ndamase organized the Democratic Party (DP), which functioned as an official opposition. Under Victor Poto's leadership from 1963 to 1966, the DP of Transkei cultivated ties with the South African Liberal Party under the famous novelist Alan Paton.[11]

After Transkei's "independence" in 1976, Kaiser Matanzima became prime minister, with Botha Sigcau, the paramount chief of Eastern Pondoland who had supported Bantu Authorities, taking on the largely ceremonial role of president. At the same time, Tutor Ndamase, son of the late Victor Poto who had died in 1972 and new paramount of Western Pondoland, left the opposition DP and joined the ruling TNIP. This sudden shift of allegiance was supposedly because the people of Western Pondoland, at a mass meeting, had decided to support the independent status of Transkei. However, political scientist Roger Southall suggests that it was rather because Tutor Ndamase wanted to enjoy "the spoils of government."[12] In 1977, Stella Sigcau, daughter of Botha Sigcau and a graduate of the University of Fort Hare – which had become a centre of protest against the state – also left the crumbling opposition to join Matanzima's cabinet. At this point, within the Transkei government, there seemed to be an alliance between the Thembu chiefs rallied around Matanzima and the Mpondo elites. This quickly broke down when, in 1978, Stella Sigcau and five members of the legislature from the Qawukeni region in Eastern Pondoland left the TNIP to eventually form the Transkei National Progressive Party (TNPP), a grouping of disenchanted Mpondo and Sotho elites that became the new official opposition.[13]

After Botha Sigcau passed away in 1978, Kaiser Matanzima arranged for himself to become president with his brother George Matanzima as a puppet prime minister. Subsequently, the Matanzimas began to ruthlessly suppress the opposition. In 1979 Mpondombini Sigcau and Ntsikayezwe Sigcau, both sons of the late paramount Botha Sigcau and brothers of Stella Sigcau, along with others, were arrested for a time because of their support for the opposition. When Mpondombini Sigcau was popularly selected as the new paramount chief of Eastern Pondoland over his brother Zwelidumile Sigcau, Kaiser Matanzima, as president, refused to accept this until 1980. By 1980, the Matanzimas had driven Sabata Dalindyebo, the legitimate Thembu paramount, into exile in Zambia, where he publicly declared his support for the outlawed ANC.[14]

In September 1987 a military coup by the Transkei Defence Force overthrew the blatantly corrupt Matanzima administration. The congress of the ruling party selected Stella Sigcau as the next president. Surprisingly, Stella Sigcau, an established homeland politician, publicly questioned the homeland system by suggesting that Transkei's "independence" was not irreversible. Her younger brother, Chief Ntsikayezwe Sigcau, went to Zambia to meet with the exiled ANC. In addition, Stella Sigcau ordered the detention of Kaiser Matanzima, the former president, because of his calls to the security forces to overthrow the Transkei government. Angered by these developments, the South African government conspired to have the Transkei Defence Force overthrow Stella Sigcau in December 1987, only eighty-six days after she had taken office. However, General Bantu Holomisa, himself a Thembu chief and head of the military council that came to administer Transkei, eventually distanced himself from the South African government and the Matanzimas. In October 1989, just a week after a major ANC gathering for the reburial of Sabata Dalindyebo who had died in exile, Holomisa released ANC cadres from prison and unbanned the South African liberation movements in Transkei.[15] Under Holomisa, Tutor Ndamase, son of the widely respected Victor Poto Ndamase and also paramount of Western Pondoland, continued to serve as ceremonial president of the Transkei.

Unfortunately, in the late 1980s and early 1990s, Pondoland was plagued by fighting between supporters of the rival ANC and PAC, which could now operate freely in the Transkei. To make matters worse, in the last days of the apartheid period, violence erupted between members of the South African National Civics Organization (SANCO) who wanted to democratize local government, and chiefs and their supporters who had enjoyed uncontested power in local administration since the late 1960s.[16]

Conclusion

After South Africa's first democratic elections in 1994, the Transkei Bantustan was reincorporated into South Africa and became part of the new Eastern Cape province. Ultimately, a compromise was achieved in which local government was democratized while at the same time "traditional leaders" or chiefs retained some authority as enshrined in the constitution. The Eastern Cape province established a House of Traditional Leaders, where representatives of the chiefs advise the provincial legislative assembly. Of course, tension between elected and hereditary institutions continues in certain areas. In Eastern Pondoland, Mpondombini Sigcau, the late Botha Sigcau's son and Stella Sigcau's younger brother, is paramount chief based at the Tribal Authority in Qawukeni, where he supervises the activities of a number of local chiefs. Stella Sigcau, as a leading member of the ANC who is said to be valued for her connections to the rural people of Pondoland, served as Minister of Public Enterprises in South Africa's first democratically elected government. Ntsikayezwe Sigcau, Mpondombini's and Stella's brother who had visited the ANC in exile, served as an ANC member of the Eastern Cape Provincial Legislature from 1994 until his death in 1997. After the death of Tutor Ndamase in February 1997, the paramountcy in Western Pondoland was not filled for some time, as the official heir had passed away before his father. Recently, Bhongolethu Ndamase became paramount chief of that area. Economically, the people of Pondoland, one of the poorest areas within South Africa's poorest province, still survive by subsistence agriculture. Since there is no significant local industry or nearby large city, people still migrate to work in either the mines around Johannesburg or the sugar cane fields of Natal. As in other areas of South Africa, the persistence of poverty and unfulfilled expectations for the post-apartheid period has contributed to the continuation of stock theft and violent crime in Pondoland. Recently, in July 1998, the Eastern Cape provincial government erected a monument at Ngquza Hill in memory of those Mpondo people who died in 1960 while fighting the apartheid government.

Appendices

Appendix 1

Cast of Characters

The Africans

Bangani	A son of Faku and full brother of Ndamase
Bangazita	A son of Faku
Bekameva	The second oldest son of Faku
Cetwa	A Bhaca sub-chief in 1848
Cingo	Faku's brother and lifelong ally
Dikiso	A son of Faku and full brother of Ndamase
Dingane	Ruler of the Zulu Kingdom from 1828 to 1840. He was killed by the Swazi after the Boer invasion of Zulu territory.
Dlanjwa	Remebered in oral history as Ndamase's best fighting man
Dliwako	The son of Madzikane who was the first Bhaca chief to take some of his people to live under the Mpondo after his father's death in 1824

Faku	King of the Mpondo people from c.1815 to 1867
Fodo	An African chief from the Boer Republic of Natalia who accompanied Boer raiders into Pondoland in the early 1840s
Gambushe	A Bomvana chief and enemy of Faku in the 1810s
Gantana	A councillor of Faku
Gastana	A councillor of Faku in the 1850s
Gezani	An Mpondomise chief in the 1850s
Gqirhana	An Mpondomise chief in the 1850s
Hintsa	Ruler of the Gcaleka who was murdered by the British in 1835
James	An African teacher at Morley mission in the 1850s
Jiqwa	A servant of Faku who accompanied missionaries to Grahamstown in 1830
Jojo	A ruler of the Xesibe and nephew of Faku
Kani	A chief of the ImiZizi in the 1860s who lived in the area ceded to Natal by Faku.
Kok, Adam	Leader of the mixed-race Griquas, moved into northern Pondoland by the British in 1863
Lochenberg, Hans	Mixed-race son of the white trader Nicholas Lochenberg and chief of a Fingo (Mfengu) group at the Buntingville mission in the late 1840s

Lochenberg, William	Another son of the trader Nicholas Lochenberg and a resident of the Palmerton mission in 1850
Ludidi	Leader of a Fingo (Mfengu) group around the Morley mission. Today, the name Ludidi is closely associated with the Hlubi people of Qumbu in Transkei.
Madzikane	Founding ruler of the Bhaca people who moved west from present-day KwaZulu/Natal into Transkei in the early 1820s
Makaula	Ncaphayi's son who became the main Bhaca ruler after his father's death in 1845
Mamanci	New name given to Nomandi upon marrying Faku. It indicates that she came from the Nei group.
Mamgcabe	Faku's mother, who became sympathetic to Christianity. She died around 1851.
Mandela	A chief who lived around the Mbashe River in 1848
Mankebe	A son of Faku
Manqayiya	Faku's first wife whom he married c.1800, and the mother of Ndamase
Matiwane	Leader of a branch of the Ngwane people destroyed by the British at the Battle of Mbolompo in 1828
Mbangata	A son of Faku and full brother of Ndamase
Mbeki	Leader of the Cwangula, a subordinate group of the Mpondo
Mbola	A nephew of Faku and one of Ndamase's sub-chiefs in Western Pondoland who led a raid of the Beecham Wood mission in 1856

Mdhlaka	Shaka's premier military commander who led an attack on the Mpondo in 1828
Mdepa	A chief of the Tshomane, who were vassals of the Mpondo Kingdom in the 1820s. Visiting missionaries were told that his mother had been the survivor of a European shipwreck.
Mdushane	A nephew of Ncaphayi who became leader of a Bhaca group in Natal
Mgcwengi	A brother of Faku
Mhlangazi	Faku's grandson and sub-chief who became a Christian in 1866
Mhlakaza	A councillor of Sarhili. As uncle of the prophetess Nongqawuse, he was a central figure in the Cattle-Killing of 1856-57.
Mhlangaso	Educated at the Lovedale mission in the Cape, he became chief councillor of Mqikela and later led the anti-colonial faction in the Mpondo civil war of 1891-94.
Mhlontlo	An Mpondomise ruler in the 1860s who was hostile to the Mpondo. He led a rebellion against colonial rule from 1880-81.
Mlanjeni	Rharhabe prophet who was prominent in the led up to the Cape-Xhosa war of 1850-53
Mlata	An Mpondomise chief in the 1850s
Moshoeshoe	Ruler of the Sotho Kingdom from c.1821 to 1870 and ally of Faku
Moshoeshoe, Nehemiah	Son of the Sotho king Moshoeshoe who led some of his people to occupy a portion of northern Pondoland in the 1860s

Mpande	Zulu king from 1840 to 1872 who remained on friendly terms first with the Boers and then with the British in Natal.
Mqeketa	Principal councillor of Ndamase in the 1860s
Mqetengo	A councillor of Faku in the 1850s
Mqikela	The great son (heir) of Faku who was born in 1831. He took over Eastern Pondoland after Faku's death in 1867 and ruled until his own passing in 1887.
Mtengwane	The right-hand (eldest) son of Ngqungqushe and half-brother of Faku. He opposed Faku's succession in c.1815.
Mtiki	An Mpondo commander under Ndamase in the 1850s
Mtirara	Son of Ngubencuka and king of the Thembu after his death
Myeki	An Mpondomise chief in the 1830s
Mzilikazi	Founding ruler of the Ndebele Kingdom which originated in present-day KwaZulu/Natal in the 1820s but eventually migrated across the South African Highveld to settle in present-day Zimbabwe by 1840
Nandi	The mother of Shaka
Ncaphayi	Right-hand son of Madzikane. He led most of the Bhaca people into the Mpondo Kingdom in 1824 and became a main ally of Faku until they split in 1840. He was killed in battle with the Mpondo in 1845.

Ndamase	Faku's eldest and right-hand son, born c.1800. He was renowned for military prowess, and in 1844 became semi-autonomous ruler of Western Pondoland until his death in 1876. In colonial documents, his name was often spelled "Damas."
Ndlambe	A chief of the Rharhabe Xhosa in the 1820s, defeated by the neighbouring Cape Colony in 1819
Ngcetane	A Tshomane chief and brother of Mdepa
Ngezana	A Bomvana chief and ally of Faku in the 1810s
Ngqungqushe	Father of Faku and king of the Mpondo from c.1780-1815
Ngoza	Ruler of the Thembu from present-day Kwa-Zulu/Natal who invaded the Mpondo Kingdom in 1819 and were destroyed. Ngoza's Thembu should not be confused with the Thembu of the present-day Transkei area who were under Ngubencuka in the 1820s.
Ngubencuka	King of the Thembu in the early 1800s until his death in 1830. Shortly before his death he married Faku's daughter, Nonesi.
Njameka	A councillor of Faku
Nogemani	A sub-chief of Ndamase in the 1850s
Nongqawuse	Teenage prophetess of the Xhosa Cattle-Killing of 1856-57
Nonkobe	One of Faku's sons
Nomandi	Faku's great wife whom he married in 1830 and mother of Mqikela

Nqeto	Ruler of the Qwabe who broke away from the Zulu Kingdom after the assassination of Shaka in 1828. The Qwabe were destroyed by the Mpondo and Bhaca in 1829.
Nqwiliso	The son of Ndamase who became ruler of Western Pondoland in 1876. In 1878 he sold Port St. John's to the British and he assisted the Cape in suppressing the Mpondomise rebellion of 1880-81.
Nogula	A Xesibe chief who was regent for Jojo after the death of Sinama
Nonesi	A daughter of Faku who married Ngubencuka, the Thembu king, around 1828
Phakani	The heir of Ngqungqushe who was usurped by Faku around 1815
Poshuli	A Sotho chief who, with Faku's permission, led some of his people to occupy portions of northern Pondoland in the 1860s
Poto, Victor	Great-grandson of Ndamase and king of Western Pondoland in the early to mid-twentieth century. He also wrote a book on the history of the Mpondo people.
Sandile	King of the Rharhabe Xhosa who fought the British of the Cape Colony in the wars of 1846-47, 1850-53 and 1877-78
Sarhili	Son of Hintsa and ruler of the Gcaleka after his father's murder in 1835. In colonial documents, his name was often spelled "Rili."
Shaka	Founding ruler of the Zulu Kingdom in c.1815 who was assassinated by his half-brother Dingane in 1828

Sigcau	Son of Mqikela and king of Eastern Pondoland from 1887 to his death in 1905. He led the victorious side in the Mpondo civil war of 1891-94 and was sympathetic to colonial intervention.
Sinama	A Xesibe chief and vassal of the Mpondo Kingdom in the 1810s
Sitata	Faku's half-brother and ally
Sobhuza	Founding ruler of the branch of the Ngwane people who moved north from KwaZulu/Natal to establish the Swazi Kingdom in the 1820s
Vadana	Regent of the Thembu after the death of Ngubencuka and ally of the Cape Colony
Vang'indaba	An ImiZizi chief who was killed by the Xesibe in c.1858

The Europeans

Addison, Major Thomas	A British officer sent to Pondoland in 1855 to investigate Mpondo complaints about the conduct of M.B. Shaw
Allsop, Rev. John	Wesleyan missionary at the Palmerton mission in the 1860s
Bain, Andrew Geddes	Visited the Mpondo Kingdom in the late 1820s as a trader from the Cape and later became famous as a road builder
Bisset, Colonel J.	British officer who commanded a force from Natal that annexed the land between the Mzimkhulu and Mtamvuna rivers (the Alfred Country) in 1866

Boyce, Rev. William B. The first Wesleyan missionary to live in Pondoland. He founded the Buntingville mission in 1830.

Cathcart, Sir George Governor of the Cape Colony from 1852 to 1854. He was killed in the Crimean War shortly after leaving the Cape.

Charters, Major Commanded the British seizure of Port Natal in 1838 and then visited the Mpondo Kingdom

Collis, Mr. A Port Natal trader

Currie, Walter Commander of the Cape's Frontier Armed and Mounted Police in the 1850s.

Davis, Rev. William A Wesleyan missionary at Clarkebury from 1831

Delancy, Captain Led a British military detachment to visit Pondoland in 1836

Dundas, Major W.B. Led a British force from the Cape into the Transkei region in 1828

Durban, Sir Benjamin Governor of the Cape Colony from 1834 to 1838

Frere, Sir Bartle British High Commissioner for South Africa and Governor of the Cape Colony in the late 1870s

Fynn, Henry Francis A Port Natal trader in the 1820s and Cape colonial agent in Pondoland in 1835 and again from 1848 to 1852

Fynn, William M.D. A brother of Henry Francis Fynn, he was Cape diplomatic agent with the Gcaleka in the 1840s and acting agent with the Mpondo in 1847.

Garner, Rev.	Wesleyan missionary at Shawbury in the 1840s
Gardiner, Captain Allen	British missionary who travelled through Pondoland in 1834-35 on his way to and from the Zulu Kingdom
Gladwin, Rev. F.P.	Wesleyan missionary in Pondoland who died in 1855
Glenelg, Lord	British Secretary for the Colonies who ordered the retrocession of conquered Xhosa territory (Queen Adelaide Province) in 1836
Gordon, Captain	Member of the colonial commission sent to Pondoland in 1851
Hancock	A resident of the Shawbury mission who helped defend the Bhaca from Mpondo attack in 1852
Harding, Walter	Member of the Natal Legislative Council who was sent to Pondoland in 1850 to conduct a commission of inquiry into allegations of stocktheft
Jenkins, Mary	After the death of her missionary husband Thomas Jenkins, she became a strong advocate of Mpondo interests until her death in 1880. Her brothers (the Whites) were traders in Pondoland.
Jenkins, Rev. Thomas	Wesleyan missionary in Pondoland from 1838 to his death in 1868. He was a close associate of Faku.
Keate, R.W.	Lieutenant-Governor of Natal from 1867 to 1872
Lochenberg, Nicholas	A trader from the Cape who operated in the Transkei region in the 1820s

MacKinnon, Colonel George	A senior British officer who served in the Cape Colony in the 1840s and 1850s.
MacLean, Colonel John	Chief Commissioner of British Kaffraria from 1852 to 1865
Maitland, Sir Peregrine	Governor of the Cape Colony from 1844 to 1846
Napier, Sir George	Governor of the Cape Colony from 1838 to 1844
Palmer, Rev. Samuel	Wesleyan missionary at Morley from 1835. He fell off his horse and died while leading refugees from Clarkebury to the Mtata River during the Cape-Xhosa War of 1846-47.
Pine, Benjamin	Lieutenant-Governor of Natal from 1850 to 1856
Pottinger, Sir Henry	Governor of the Cape in 1847
Pretorius, Commandant	Led a large Boer raiding party from Natalia against the Bhaca in 1840
Retief, Piet	A leader of the Boers during their trek from the Cape Colony, killed on the orders of the Zulu king Dingane in 1838.
Rhodes, Cecil	Premier of the Cape from 1890 to 1896
Satchell, William	Wesleyan assistant missionary at Buntingville in the 1830s. He later served as a missionary in the West Indies for 21 years.
Shaw, Mathew B.	Son of William Shaw and colonial resident with the Mpondo from 1852 until he was dismissed in 1855

Shaw, William	Director of the Wesleyan Methodist Missionary Society in South Africa
Shepstone, John	Son of Rev. William Shepstone and member of the colonial commission sent to Pondoland in 1851
Shepstone, Theophilus	Son of Rev. William Shepstone and a colonial official in the Cape and Natal. He was Natal's Secretary of Native Affairs in the 1850s.
Shepstone, Rev. William	A Wesleyan missionary who founded the Morley mission in the 1820s
Shrewsbury, Rev. William	Wesleyan missionary with the Gcaleka from 1827 to 1834
Smith, Captain Thomas	British officer who commanded a military expedition from the Cape in 1841 which was meant to protect the Mpondo Kingdom from the Boers of Natalia. Eventually, this force marched up the coast to conduct the annexation of Natal in 1842-43.
Smith, Sir Harry	British commander in the Cape during the Cape-Xhosa War of 1835 and governor of the Cape Colony from 1847 to 1852
Somerset, Colonel Henry	British commander of the Cape Mounted Rifles who led a colonial force into Transkei to destroy Matiwane's Ngwane at the Battle of Mbolompo in 1828
Stockenstrom, Andries	Lieutenant-governor of the Eastern Districts of the Cape from 1837 to 1839
Tainton, R.	A "mechanic missionary" who was with his family at the Buntingville mission in 1835

Thackwray, William	A trader from the Cape who operated in Pondoland in the 1820s
Thomas, Rev. James	Wesleyan missionary who was murdered by an Mpondo man in 1856
Toohey, D.C.	A Port Natal trader
Uys, Cobus	Led a Boer raiding party from Natalia into Mpondo territory in 1840
van Breda, Servas	A Boer representative from Natalia who visited the Mpondo Kingdom
van Rooyan, Dirk	A Boer representative from Natalia who visited the Mpondo Kingdom
Warden, Captain H.D.	A British officer who lead the Thembu against the Gcaleka in the Cape-Xhosa War of 1835
Warner, J.C.	Originally a Wesleyan missionary, he served as Cape government agent with the Thembu from 1852 to 1864.
White, Alfred	A trader in Pondoland and brother of Mary Jenkins
Wilson, H.A.	Resident magistrate in the Alfred Country in 1866
Wodehouse, Sir Phillip	Governor of the Cape Colony from 1862 to 1870

Appendix 2

List of Terms

Alfred Country

The name given to the land between the Mzimkhulu and Mtamvuna rivers which was annexed by Natal in 1866

Amatolas

Mountains located between the Keiskamma and Kei rivers. They were the heartland and military stronghold of the Rharhabe state throughout its wars with the British of the Cape. Also refers to a group of San (Bushmen) living near Pondoland in the 1840s who were allegedly stealing livestock from Natal settlers

Beecham Wood

A Wesleyan mission in Mpondomise territory, founded in 1856

Bhaca

An African group that originated from present-day KwaZulu/Natal, but moved west toward the Mpondo Kingdom in the 1820s where they settled and adopted the Xhosa language. Under the rulership of Ncaphayi, the Bhaca became a semi-autonomous tributary state and important military ally of the Mpondo until 1840 when the Boers of Natalia blamed them for stocktheft.

Boers

Dutch-speaking settlers whose descendants had arrived in the Cape in the late 1600s and 1700s. The word actually means "farmer."

Bomvana

A Xhosa-speaking group who lived just over the southwest boundary of the Mpondo Kingdom

British Kaffraria	This was the name given to the area between the Keiskamma and Kei rivers, inhabited by the Rharhabe and Gqunukhwebe, which was conquered by the British in 1847 and made into a separate colony from the Cape, but administered by the Cape's governor.
Buntingville	Founded in 1830, this Wesleyan mission in the Mpondo Kingdom was located on the Mngazi River.
Butterworth	A Wesleyan mission established in 1827 and located within the Gcaleka state
Cele	An Mpondo sub-group
Clarkebury	A Wesleyan mission founded in 1830 and located in the Thembu Kingdom
Commando	A group of armed men
Cwangula	An Mpondo sub-group
Cwera	An Mpondo sub-group
Delagoa Bay	Location of the present-day city of Maputo in Mozambique, a Portuguese trading centre in the 1800s
Durban	The name given by the British to Port Natal after their annexation of Natal in 1843
Fingo (Mfengu)	A term referring to Xhosa-speaking people living in and around the Cape Colony who were closely allied with the British, provided labour to settler farms and had adopted Christianity

Fort Beaufort	A Cape colonial town established by the British in 1823 in the Kat River Valley as a military post to guard the border with the Xhosa states
Fynn's People	A mysterious African group who lived around the Mzimkhulu River and considered Henry Francis Fynn to be their leader. They were former soldiers in Fynn's private army in the 1820s and some were his children by his numerous African wives.
Gcaleka	A precolonial state of Xhosa-speaking people located on the east bank of the Kei River and far west of the Mpondo Kingdom
Gingqi	A Xhosa-speaking group who inhabited an area of Pondoland west of the Mzimvubu River
Gqunukhwebe	A precolonial state of Xhosa-speaking people located near the coast between the Fish and Kei rivers close to the Cape Colony. They were conquered by the British in the war of 1846-47.
Grahamstown	A British colonial town in the eastern part of the Cape Colony. It began as a British military camp in 1811 and officially became a town, capital of the Albany District, in 1814.
Griqua	A Dutch-speaking group of mixed racial origin who militarily dominated the South African Highveld in the 1820s. In 1863 the British settled a group of Griqua in the northeastern section of the Mpondo Kingdom. This area became called Griqualand East and contains the modern town of Kokstad, named after the Griqua leader Adam Kok.

Idutywa

A mission/colonial outpost founded in the 1850s

ImiZizi

A vassal state of the Mpondo Kingdom located near the Mzimkhulu River, not to be confused with the AmaZizi who are generally considered part of the Fingo (Mfengu) people.

Jali

An Mpondo sub-group

Kaffirs

Today, this is regarded as a highly offensive, racist way of referring to black South Africans. However, in the nineteenth century it was a non-derogatory, colonial term for Xhosa-speaking Africans.

Kathlamba Mountains

African term for the Drakensberg Mountains running north of the Mpondo Kingdom

Kei

A major river to the west of the Mpondo Kingdom. The area to the east of the Kei but west of present-day KwaZulu/Natal was/is commonly referred to as Transkei.

Keiskamma

A small river located just to the east of the Fish River and near the Cape Colony. It became the border between the Cape Colony and the Xhosa states in 1819 and was later incorporated into British Kaffraria when the area was conquered by the British in 1847.

Khoikhoi

Indigenous people of the Cape who were absorbed into both Cape colonial society as "Coloureds" and various Xhosa-speaking groups. In the 1800s the Cape Mounted Rifles was a British cavalry unit based in the Cape Colony and made up primarily of Khoikhoi.

Khoisan	A collective term for both the Khoikhoi and San people
King William's Town	Capital of British Kaffraria
Konjwayo	An Mpondo group who lived west of the Mzimvubu River
Korana	Similar to the Griqua, these people dominated the Highveld in the 1820s.
Libode	A present-day town in Western Pondoland which is part of the Eastern Cape Province of South Africa
Lobola	A Xhosa term meaning the cattle given to a bride's family by her intended husband
Lusikisiki	A present-day town in Eastern Pondoland, part of the Eastern Cape Province of South Africa
Mbashe	A river to the west of the Mpondo state
Mbolompo	A place along the upper Mtata River where a British army accompanied by Thembu and Mpondo warriors destroyed Matiwane's Ngwane in 1828
Mbulu	A vassal chiefdom of the Mpondo state
Mdumbi	A river in Western Pondoland
Mfundisweni	A Wesleyan mission established in 1862 in the north of Eastern Pondoland
Morley	A Wesleyan mission founded in 1829 on the lower Mtata River. It was on the western boundary of the Mpondo Kingdom.

Mpondo	Refers to Xhosa-speaking people living between the Mtata and Mzimkhulu rivers who were organized into a centralized state under Faku
Mpondomise	A Xhosa-speaking people who, in the time of Faku, lived to the northwest of the Mpondo Kingdom
Mtamvuna	A river in the east of the Mpondo Kingdom which eventually became its border with the British Colony of Natal in the early 1860s
Mtata	A river which marked the western boundary of the Mpondo Kingdom
Mthethwa	A precolonial African state in what is now the KwaZulu/Natal province of South Africa. It was absorbed into the emerging Zulu Kingdom in the 1810s
Mtwa	An Mpondo sub-group
Mzimhlava	A minor river in the eastern and inland part of the Mpondo Kingdom
Mzimkhulu	A major river which marked the eastern boundary of the Mpondo Kingdom
Mzimvubu	A large river which was regarded as marking the centre of the Mpondo Kingdom under Faku, but which today divides the areas of Eastern and Western Pondoland
Natalia	The republic set up by the Trekkers in present-day KwaZulu/Natal after they defeated the Zulu Kingdom in the late 1838. It was seized by the British in 1843 and became the Colony of Natal.

Nguni	A term which refers to a number of closely related, mutually intelligible African languages, including IsiXhosa, IsiZulu, SiSwati (the language of the Swazi) and SiNdebele (the language of the Ndebele). Generally, Southern Nguni refers to IsiXhosa and Northern Nguni to IsiZulu and its variants.
Nci	An Mpondo sub-group
Ndebele	The people, led by Mzilikazi, who originated in present-day KwaZulu/Natal and moved onto the Highveld in the 1820s. In the late 1830s they were attacked by Boer Trekkers and moved further north into present-day Zimbabwe. They spoke/speak a variant of the Northern Nguni or Zulu language.
Ndela	A vassal chiefdom of the Mpondo state
Ndwandwe	A precolonial state which was eventually conquered by the Zulu Kingdom in the 1820s
Ngwane	After the emergence of the Zulu Kingdom, the Ngwane split into two groups. One under Sobhuza went north to settle in a mountainous area where it formed the nucleus of the Swazi Kingdom, and the other under Matiwane went west to be destroyed by the British at the Battle of Mbolompo in 1828.
Ntshangasi	A small chiefdom within the Mpondo state, neighbour of the Xesibe
Ntusi	An Mpondo sub-group

Nyandeni	The great place (capital) of Western Pondoland
Osborn Mission	A Wesleyan mission in Pondoland
Palmerton	A Wesleyan mission established in 1845 in the Mpondo Kingdom. It was eventually named in memory of Rev. S. Palmer, who died in 1846.
Pietermaritzburg	A town which started as the capital of the Republic of Natalia and after 1843 became the capital of the British Colony of Natal
Pondoland	The common name given to the area inhabited by the Mpondo people
Port Natal	Located on the site of the present-day city of Durban in KwaZulu/Natal, in the early nineteenth century this was a trading centre within Zulu territory which was patronized by British seagoing merchants who wanted to acquire ivory and possibly slaves.
Port St. John's	The mouth of the Mzimvubu River which European seafaring traders began using as a somewhat regular port of call from the 1820s
Qawukeni	Great Place (capital) of the Mpondo Kingdom located near the present-day town of Lusikisiki in Eastern Pondoland
Qora	A river to the west of the Mpondo state
Queen Adelaide Province	The area between the Keiskamma and Kei rivers, inhabited by the Rharhabe and Gqunukhwebe states, which was conquered by the British at the Cape in 1835 but abandoned in 1837 on the orders of the British Colonial Office in London

Qwabe	A Zulu-speaking group under Nqetho, who left the Zulu Kingdom after the murder of Shaka only to be destroyed by the Mpondo and Bhaca in 1829
Rharhabe	A precolonial state of Xhosa-speaking people located around the Amatola Mountains between the Fish and Kei rivers, and close to the Cape Colony. They were conquered by the British in the war of 1846-47.
San	Indigenous people of the Cape who lived by hunting and gathering. Also called Bushmen, many of them were absorbed into Xhosa-speaking communities and others were hunted down by European settlers. By the mid-nineteenth century the San had already been marginalized, but small independent groups did continue to exist in isolated areas of what is now the Eastern Cape.
Shangaan	A precolonial people who lived in what is now northeast South Africa and Mozambique
Shawbury	Established in 1840, this was a Wesleyan mission in the Bhaca area.
Sotho	This term can refer to the Sotho people who inhabited a section of the Drakensberg Mountains and Highveld north of the Mpondo Kingdom. During Faku's lifetime the main Sotho king was Moshoeshoe. The term can also refer to the language (called seSotho) spoken by these people who today inhabit Lesotho and South Africa's Free State province.

Thembu	A precolonial state of Xhosa-speaking people located to the northwest of the Mpondo Kingdom
Thukela	A river to the northeast of the Mpondo Kingdom in what is now the province of KwaZulu/Natal
Transkei	See Kei River
Trekkers	Also called Voortrekkers, these were Dutch-speaking settlers (Boers) who left British rule at the Cape in the late 1830s to establish independent Republics in Natal and the interior of South Africa. To trek means "to pull," which refers to the Boers pulling their wagons across long distances.
Tshomane	A small tributary state of the Mpondo Kingdom, located on the latter's western boundary of the Mtata River
Tsolo	A town in the eastern part of Transkei in the present-day Eastern Cape province
Tswana	The people who inhabit present-day Botswana and north west South Africa
Umzi	A Xhosa term for a homestead. The plural is ImiZizi.
Volksraad	A Boer or Trekker legislature
Xesibe	A precolonial state of Xhosa-speaking people located on the northern fringes of the Mpondo Kingdom

Xhosa

Refers to an African language (called IsiXhosa) spoken mostly in the Eastern Cape province of today's South Africa. Historically, people of many different precolonial states (including the Mpondo Kingdom) spoke dialects of the Xhosa language. Xhosa can also be used to refer to particular African states which were located near the border of the Cape Colony in the early to mid-1800s such as the Rharhabe Xhosa and Gcaleka Xhosa. The people of these Xhosa states are referred to as AmaXhosa. The Mpondo people speak the Xhosa language, but are not associated with the Xhosa states and do not call themselves AmaXhosa.

Zulu

Refers to an African language (IsiZulu) spoken today by most people in KwaZulu/Natal. Today, Zulu-speaking people call themselves AmaZulu. Historically, Zulu refers to the Zulu Kingdom which was founded by Shaka northeast of the Mpondo Kingdom (in present-day KwaZulu/Natal) from c.1815. However, in the 1800s, both the inhabitants of the Zulu Kingdom and its close neighbours spoke what is today called IsiZulu (the Zulu language), but not all people who call themselves Zulu today had ancestors who lived within the historic Zulu Kingdom.

Appendix 3

Chronology of Major Events

c.1780	Faku's birth
c.1800	Birth of Ndamase, Faku's first son
1811	British army push western Xhosa east of the Fish River
c.1815	Succession of Faku as Mpondo ruler
c.1815	Rise of the Zulu Kingdom
1819	Colonial border moved east to the Keiskamma River
c.1820	Ngoza's Thembu invade the Mpondo Kingdom
1820	British settlers arrive in the Cape Colony
1820s	Faku bans circumcision
1824	Zulu attack on the Mpondo is defeated
1824	Bhaca make an alliance with the Mpondo Kingdom
1824	Faku moves his great place west of the Mzimvubu River
1824-25	H.F. Fynn travels to Mpondo Kingdom from Port Natal
1826	Mpondo attack Bomvana
1827	H.F. Fynn establishes post on the Mzimkhulu River
1828	The Zulu and H.F. Fynn attack the Mpondo
1828	British, Mpondo, Thembu and Gcaleka destroy the Ngwane at Mbolompo
1828	Mpondo attack the Xesibe

1828	Assassination of Shaka, the Zulu king
1829	Nicholas Lochenberg and Francis Farewell are killed by the Qwabe
1829	Establishment of the Morley mission with the Tshomane
1829	Mpondo and Bhaca destroy the Qwabe
1830	Establishment of the Buntingville mission with Faku
1831	Mpondo attack the Tshomane
1831	Birth of Mqikela, Faku's heir
1833	Zulu raids on Mpondo and Bhaca
1834	Mpondo attack Mpondomise near the Morley mission
1834-35	Cape-Xhosa war; colonial forces attack Gcaleka east of Kei River
1835	H.F. Fynn sent to Pondoland from the Cape to enlist Mpondo and Thembu support in the war
1836	Mpondo attacks on Thembu and Bomvana
1836-40s	Boer trekkers establish republics in the South African interior (eventually the Orange Free State and Transvaal)
1837	Boer trekkers from the Cape move into Zulu territory
1838	Mpondo raids on the Thembu
1838	British occupation of Port Natal
1838	Boers defeat the Zulu at the Battle of Blood River
1839	British withdraw from Port Natal

1839	Trekkers establish Republic of Natalia
1840	Faku moves his great place east of the Mzimvubu
1840	Boers raid the Bhaca and threaten Faku; Mpondo-Bhaca alliance breaks down
1841	British soldiers sent to Mpondo Kingdom
1842	British soldiers from Pondoland occupy Natal
1843	British annexation of Natal
1844	Treaty between the Mpondo and British
1845	Bhaca and Xesibe attack the Mpondo
1845	Establishment of the Palmerton mission in Pondoland
1845	Movement of Ndamase west of the Mzimvubu River
1846-47	Cape-Xhosa war; colonial conquest of western Xhosa to the Kei River; colonial attacks on Gcaleka
1847	Missionary stops Faku from attacking Gcaleka on British request
1848	British annex Boer republics in the interior
1848	H.F. Fynn appointed colonial resident with Faku
1849	Mpondo attack the Bhaca on H.F. Fynn's request
1850	Harding commission in Pondoland; Faku ceded land between the Mzimkhulu and Mtamvuna rivers to Natal
1850	Harding commando and Fynn extort 1,000 cattle from Faku as compensation for alleged stock theft
1850-53	Rebellion of Rharhabe Xhosa in British Kaffraria; colonial attacks on the Gcaleka ·

1851	Faku sends envoys to Rharhabe rebels
1851-52	Faku agrees to British demands that he attack the Gcaleka, but his army cannot cross the flooded Mzimvubu River; Ndamase leads raid of the Gcaleka
1852	Dismissal of H.F. Fynn as colonial resident with Faku; appointment of M.B. Shaw as colonial agent with Mpondo and Thembu
1852	Mpondo raids on the Bhaca near the Shawbury mission
1852	In Sand River Convention the British recognize the independence of the Transvaal Boers
1854	Failed attempt by Theophilus Shepstone to make himself ruler of an African chiefdom within Pondoland
1854	In the Bloemfontein Convention the British give independence to the Free State Boers
1855	Dispute between M.B. Shaw and Ndamase/Faku over settlement of colonial Africans along Mdumbi River
1856	Dismissal of M.B. Shaw
1856-57	Expansion of settlers in the Cape and British Kaffraria because of Xhosa Cattle-Killing; Faku rejects Cattle-Killing prophecies; Gcaleka driven east by colonial police
1861-62	Cape officials convince Faku to cede the northern part of his territory
1862	Sotho chiefs move their people south into northern part of Mpondo Kingdom
1863	Griqua move into northeast part of Mpondo Kingdom, which becomes Griqualand East
1865-66	Faku and Mqikela refuse to cede Port St. John's to the British

1866	Natal annexes land between the Mzimkhulu and Mtamvuna as the "Alfred Country"
1866	Ndamase at war with the Mpondomise
1866	Mqikela leads disastrous attack on the Bhaca
1867	Death of Faku; Mqikela becomes king of the Mpondo
1868	Death of the Reverend Thomas Jenkins
1868	In the face of aggression from the Boers of the Free State, Moshoeshoe's Sotho Kingdom agrees to come under British protection.

Notes

Preface

1 The term "Boer" will be used to refer generally to nineteenth-century white settlers who spoke a variant of the Dutch language and were the descendants of Dutch, German and French people who had come to the Cape from the late 1600s. The term "Boer" is not derogatory, but simply means farmer in Dutch. The term "trek-boer," literally meaning "pulling farmers" or farmers who moved east out of the Cape Colony, usually refers to the 1700s and is not appropriate for the early to mid-1800s, when colonial borders became more rigidly defined. "Voortrekkers" will not be used, as it is meant specifically for those "Boers" who left the Cape in the late 1830s on what has become called the "Great Trek." The term "Voortrekker" was not used at the time and is a creation of twentieth-century Afrikaner nationalism. The terms "Afrikaner" and "Afrikaans" will not be used because they also did not exist in the subject period and were developed later to emphasize the length of time that descendants of Dutch settlers had lived in Africa: in other words, to claim that they were in fact "Africans" with the same ties to the land as indigenous people. When I refer specifically to those Boers who left the Cape in the late 1830s I will use the term "trekker."

Introduction

1 Margaret H. Lister (ed.), *The Journals of Andrew Geddes Bain* (Cape Town: Van Riebeeck Society, 1949), p. 105.

2 P. R. Kirby (ed.), *Andrew Smith and Natal* (Cape Town: Van Riebeeck Society, 1955), p. 108.

3 Allen F. Gardiner, *Narrative of a Journey to the Zoolu Country* (London: William Crofts, 1836), p. 14.

4 C. Brownlee, *Reminiscences of Kaffir Life and History* (Lovedale: Lovedale Press, 1896), p. 115. See also G. Theal, *History of South Africa,* vol. 10 (London: George Allen and Unwin, 1919), pp. 173-77.

5 Victor Poto Ndamase, *AmaMpondo: Ibali ne Ntlalo* (Lovedale: Lovedale Press, n.d.).

6 J.H. Soga, *The South-Eastern Bantu* (Johannesburg: Witwatersrand University Press, 1930), p. 308.

7 Ibid.

8 D.G.L. Cragg, "Faku," in W.J. de Kock (ed.), *Dictionary of South African Biography,* vol. 1 (Pretoria: Human Sciences Research Council, 1968), pp. 284-85. See also

D.G.L. Cragg, "The Relations of the AmaMpondo and the Colonial Authorities 1830-1886, with Special Reference to the Role of Wesleyan Missionaries," D.Phil. thesis, Oxford, 1959. Dora Taylor (a.k.a. N. Majeke), *The Role of Missionaries in Conquest* (Johannesburg: Society of Young Africa, 1952).

9 J.D. Omer-Cooper, *The Zulu Aftermath* (London: Longman, 1966), p. 158.

10 Ibid., p. 163.

11 W. Beinart, *The Political Economy of Pondoland, 1860-1930* (Johannesburg: Ravan Press, 1982), p. 11.

12 Interview with Lombekiso Masobhuza Sigcau (nee Dlamini), 14 July 1997, Qawukeni Great Place, Lusikisiki.

13 Julian Cobbing, "The Mfecane as Alibi: Thoughts on the Battles of Dithakong and Mbolompo," *Journal of African History* 29, 3 (1988): 487-519. For criticism of Cobbing see C. Hamilton (ed.), *The Mfecane Aftermath* (Johannesburg: Witwatersrand University Press, 1995).

14 For more on H.F. Fynn and his writing see J. Pridmore, "The Production of H.F. Fynn, c.1830-1930," in D.R. Edgecombe, J. Laband and S. Thompson (eds.), *The Debate on Zulu Origins* (Pietermaritzburg: University of Natal Press, 1992); and D. Wylie, "Proprietor of Natal: Henry Francis Fynn and the Mythography of Shaka," *History in Africa* 22 (1995): 408-37.

15 For more on the *James Stuart Archive* see J. Cobbing, "A Tainted Well: The Objectives, Historical Fantasies and Working Methods of James Stuart, with Counter-Argument," *Journal of Natal and Zulu History* 11 (1988): 115-54; J. Wright, "Making the James Stuart Archive," *History in Africa* 23 (1996): 333-50.

16 For these traditions see interviews quoted in subsequent chapters.

Chapter 1

1 Soga, *South-Eastern Bantu*, pp. 300-301; for the *Grosvenor* see Andrew Steedman, *Wanderings and Adventures in the Interior of Southern Africa*, vol. 2 (London: Longman, 1835), p. 256; for Faku's mother see Ndamase, *AmaMpondo*, p. 141.

2 Ndamase, *AmaMpondo*, p. 141.

3 Kevin Shillington, *History of Africa* (London: MacMillan, 1995), pp. 223-25.

4 Soga, *South-Eastern Bantu*, p. 305.

5 Ndamase, *AmaMpondo*, p. 6.

6 Ibid.

7 Interview with Mr. Merriman Mawethu Laqwela, 15 July 1997, Gemvale, Lusikisiki.

8 Ndamase, *AmaMpondo*, pp. 17-21. In his list of the wives of various Mpondo kings, Ndamase places Mamgcambe as the great wife of Ngqungqushe. See p. 141. For "Umkhulu" (recorded as Umkalu) see Steedman, *Wanderings and Adventures*, p. 284.

9 J.B. Peires, *The House of Phalo: A History of the Xhosa People in the Days of Their Independence* (Johannesburg: Ravan Press, 1981), p. 86.

10 Ibid.

11 For Mtengwane see Ndamase, *AmaMpondo*, p. 4. For Mtengwane as the right-hand son see Soga, *South-Eastern Bantu*, genealogy between pp. 300-301. For the defection to the Xesibe see Ibid., p. 308. For the oral account see interview with Mr. Laqwela.

12 Cobbing, "The Mfecane as Alibi"; E. Eldredge, "Sources of Conflict in Southern Africa, ca. 1800-30: The Mfecane Reconsidered," *Journal of African History* 33, 1 (1992): 1-35.

13 Cragg, "Amampondo and the Colonial Authorities," pp. 22-23. For the visit of Mdepa see H. Fast (ed.), *The Journal and Selected Letters of the Rev. William Shrewsbury, 1826-35* (Johannesburg: Witwatersrand University Press, 1994), pp. 60-61.

14 J. Cobbing, "Grasping the Nettle: The Slave Trade and the Early Zulu," in Edgecombe, Laband and Thompson (eds.), *Zulu Origins*, pagination irregular; and J. Wright, "Political Transformation in the Thukela-Mzimkhulu Region in the Late Eighteenth and Early Nineteenth Centuries", in Hamilton, *Mfecane Aftermath*, pp. 163-81.

15 C. de B. Webb and J.B. Wright (eds.), *The James Stuart Archive of Recorded Oral Evidence Relating to the History of the Zulu and Neighbouring Peoples* (Durban: Killie Campbell Africana Library, 1976), vol. 1, pp. 298-99, evidence of Lunguza ka Mpukane, 11, 3, 1909. See also Soga, *South-Eastern Bantu*, pp. 318-19.

16 *James Stuart Archive*, vol. 4, p. 17; evidence of Mqaikana ka Yenge, 11, 5, 1916.

17 Ibid. For the first account see vol. 3, pp. 43-44; evidence of Mbovu ka Mtshumayeli, 25, 9, 1904 and p. 66; evidence of Mcotoyi ka Mnini, 16, 4, 1905; for the second account see vol. 2, p. 272; evidence of Maziyana ka Mahlabeni, 22, 4, 1905.

18 Omer-Cooper, *Zulu Aftermath*, p. 157.

19 For Ndamase see M. Hunter, *Reaction to Conquest: Effects of Contact with Europeans on the Pondo of South Africa* (London: Oxford University Press, 1936), p. 402. Hunter derived this information from oral informants, but did not list them. For the quotation see Soga, *South-Eastern Bantu*, p. 318.

20 Webb and Wright, *The James Stuart Archive*, vol. 2, pp. 272-73; evidence of Maziyana ka Mahlabeni, 22, 4, 1905.

21 Ibid, p. 272.

22 J. Stuart and D. Malcolm (eds.), *Diary of Henry Francis Fynn* (Pietermaritzburg: Shuter and Shooter, 1969), p. 63.

23 Ibid, p. 116.

24 V. W. Gamede, "The Oral History of the Bhaca of Umzimkhulu," MA thesis, University of Transkei, 1992, p. 107 and p. 110. See also W.D. Hammond-Tooke, *Bhaca Society* (London: Oxford University Press, 1962), p. 6.

25 Soga, *South-Eastern Bantu*, pp. 308-309.

26 Malcolm, *Diary of Fynn*, p. 130.

27 Omer-Cooper, *Zulu Aftermath*, p. 159; Beinart, *Political Economy of Pondoland*, pp. 10-11.

28 For the quotations see Cobbing, "Mfecane as Alibi," p. 510-11, citing Dundas to Somerset (?), 15 August 1828, in M.J. van Warmelo (ed.), *History of Matiwane and the AmaNgwane Tribe* (Pretoria: Government Printer, 1938), p. 243; for Farewell and Ogle, Cobbing cites N. Isaacs, *Travels and Adventures in Eastern Africa*, vol. 1 (London: Edward Churton, 1836), pp. 227-28. For the great place burned down see Noel Mostert, *Frontiers: The Epic of South Africa's Creation and the Tragedy of the Xhosa People* (New York: Alfred Knopf, 1992), p. 56. For a critique of Cobbing's revision see Jeff Peires, "Matiwane's Road to Mbholompo: A Reprieve for the Mfecane," in Hamilton, *Mfecane*, pp. 213-39. While Cobbing claims that Fynn was the primary leader of the 1828 attack, Peires believes that Fynn simply led a small contingent within Shaka's army. I support the concept that Fynn worked for Shaka as a mercenary in this attack, but point out that Peires has seriously underestimated the potential size of Fynn's force and the effectiveness of its firearms in this campaign. Just as they had done against the Ndwandwe in 1826, Fynn's detachment may have been smaller than the rest of the Zulu army, but its firepower was the most important

element of Shaka's operation. Of course, there are other possibilities which are difficult to prove; Shaka and Fynn may have been cooperating as equals in a joint raid, or Shaka might have been working for Fynn.

29 John Laband, *Rope of Sand: The Rise and Fall of the Zulu Kingdom in the Nineteenth Century* (Johannesburg: Jonathan Ball, 1995), p. 45.

30 Ibid., p. 34.

31 Webb and Wright, *The James Stuart Archive*, for the quotations see vol. 2, p. 249; evidence of Mayinga ka Mbekuzana, 8, 7, 1905; for a similar version see vol. 3, p. 44; evidence of Mbovu ka Mtshumayeli, 25, 9, 1904; for the Mkandhlu regiment see vol. 4, p. 27; evidence of Mqaikana ka Yenge, 14, 5, 1916; for the poisoned assegais see vol. 4, p. 82; evidence of Mtshapi ka Noradu, 9, 4, 1918.

32 Ibid., vol. 1, p. 186; evidence of Jantshi ka Nongila, 16, 2, 1903; vol. 2, p. 274; evidence of Maziyana ka Mahlabeni, 22, 4, 1905.

33 For the first account see interview with Laqwela; for the second see interview with Mr. Arthur Lizo Luwaca, 13 July 1997, Bridge Farm, Libode.

34 Brownlee, *Reminiscences*, pp. 105-106.

35 Steedman, *Wanderings and Adventures*, vol. 2, p. 260, Journal of the Rev. William Shaw dated 27 June 1828.

36 Ndamase, *AmaMpondo*, p. 10.

37 F.P. Gladwin, "Historical Sketch of the Mpondomise Tribe as Taken from Vete, the Son of Umziziba (1883)," in Frank Brownlee (ed.), *The Transkeian Native Territories: Historical Records* (Lovedale: Lovedale Press, 1923), p. 114; for Faku's daughter see p. 22.

38 Cobbing, "Mfecane as Alibi," pp. 500-503. For Ngwane going to Faku see Webb and Wright, *The James Stuart Archive*, vol. 2, p. 267; evidence of Maziyana ka Mahlabeni, 21,4,1905. Fast, *Journal of Shrewsbury*, for Dundas's female prisoners see p. 90 and for Shrewsbury buying a pregnant women see p. 92.

39 Lister, *Journal of Bain*, pp. 83-84.

40 S. Kay, *Travels and Researches in Caffraria* (London: John Mason, 1833), pp. 385. For Butterworth see Fast, *Journal of Shrewsbury*, p. 200, n. 159. For the wounding of Nqeto see Steedman, *Wanderings and Adventures*, vol. 1, p. 276 and Webb and Wright, *The James Stuart Archive*, vol. 3, p. 37, evidence of Mbovu ka Mtshumayeli, 16, 9, 1904.

41 Celia Sadler (ed.), *Never a Young Man: Extracts from the Letters and Journals of the Rev. William Shaw* (Cape Town: H.A.U.M., 1967), p. 82. Fast, *Journal of Shrewsbury*, p. 102.

42 Steedman, *Wanderings and Adventures*, vol. 1. For the guns and ammunition see p. 278 and for Farewell's statement to Shrewsbury see p. 274.

43 For the Farewell incident see Steedman, *Wanderings and Adventures*, vol. 1, pp. 275-76. For the tradition see Webb and Wright, *The James Stuart Archive*, vol. 2, p. 268; evidence of Maziyana ka Mahlabeni, 21, 4, 1905.

44 Sadler, *Never a Young Man*, pp. 79-80.

45 Soga, *South-Eastern Bantu*, pp. 311-14. For Mpondo superior numbers see Webb and Wright, *The James Stuart Archive*, vol. 1, p. 105; evidence of Dinya ka Zokozwayo, 29, 3, 1905.

46 Fast, *Journal of Shrewsbury*, p. 121.

47 Malcolm, *Diary of Fynn*, pp. 171-72. For a similar oral tradition see Webb and Wright, *The James Stuart Archive*, vol. 3, p. 38; evidence of Mbovu ka Mtshumayeli, 16, 9, 1904.

48 William Taylor, *Christian Adventures in South Africa* (London: Jackson, Walford and Hodder, 1867), p. 323.

49 For the rumour about no Mpondo fatalities see Fast, *Journal of Shrewsbury*, p. 112. For the praise-name see Kirby, *Andrew Smith and Natal*, p. 102 and Steedman, *Wanderings and Adventures*, vol. 2, p. 275.

50 Malcolm, *Diary of Fynn*, p. 173.

51 Steedman, *Wanderings and Adventures*, vol. 2; for the population estimates see p. 268; for the quotation see p. 270.

52 Kirby, *Andrew Smith and Natal*, p. 102.

53 Ibid., p. 105.

54 Ibid., p. 103 and p. 121.

55 Lister, *Journal of Bain*, p. 104.

56 Steedman, *Wanderings and Adventures*, vol. 2, p. 208.

57 For bride price see Beinart, *Political Economy of Pondoland*, p. 15; for men working in the fields see Steedman, *Wanderings and Adventures*, vol. 1, pp. 261-62.

58 Ibid., pp. 268-69.

59 Kirby, *Andrew Smith and Natal*, p. 121.

60 Steedman, *Wanderings and Adventures*, vol. 2, p. 280.

61 Peiter Jolly, "Interaction Between South-Eastern San and Southern Nguni and Sotho Communities, c.1400 to c.1880," *South African Historical Journal* 35 (November 1996): 48.

62 (NA) A1382 FP, vol. 4, Fynn to H. Smith, 10 August 1848.

63 For Mpondo military organization see Webb and Wright, *The James Stuart Archive*, vol. 2. pp. 63 and 65, evidence of Mcotoyi ka Mnini, 16, 4, 1905. For the date of the ban on circumcision see Lister, *Journals of Bain*, p. 104, n. 54; for the oral evidence from the early 1900s see Hunter, *Reaction to Conquest*, pp. 165 and 396. For vulnerability to attack see Webb and Wright, *The James Stuart Archive*, vol. 3, p. 248, evidence of Mmemi ka Nguluzane, 16, 10, 1904. For recent oral evidence about Mqikela's poor health see interview with Paramount Chief Sigcau. For the compromise view see interview with Mr. Laqwela. Mr. Laqwela favours the explanation that an unidentified son of Faku was sick. For the quotation see interview with Mr. Luwaca.

64 For this point I am indebted to Dr. Wellington Sobahle of the Department of African Studies, University of Fort Hare.

65 Gladwin, "Mpondomise," in Brownlee, *The Transkeian Native Territories*, p. 114. While "Mfecane" is the term applied to the conventional historical concept that the growth of Shaka's Zulu kingdom caused a wave of state formation and migration in early-nineteenth-century southern Africa, informant may have been referring to groups of refugees/raiders who allegedly fled from Shaka's rampaging armies.

Chapter 2

1 Interview with Mr. Pondolwendlovu Ndamase, 11 July 1997, Fort Gale, Umtata; interview with Paramount Chief Sigcau; interview with Mr. Laqwela.

2 Steedman, *Wanderings and Adventures*, vol. 2, pp. 265-66, "Extracts from the Journal of W.B. Boyce." Sadler, *Never a Young Man*, pp. 82-83.

3 Steedman, *Wanderings and Adventures*, vol. 2, p. 270, "Journal of Boyce." Sadler, *Never a Young Man*, p. 84.

4 Steedman, *Wanderings and Adventures*, pp. 272-73, "Journal of Boyce."

5 Ibid., pp. 271-73. For the chiefs' role see Taylor, *Christian Adventures*, p. 325 and p. 329.

6 Steedman, *Wanderings and Adventures*, p. 275.

7 Ibid., p. 276.

8 Ibid., pp. 276-79.

9 Ibid., p. 282.

10 Laband, *Rope of Sand*, p. 75.

11 Steedman, *Wanderings and Adventures*, vol. 2, p. 284, "Journal of Boyce."

12 Ibid., p. 286.

13 Ibid.

14 Ibid., pp. 287-88.

15 Ibid., p. 288.

16 For Mamanci's origin, the role of Ndamase and Bekameva as well as the meaning of Mqikela see interviews with Mr. P. Ndamase, Paramount Chief Sigcau, Chief Mfolozi and Mr. Luwaca. For the date of Mqikela's birth see Steedman, *Wanderings and Adventures*, vol. 2, "Journal of Boyce," pp. 288-89.

17 Steedman, *Wanderings and Adventures*, vol. 2, "Journal of Boyce," pp. 288-89.

18 Kirby, *Andrew Smith and Natal*, p. 110.

19 Cragg, "AmaMpondo and Colonial Authorities," p. 35.

20 Steedman, *Wanderings and Adventures*, vol. 2, p. 292, "Extract from the Journal of Mr. S. Palmer, 24 June 1834."

21 A.T. Bryant, *Olden Times in Zululand and Natal* (London: Longmans, Green and Co., 1929), pp. 398-99.

22 Steedman, *Wanderings and Adventures*, vol. 2, pp. 292-302, "Journal of Palmer."

23 Ibid., pp. 306-307.

24 Ibid., p. 309.

25 Cragg, "AmaMpondo and Colonial Authorities," p. 37.

26 For Fynn's appointment see Stuart and Malcolm, *Diary of Fynn*, p. 335. For Read's comment see Wylie, "Proprietor of Natal," p. 418.

27 Gardiner, *Journey to the Zoolu Country*, pp. 13-15.

28 G.M. Theal (ed.), *Documents Relating to the Kaffir War of 1835* (London: Government of the Union of South Africa, 1912). For D'Urban's message see pp. 72-73, D'Urban to Davis, 21 February 1835; for Faku's answer see pp. 132-33, D'Urban to Fakoo [sic], 22 April 1835.

29 Stuart and Malcolm, *Diary of Fynn*, pp. 235-36.

30 Fast, *Journal of Shrewsbury*. For prisoners see p. 176; for quotation see p. 169.

31 For the three quotations in this paragraph see (NA) A1382 FP, Vol 6, Satchell to Smith, 29 April 1835.

32 Theal (ed.), *The War of 1835*, pp. 146-47, D'Urban to Faku, 6 May 1835.

33 (NA) A1382 FP, Vol 6, Memorandum: D'Urban to Fynn, 6 May 1835.

34 Gardiner, *Zoolu Country*, pp. 368-69.

35 For Dingane and Gardiner see N. Etherington, "Christianity and African Society in Nineteenth Century Natal," in A. Duminy and B. Guest (eds.), *Natal and Zululand from Earliest Times to 1910: A New History* (Pietermaritzburg: University of Natal Press, 1989), pp. 275-77; see also Laband, Rope of Sand, p. 76. For the quotations see Gardiner, *Zoolu Country*, p. 364-66.

36 Gardiner, *Zoolu Country*, pp. 368-70.

37 J.M. Berning (ed.), *The Historical Conversations of Sir George Cory* (Cape Town: Maskew Miller Longman, 1989), pp. 78-79, interview with Sir Walter Stanford, June 1929, also see n. 160.

38 Gardiner, *Zoolu Country*, pp. 372-73.

39 Ibid., p. 380.

40 Brownlee, *Transkeian Territories*, p. 67, extract from "Blue Book on Native Affairs, 1885."

41 Ibid.

42 Ibid., p. 68.

43 Cragg, "AmaMpondo and Colonial Authorities," p. 40.

44 WMMS, SA Box 7, J. Cameron to Secretaries, 24 May 1836, as quoted in Beinart, *Pondoland*, p. 11.

Chapter 3

1 Norman Etherington, "Old Wine in New Bottles: The Persistence of Narrative Structures in the Historiography of the Mfecane and Great Trek," in Hamilton, *Mfecane Aftermath*, pp. 35-50.

2 Cragg, "AmaMpondo and Colonial Authorities", p. 43.

3 J.C. Chase (ed.), *The Natal Papers*, vol. 2, (Cape Town: C. Struik, 1968), p. 45, Natal Council to Napier, 1838.

4 J. Bird (ed.), *The Annals of Natal* (Cape Town: C. Struik, 1965), vol. 1, p. 552, evidence of D.C. Toohey, Kafir Commission 1852.

5 (Wits) JP, W. Shaw to T. Jenkins, 2 November 1838.

6 (CA) CO 48/100, Charters to Shaw, 9 November 1838.

7 (CA) CO 48/200, Charters to Napier, 27 February 1839.

8 Bird, *The Annals of Natal*, vol. 1, p. 434, Charters to Napier, 12 December 1838.

9 Ibid., p. 437, Charters to Faku, 11 December 1838.

10 Ibid., p. 502, Napier to Lord Glenelg, 4 February 1839; p. 513, Captain Jervis to Napier, 30 March 1839.

11 (CA) CO 48/200, Charters to Napier, 27 February 1839.

12 Laband, *Rope of Sand*, p. 123.

13 Beinart, *Pondoland*, p. 12.

14 Ndamase, *AmaMpondo*, p. 157. For the missionaries see below in this chapter.

15 Cragg, "AmaMpondo and Colonial Authorities," p. 58, n. 116.

16 Chase, *Natal Papers*, vol. 2, p. 142, extract from the *Grahamstown Journal* 24 June 1840.

17 Hammond-Tooke, *Bhaca Society*, p. 7.

18 Chase, *Natal Papers*, vol. 2, p. 173, J. Prinsloo (President of the Volksraad) to Napier, 7 April 1841.

19 Ibid. See also Bird, *Annals of Natal*, vol. 1, p. 249, Journal of the Late Charl Celliers.

20 (CA) CO 48/211, Journal of Missionaries, enclosed in Napier to Russell, 21 January 1841. See also Cragg, "AmaMpondo and Colonial Authorities," p. 55.

21 Cragg, "AmaMpondo and Colonial Authorities," pp. 56-57.

22 Bird, *Annals of Natal*, vol. 1, p. 639, "Council of the People" to Napier, 7 April 1841.

23 (CA) CO 48/211, Journal of Missionaries, enclosed in Napier to Russell, 21 January 1841.

24 Ibid.

25 Brownlee, *Transkeian Territories*, p. 70, Faku to Napier, 5 January 1841. Palmer, Garner and Jenkins signed the letter as witnesses.

26 Cragg, "AmaMpondo and Colonial Authorities," p. 62.

27 Ibid., p. 63.

28 For Shaw's visit to Faku see (Wits) JP, Shaw to Jenkins, 1 February 1841; for the Mngazi post see Brownlee, *Transkeian Territories*, p. 70.

29 Bird, *Annals of Natal*, vol. 1, p. 639, Volksraad to Napier, 7 April 1841.

30 (Wits) JP, Shaw to the editor of the *Grahamstown Journal*, 3 August 1841.
31 For Shaw's prediction see (Wits) JP, Shaw to Jenkins, 29 September 1841; for Napier see Bird, *Annals of Natal*, vol. 1, p. 659, Proclamation by Napier, 2 December 1841; for Smith's departure see (Wits) JP, Smith to Jenkins, 1 April 1842.
32 (Wits) JP, Shaw to Jenkins, 30 April 1844 and Shaw to Jenkins, 1 August 1844.
33 Brownlee, *Transkeian Territories*, p. 95, "The Maitland Treaty." See also Cragg, "AmaMpondo and Colonial Authorities," p. 77. While the treaty states that "Umciwengi" was a brother of Faku, Victor Poto Ndamase says that Mgcwengi was a half-brother of Ngqungqushe, Faku's father.
34 Quotations in the four previous paragraphs are from Brownlee, *Transkeian Territories*, pp. 92-95, "The Maitland Treaty," 23 November 1844.
35 Cragg, "AmaMpondo and Colonial Authorities," chap. 5.

Chapter 4

1 Hunter, *Reaction to Conquest*, p. 379. Quoted from Ndamase, *AmaMpondo*. Mqikela's alleged sickliness is discussed in chap. 1.
2 Interview with Paramount Chief Sigcau; interview with Mr. Laqwela; for the variation see interview with Mr. Luwaca; for Ndamase's brothers see interview with Mr. P. Ndamase.
3 Taylor, *Christian Adventures*, p. 343.
4 Peter Sanders, *Moshoeshoe: Chief of the Sotho* (London: Heinneman, 1975), p. 244.
5 (Wits) JP, Jenkins to H. Fynn, 31 January 1845.
6 (Wits) JP, Captain T.C. Smith to Jenkins, 20 April 1845.
7 (Wits) JP, Shaw to Jenkins, 3 September 1845. For the details of Ncaphayi's death see Gamede, "Oral History of the Bhaca," p. 111.
8 Cragg, "AmaMpondo and Colonial Authorities," pp. 95-96.
9 Brownlee, *Transkeian Territories*, p. 99, "History of the AmaXesibe since 1840, as Narrated by the Pondos during a Meeting Held at Ngozi on 27th, 28th and 29th May 1880."
10 (Wits) JP, "Diary of the Reverend Thomas Jenkins," 2 June 1845.
11 (Wits) JP, Shaw to Jenkins, 3 September 1845.
12 Cragg, "AmaMpondo and Colonial Authorities," p. 123.
13 (Wits) JP, Shaw to Wesleyans, 18 August and 26 September 1846; Cragg, "AmaMpondo and Colonial Authorities," pp. 106-107 and p. 120. For the rumour about Shepstone see John Frye (ed.), *The War of the Axe and the Xhosa Bible: The Journal of the Rev. J.W. Appleyard* (Cape Town: C. Struik, 1971), p. 88; according to the editor of Appleyard's journal, Faku was not involved in the war.
14 (Wits) JP, Shaw to Wesleyans, 23 December 1846.
15 Berning, *George Cory*, p. 40.
16 (Wits) JP, "Diary of Jenkins," 10 February - 6 April 1847.
17 (Wits) JP, "Diary of Jenkins," 11 - 22 April 1847. For the letter to Pottinger see (Wits) JP, Shaw to Wesleyans, 25 September 1847.
18 (CA) CO 48/285, Smith to Faku, 3 April 1848, enclosed in Smith to Grey, 20 April 1848.
19 (NA) A1382 FP, vol 2, Order for presents for Faku, 8 June 1848, signed by Colonel G. MacKinnon.
20 (NA) A1382 FP, vol. 4, Fynn to Southey, 29 July 1848.
21 Ibid.
22 (NA) A1382 FP, vol. 4, Fynn to Smith, 10 August 1848.

23 (NA) A1382 FP, vol. 4, Fynn to Smith, 10 August 1848; see also (NA) A1382 FP, vol. 8, Smith to Faku, 20 June 1848.

24 (NA) A1382 FP, vol. 4, Fynn to Moodie, 4 October 1848.

25 Ibid.

26 (NA) A1382 FP, vol. 4, Fynn to Southey, 16 October 1848, and Fynn to Southey, 5 December 1848. It is difficult to assess Jenkins's opinion of this arrangement as his diary does not contain entries for 1848 and his letters from the same period do not mention this issue. However, as stated later in this chapter, he later advised Faku to prevent Fynn from settling "Government People" within Mpondo territory.

27 (Wits) JP, Fynn to Jenkins, 2 May 1849, enclosed in "Diary of Jenkins".

28 Cragg, "AmaMpondo and Colonial Authorities," pp. 124-26; (Wits) JP, "Diary of Jenkins," 1 May - 3 June 1849; (NA) A1382 FP, vol. 4, Fynn to Moodie, 13 January 1849, 17 March 1849, 12 May 1849; *Grahamstown Journal*, 26 May 1849, 9 June 1849, 23 June 1849.

29 (Wits) JP, Shaw to Jenkins, 1 January 1849.

30 (Wits) JP, Jenkins to Shaw, 1 May 1849. Emphasis is original.

31 (Wits) JP, Jenkins to Fynn, 7 May 1849; P.P. 1850 XXXVIII (1292), "Fynn's Report" in Moodie to Montagu, 24 July 1849; Cragg, "AmaMpondo and Colonial Authorities," pp. 141-43.

32 (Wits) JP, Shaw to Jenkins, 25 May 1849.

33 (Wits) JP, "Diary of Jenkins," 11 June and 8 July 1849. For Jenkins's message to Faku see (NA) A1382 FP, vol. 8, Jenkins to Faku, 3 July 1849.

34 (Wits) JP, Shaw to Jenkins, 16 August 1849. Emphasis in original.

35 Ibid. Emphasis in original.

36 (Wits) JP, Harding to Jenkins, 6 March 1850.

37 (Wits) JP, Harding to Jenkins, 29 March 1850.

38 (Wits) JP, "Diary of Jenkins," 1 April 1850.

39 (Wits) JP, "Diary of Jenkins," 1 April 1850. See also (NA) A1382 FP, vol. 4, Fynn to Garvock, 17 May 1850.

40 (Wits) JP, M.B. Shaw to Jenkins, 4 April 1850.

41 (Wits) JP, "Diary of Jenkins," 11 April 1850.

42 (CA) CO 179/57, "Treaty entered into by the Honourable Walter Harding and Faku, Paramount Chief of the Amaponda Nation," 11 April 1844, and Harding to Moodie, 2 April and 12 June 1850, enclosed in Scott to Newcastle, 21 November 1860.

43 (Wits) JP, "Diary of Jenkins," 11 April 1850.

44 (Wits) JP, William Shaw to Jenkins, 22 May 1850.

45 Cragg, "AmaMpondo and Colonial Authorities," pp. 129-30.

46 For the quotations see (Wits) JP, Shaw to Jenkins, 7 June 1850, and "Diary of Jenkins," 4 May to 2 July 1850. For Fynn role see (NA) A1382 FP, Fynn to Garvock, 29 May 1850.

47 (CA) CO 48/407, Pine to Smith, 23 November 1850.

48 (NA) A1382 FP, vol. 4, Fynn to Harding, 17 September 1850, this letter does not say that Fynn explained the reason why the cattle were being demanded; Fynn to MacKinnon, 25 September 1850 also fails to state that the resident fully explained the reason behind the demand.

49 (Wits) JP, Harding to Jenkins, 20 September 1850 and "Diary of Jenkins," 20-23 September and 2 November 1850; see also Cragg, "AmaMpondo and Colonial Authorities," p. 147.

50 (Wits) JP, "Diary of Jenkins," 17 June 1850 and Harding to Jenkins, 20 September 1850.

51 (CA) CO 48/407, Faku to Colonial Government, 7 October 1850, enclosed in Grey to Newcastle, 6 March 1861. For another copy see (NA) A1382 FP, vol. 4, Faku to Colonial Government, 7 October 1850, enclosed in Fynn to Harding, 7 October 1850.

52 (CA) CO, 48/407, Pine to Faku, 2 November 1850; Pine to Smith, 23 November 1850. See also Cragg, "AmaMpondo and Colonial Authorities," pp. 149-50.

53 Jolly, "San, Nguni and Sotho Communities," p. 54. Jolly cites P. Vinnicombe, People of the Eland (Pietermaritzburg: University of Natal Press, 1976), p. 64.

54 (Wits) JP, "Diary of Jenkins," 28 October - 2 November 1850.

55 Cragg, "AmaMpondo and Colonial Authorities," p. 154.

56 (Wits) JP, "Diary of Fynn," 15 and 16 November 1850.

57 (CA) CO 48/461, Faku to Pine, 16 November 1850.

58 (Wits) JP, "Diary of Jenkins," 9 December 1850.

59 (Wits) JP, "Diary of Jenkins," 24 December 1850; Shaw to Jenkins, 6 December 1850.

60 (Wits) JP, Pine to Jenkins, 23 December 1850; "Diary of Jenkins," 6 January 1851. (CA) GH 8/23, Pine to Fynn, 20 January 1851.

61 For the quotation see (NA) A1382 FP, vol. 4, Fynn to Garvock, 26 January 1851; for the Natal force see Cragg, "AmaMpondo and Colonial Authorities," pp. 109-110.

62 (Wits) JP, "Diary of Jenkins," 13 January to 26 March 1851. Emphasis is original.

63 (NA) A1382 FP, vol. 4, Fynn to Moodie, 21 April 1851.

64 (CA) BK 433, W. Fynn to G. MacKinnon, 7 December 1850.

65 (Wits) JP, "Diary of Jenkins," 14 April 1851.

66 (Wits) JP, "Diary of Jenkins," Jenkins to Shepstone, 3 and 20 May 1851.

67 Taylor, *Christian Adventures*, p. 439.

68 (CA) CO 48/374, Addison to Maclean, 14 December 1855. (CA) BK 77, Copy of Lease, 20 September 1851. (Wits) JP, Evidence Given By the Rev. Thomas Jenkins Before Major Addison on the Umdumbi Collision Enquiry, no date; Jenkins to M.B. Shaw, 18 September 1855.

69 (Wits) JP, William Shaw to Jenkins, 30 September 1851; "Diary of Jenkins," 16 March 1852.

70 (NA) A1382 FP, vol. 4, Fynn to Garvock, 25 September 1851.

71 (NA) A1382 FP, vol. 4, Fynn to Moodie, 13 October 1851.

72 (NA) A1382 FP, vol. 4, Fynn to Moodie, 21 October 1851; and Fynn to Garvock, 24 October 1851.

73 (Wits) JP, Smith to Faku, 27 November 1851.

74 (Wits) JP, "Diary of Jenkins," 6 December 1851.

75 Previous three paragraphs based on (Wits) JP, "Diary of Jenkins," 9 December 1851 - 15 January 1852; M.B. Shaw to Jenkins, 23 and 24 December 1851. PP 1852-3 LXVI (1635), MacKinnon to Somerset, 4 January 1852, enclosed in Smith to Grey, 13 January 1852. Cragg, "AmaMpondo and Colonial Authorities," pp. 112-13. For Fynn's illness see (NA) A1382 FP, vol. 5, Fynn to Cathcart, 26 July 1853.

76 (Wits) JP, M.B. Shaw to Jenkins, 16 February 1852; "Diary of Jenkins," 16 March 1852.

77 (Wits) JP, "Diary of Jenkins," 21 April 1852.

78 (Wits) JP, "Diary of Jenkins," 21 April 1852.

79 PP, 1852-3 LXVI (1635) Cathcart to Pakington, 15 August 1852. (Wits) JP, "Diary of Jenkins," 20 July - 10 August 1852; M.B. Shaw to Jenkins, 23 and 28 July 1852.

80 Cragg, "Faku," p. 284.

Chapter 5

1 (Wits) JP, "Diary of Jenkins," 4 - 13 September 1852; William Shaw to Jenkins, 23 October 1852.

2 (Wits) JP, M.B. Shaw to Jenkins, 23 October and 5 November 1852. Emphasis is original.

3 (Wits) JP, Jenkins to M.B. Shaw, 3 February 1853; M.B. Shaw to Jenkins, 8 January 1854. George Cathcart, *Correspondence of Sir George Cathcart* (London: John Murray, 1856), p. 350, May 1853.

4 PP, 1852-3 LXII (1697), Shepstone to Secretary to Government (Natal), 9 December 1851 enclosed in Pine to Smith, 27 February 1852.

5 (CA) CO, 179/35, Memorandum by Shepstone, 23 January 1854. Also see Cragg, "AmaMpondo and Colonial Authorities," pp. 208-209.

6 (Natal) SP, Shepstone to Cato, 21 May 1854. (CA) CO 179/49, Declarations by Native Chiefs, enclosed in Scott to Labouchere, 3 June 1858. (Natal) SNA, 1/1/5, Shepstone to Colonial Secretary, 16 August 1854. (Wits) JP, Jenkins to William Shaw, 21 August 1854. (CA) CO 179/49, Memorandum of Agreement Between Faku and Shepstone, 20 July 1854, enclosed in Scott to Labouchere, 3 June 1858. Cragg, "AmaMpondo and Colonial Authorities," pp. 213-17.

7 (Wits) JP, T. Shepstone to Jenkins, 27 February 1855. (CA) CO 179/37, M.B. Shaw to Maclean, 28 May 1855 and Grey to Russell, 19 July 1855. Cragg, "AmaMpondo and Colonial Authorities," pp. 220-31.

8 (CA) BK 77, Garner to Maclean, 20 October 1855 and M.B. Shaw to Maclean, 3 August 1855. (CA) CO 48/367, A.S. White to Maclean, 20 July 1855.

9 (CA) 48/374, Evidence enclosed in Addison to Maclean, 14 December 1855. (CA) BK 77, M.B. Shaw to Maclean, 22 November 1854.

10 Sadler, *Never a Young Man*, p. 136; for the description of Faku see W. Shaw, *Memoir of the Rev. William Shaw* (London: Wesleyan Conference Office, 1874), pp. 241.

11 (Wits) JP, C. White to Jenkins, 5 July 1855 and Jenkins to William Shaw, 18 July 1855.

12 (Wits) JP, C. White to Jenkins, 11 and 16 July 1855; and Jenkins to William Shaw, 18 July 1855.

13 (Wits) JP, Jenkins to M.B. Shaw, 7 August 1855; Jenkins to Maclean, 8 August 1855.

14 (Wits) JP, Maclean to Jenkins, 28 and 29 August 1855.

15 (CA) BK 77, Maclean to Addison, 4 October 1855 and Addison to Maclean, 14 December 1855. (Wits) JP, Addison to Jenkins, 3 November 1855; Evidence Given by Jenkins before Major Addison, no date; "Diary of Jenkins," October 1855. (CA) CO 48/374, Grey to Labouchere, 6 June 1856.

16 (Wits) JP, Jenkins to William Shaw, 6 February 1856; Jenkins to Maclean, 14 May 1856; Extract from Maclean to Grey, 15 June 1856; Jenkins to Travers, 11 October 1856. (CA) CO 48/380, Maclean to Liddle, 15 June 1856.

17 (Wits) JP, Jenkins to Thomas, 10 June 1856.

18 Cragg, "AmaMpondo and Colonial Authorities," p. 190. (Wits) JP, Jenkins to Maclean, 31 May 1856 (This letter was probably misdated as it discusses the Thomas murder which did not take place until June.); Jenkins to Maclean, 25 June 1856, written from Buntingville; "Report of a Meeting of the Pondos to Consider the Question of Reparations on the Death of the Rev. J.S. Thomas," 25 June 1856.

19 (Wits) JP, Jenkins to Maclean, 7 July 1856; Chief Faku to Sir George Grey, 7 July 1856; Jenkins to Brother Missionaries, n.d.

20 (Wits) JP, Maclean to Jenkins, 10 July 1856; Jenkins to Maclean, 5 September 1856;

Jenkins to Travers, 11 October 1856; Jenkins to Maclean, 6 December 1856; Jenkins to Maclean, 30 December 1856; Jenkins to Brother Missionaries, no date.

21 Taylor, *Christian Adventures*, p. 444. For more on the Cattle-Killing see J. Peires, *The Dead Will Arise: Nongqawuse and the Great Xhosa Cattle-Killing Movement of 1856-57* (Johannesburg: Ravan Press, 1989); and Timothy J. Stapleton, "Reluctant Slaughter: Rethinking Maqoma's Role in the Xhosa Cattle-Killing," *International Journal of African Historical Studies* 26, 2 (1993): 345-69.

22 (Wits) JP, Maclean to Jenkins, 20 May 1858, 9 May 1859, 7 June 1859,17 November 1859.

23 For the two previous paragraphs see Brownlee, *Transkeian Territories*, pp. 100-107, statements by Mqikela in 1880 and Jojo in 1874.

24 (Wits) JP, Jenkins to Shepstone, 30 March 1860.

25 (CA) GH 8/25, Brownlow to Jenkins, 21 November 1860; Jenkins to Maclean, 26 December 1860. (Wits) JP, Maclean to Jenkins, 1 March 1860.

26 (CA) CO 48/407, Currie to Grey, 18 March and 8 April 1861. For the border see (CA) CO 179/59, White to Cato, 22 March 1861; CO 48/461, Minutes of Meeting, 28 March 1872. For a hint that Currie used intimidation see CO 48/461, Barley to Kimberley, 23 August 1872.

27 (CA) GH 8/48, Jenkins to Wodehouse, 28 March 1862 enclosed in Milward to Barkly, 2 January 1873; CO 48/412, Instructions to Currie, 18 January 1861; (Wits) JP, Currie to Jenkins, 25 January and 1 April 1861; Cragg, "AmaMpondo and Colonial Authorities," pp. 265-66.

28 For Mfundisweni see D. Cragg, "Thomas Jenkins," in W.J. de Kock (ed.), *Dictionary of South African Biography*, vol. 1, (Pretoria: Human Sciences Research Council, 1968), p. 408. For the Sotho and Griqua movements see A.E. du Toit, *The Cape Frontier: A Study of Native Policy with Special Reference to the Years 1847-66* (Pretoria: Archives Year Book, 1954), p. 163. For Jojo see Brownlee, *Transkeian Territories*, p. 104.

29 Taylor, *Christian Adventures*, pp. 440-42. Jenkins, who told this story to Taylor in 1866, said that it had happened "a few years ago." Unfortunately, the section of Jenkins's diary which would have covered this incident was destroyed and none of his other correspondence refers to it.

30 Cragg, "AmaMpondo and Colonial Authorities," pp. 273-80. For firearms and liquor being landed see (CA) BK 91, Jenkins to Maclean, 26 December 1860; and (CA) GH 18/6, Jenkins to Grey, 15 August 1860.

31 (Wits) JP, Jenkins to T. Shepstone, 26 April 1865; for the quotation see Wodehouse to Jenkins, 4 May 1865. Emphasis is original.

32 Sanders, *Moshoeshoe*, p. 282.

33 (Wits) JP, Jenkins to Warner, 14 August 1865. Emphasis is original.

34 (Wits) JP, Jenkins to Wodehouse, 9 December 1865.

35 Ibid. Emphasis is original.

36 Ibid. (Wits) JP, Bisset to Jenkins, 7 January 1866.

37 (Wits) JP, Colonel Bisset to Jenkins, 27 December 1865, emphasis is original; Shepstone to Jenkins, 27 September 1865.

38 (Wits) JP, Shepstone to Jenkins, 7 January 1866; Bisset to Jenkins, 7 January 1866.

39 (Wits) JP, Shepstone to Jenkins, 17 February 1866; Jenkins to Shepstone, 24 February 1866; Wilson to Jenkins, 16 April 1866; Wilson to Jenkins, 15 May 1866.

40 (Wits) JP, Wodehouse to White, 18 April 1866.

41 Cragg, "Faku," p. 283.

42 For the previous three paragraphs see (Wits) JP, White to Wodehouse, 4 July 1866.

43 Taylor, *Christian Adventures*, pp. 347, 352-54, 364 and 373.

44 Ibid., pp. 386-87. For the oral traditions see Gamede, "Oral History of the Bhaca," pp. 69-70. For the quotation about the calf see A.M. Makaula, "A Political History of the Bhaca from Earliest Times to 1910," (MA thesis, Rhodes University, 1988), p. 111. For the Mpondo oral account see interview with Mr. Laqwela.

45 (Wits) JP, White to Wodehouse, 29 September 1866.

46 (Wits) JP, Wodehouse to White, 12 October 1866; Cragg, "AmaMpondo and Colonial Authority," p. 284.

47 For the oral history see interview with Mr. Laqwela. For the rest of the paragraph see (Wits) JP, Adam Kok to Faku, 29 March 1866 (Translated from Afrikaans by Prof. M.J. Prins of the University of Fort Hare.); J.C. Warner to Jenkins, 29 January 1867; Adam Kok to Jenkins, 21 February 1867; Wilson to Jenkins, 29 July 1867.

48 Taylor, *Christian Adventures*, pp. 462-63.

49 Cragg, "AmaMpondo and Colonial Authorities," p. 292. For Faku's inability to eat see interview with Paramount Chief Sigcau.

50 (Wits) JP, Wilson to Jenkins, 22 August 1867; Wilson to Jenkins, 10 November 1867; Allsop to Shepstone, 15 November 1867. For the hut see Taylor, *Christian Adventures*, p. 433. For the cattle kraal see interview with Chief Mnakwa Mqabalaki, 15 July 1997, the site of Faku's grave near Qawukeni Great Place, Lusikisiki.

51 (Wits) JP, Shepstone to Jenkins, 9 December 1867; Keate to Mqikela, 9 December 1867.

52 Ibid.

Afterword

1 For further reading consult Beinart, *Pondoland*, pp. 31-41; and Cragg, "AmaMpondo and Colonial Officials," pp. 296-440.

2 Beinart, *Pondoland*, pp. 104-109.

3 William Beinart and Colin Bundy, *Hidden Struggles in Rural South Africa: Politics and Popular Movements in the Transkei and Eastern Cape 1890-1930* (Johannesburg: Ravan Press, 1987), pp. 308-14.

4 Beinart, *Pondoland*, p. 120.

5 "Briefing Document for Commissioners and Council Members," South African Truth and Reconciliation Commission (TRC), Lusikisiki Public Hearings, 10-12 March 1997, p. 4.

6 Statement of Mr. Clement Gxabu, TRC, Lusikisiki, p. 35.

7 "Briefing Document," TRC, Lusikisiki, p. 5.

8 Statement of Mr. Gxabu, TRC, Lusikisiki, p. 14.

9 Statement of Mr. S. Silangwe, TRC, Lusikisiki, p. 22.

10 "Briefing Document," TRC, Lusikisiki, p. 6. For accounts of the Pondoland Revolt see Govan Mbeki, *South Africa: The Peasants' Revolt*, Baltimore: (Penguin, 1964); and Sean Redding, "Government Witchcraft, Taxation, the Supernatural, and the Mpondo Revolt in Transkei, South Africa, 1955-1963," *African Affairs* 95, 381 (1996): 555-79.

11 Roger Southall, *South Africa's Transkei: The Political Economy of an "Independent" Bantustan* (New York: Monthly Review Press, 1983); for the election see p. 118, for Sigcau's farm see p. 143, and for the arrest of candidates in Pondoland see p. 127. Also see G. Carter, T. Karis and N. Stultz, *South Africa's Transkei: The Politics of Domestic Colonialism* (Evanston: Northwestern University Press, 1967), pp. 134-35.

12 Ibid., p. 128.

13 Ibid., pp. 257-61.

14 Ibid., pp. 259-60 and p. 277.

15 J.B. Peires, "The Implosion of Transkei and Ciskei," *African Affairs* 91 (1992): 367-371.

16 "Briefing Document," TRC, Lusikisiki, p. 9.

Bibliography

Oral Sources

Mr. Merriman Mawethu Laqwela, Lusikisiki
Mr. Arthur Lizo Luwaca, Libode
Mr. Mlimandlela Ndamase, Umtata
Mr. Pondolwendlovu Ndamase, Umtata
Mr. Sithembele Ndamase, Umtata
Mr. Vuyani Ndamase, Umtata
Mr. Xhalinlonda Ndamase, Umtata
Mr. Zwelicacile Ndamase, Umtata
Chief Pronnly Sikilimba Mfolozi, Lusikisiki
Chief Mnakwa Mqabalaki, Lusikisiki
Paramount Chief Justice Mpondombini Sigcau, Lusikisiki
Princess Lombekiso Masobhuza Sigcau, Lusikisiki
Mrs. Stella Sigcau, Lusikisiki

Archival Sources

William Cullen Library, University of the Witwatersrand:
A56, The Reverend Thomas Jenkins Papers and Diary, 1838-1880.

State Archives, Cape Town:
Colonial Office (CO) 48/285-461, 179/35-59; Correspondence. British Kaffraria (BK) 77, Transkeian Magistrate, 1854-56.

Natal Archives, Pietermaritzburg:
The Fynn Papers A1382:   Vol 4, Letters Despatched
Vol 5, Letters Despatched
Vol 6, Other Letters
Vol 8, Messages to/from Chiefs
Vol 11, Notes on Pondoland and Faku
Vol 12, The Bushman Affair
Shepstone Papers (SP) 14, Letters from T. Shepstone to G. Cato.
Secretary of Native Affairs (SNA) 1/1/5, T. Shepstone to Colonial Secretary.

British Parliamentary Papers:

1852-53, LXVI (1635) Correspondence re. Kaffir Tribes.
1852-53, LXII (1697) Natal, Correspondence, 1851-53.
Truth and Reconciliation Commission (TRC):
"Briefing Document for Commissioners and Committee Members," Lusikisiki Public Hearings, 10-12 March 1997.

Newspapers

The Grahamstown Journal.

Books

Beinart, W. *The Political Economy of Pondoland, 1860-1930.* Johannesburg: Ravan Press, 1982.

Beinart, W. and C. Bundy. *Hidden Struggles in Rural South Africa: Politics and Popular Movements in the Transkei and Eastern Cape.* Johannesburg: Ravan Press, 1987.

Berning, J. M. (ed.). *The Historical Conversations of Sir George Cory.* Cape Town: Maskew Miller Longman, 1989.

Bird, J. (ed.). *The Annals of Natal.* Cape Town: C. Struik, 1965.

Brownlee, C. *Reminiscences of Kaffir Life and History.* Lovedale: Lovedale Press, 1896.

Brownlee, F. (ed.). *The Transkeian Native Territories: Historical Records.* Lovedale: Lovedale Press, 1923.

Bryant, A.T. *Olden Times in Zululand and Natal.* London: Longmans, Green and Co., 1929.

Carter, G., T. Karis, and N. Stultz. *South Africa's Transkei: The Politics of Domestic Colonialism.* Evanston: Northwestern University Press, 1967.

Cathcart, G. *Correspondence of Sir George Cathcart.* London: John Murray, 1856.

Chase, J.C. (ed.). *The Natal Papers.* Cape Town: C. Struik, 1968.

Cingo, W.D. *Ibali LamaMpondo, Bhaca, Xesibe nama Mpondomise.* Palmerton: Palmerton Mission Press, 1925.

Davenport, T.R.H. *South Africa: A Modern History.* Toronto: University of Toronto Press, 1989.

Du Toit, A.E. *The Cape Frontier: A Study of Native Policy with Special Reference to the Years 1847-66.* Pretoria: Archives Year Book, 1954.

Eldredge, E. *A South African Kingdom: The Pursuit of Security in Nineteenth Century Lesotho.* Cambridge: Cambridge University Press, 1993.

Fast, H. (ed.). *The Journal and Selected Letters of the Rev. William Shrewsbury, 1826-35.* Johannesburg: Witwatersrand University Press, 1994.

Frye, J. (ed.). *The War of the Axe and the Xhosa Bible: The Journal of the Rev. J.W. Appleyard.* Cape Town: C. Struik, 1971.

Galbraith, J.S. *Reluctant Empire: British Policy on the South African Frontier 1834-54.* Berkeley: University of California Press, 1963.

Gardiner, A.F. *Narrative of a Journey to the Zoolu Country.* London: William Crofts, 1836.

Hammond-Tooke, W.D. *Bhaca Society.* London: Oxford University Press, 1962.

Hunter, M. *Reaction to Conquest: Effects of Contact with Europeans on the Pondo of South Africa.* London: Oxford University Press, 1936.

Isaacs, N. *Travels and Adventures in Eastern Africa.* London: Edward Churton, 1836.

Kay, S. *Travels and Researches in Caffraria*. London: John Mason, 1833.

Kirby, P.R. (ed.). *Andrew Smith and Natal*. Cape Town: Van Reibeeck Society, 1955.

Laband, J. *Rope of Sand: The Rise and Fall of the Zulu Kingdom in the Nineteenth Century*. Johannesburg: Jonathan Ball, 1995.

Lister, M.H. (ed.). *The Journals of Andrew Geddes Bain*. Cape Town: Van Riebeeck Society, 1949.

Majeke, N. *The Role of Missionaries in Conquest*. Johannesburg: Society of Young Africa, 1952.

Mbeki, G. *South Africa: The Peasants' Revolt*. Baltimore: Penguin, 1964.

Mostert, N. *Frontiers: The Epic of South Africa's Creation and the Tragedy of the Xhosa People*. New York: Alfred Knopf, 1992.

Ndamase, V.P. *AmaMpondo: Ibali ne Ntlalo*. Lovedale: Lovedale Press, [late 1920s].

Omer-Cooper, J.D. *The Zulu Aftermath*. London: Longman, 1966.

Peires, J. *The Dead Will Arise: Nongqawuse and the Great Xhosa Cattle-Killing Movement of 1856-57*. Johannesburg: Ravan Press, 1989.

——*The House of Phalo: A History of the Xhosa People in the Days of Their Independence*. Johannesburg: Ravan Press, 1981.

Sadler, C. (ed.). *Never a Young Man: Extracts from the Letters and Journals of the Rev. William Shaw*. Cape Town: H.A.U.M., 1967.

Sanders, P. *Moshoeshoe: Chief of the Sotho*. London: Heinemann, 1975.

Shaw, W. *The Story of My Mission in South-East Africa*. London: Hamilton, Adams and Co., 1860.

——*Memoir of the Rev. William Shaw*. London: Wesleyan Conference Office, 1874.

Shillington, K. *History of Africa*. London: MacMillan, 1995.

Soga, J.H. *The South-Eastern Bantu*. Johannesburg: Witwatersrand University Press, 1930.

Southall, R. *South Africa's Transkei: The Political Economy of an "Independent" Bantustan*. New York: Monthly Review Press, 1983.

Stapleton, T.J. *Maqoma: Xhosa Resistance to Colonial Advance, 1798-1873*. Johannesburg: Jonathan Ball, 1994.

Steedman, A. *Wanderings and Adventures in the Interior of Southern Africa*. Vols. 1 and 2. London: Longman, 1835.

Stuart, J. and Malcolm, D. (eds.). *Diary of Henry Francis Fynn*. Pietermartizburg: Shuter and Shooter, 1969.

Taylor, W. *Christian Adventures in South Africa*. London: Jackson, Walford and Hodder, 1867.

Theal, G.M. *History of South Africa*. Vols. 1-10. London: George Allen and Unwin, 1897-1919.

Theal, G.M. (ed.). *Documents Relating to the Kaffir War of 1835*. London: Government of the Union of South Africa, 1912.

Thompson, L. *Survival in Two Worlds: Moshoeshoe of Lesotho*. Oxford: Oxford University Press, 1975.

Van Warmelo, M.J. (ed.). *History of Matiwane and the AmaNgwane Tribe*. Pretoria: Government Printer, 1938.

Vinnicombe, P. *People of the Eland*. Pietermaritzburg: University of Natal Press, 1976.

Webb, C. de B. and J. Wright (eds.). *The James Stuart Archive of Recorded Oral Evidence Relating to the History of the Zulu and Neighbouring Peoples*. Vols. 1-4. Pietermaritzburg: Killie Campbell Africana Library, 1976-86.

Wright, J.B. *Bushmen Raiders of the Drakensberg 1840-1870: A Study of Their Conflict with Stock-Keeping Peoples in Natal*. Pietermaritzburg: University of Natal Press, 1971.

Articles and Chapters

Cobbing, J.R.D. "A Tainted Well: The Objectives, Historical Fantasies and Working Methods of James Stuart, with Counter-Argument." *Journal of Natal and Zulu History* 11 (1988): 115-54.

——."Grasping the Nettle: The Slave Trade and the Early Zulu." In D.R. Edgecombe, J. Laband and P. Thompson (eds.), *The Debate on Zulu Origins*. Pietermaritzburg: University of Natal Press, 1992.

——."The Mfecane as Alibi: Thoughts on the Battles of Dithakong and Mbolompo. " *Journal of African History* 29, 3 (1988): 487-519.

Cragg, D.G.L. "Correspondence Relative to the Attack on the Chief Ncaphayi," *Journal of the Methodist Historical Society of South Africa* (October 1960 and April 1961).

——."Faku," and "Thomas Jenkins." In W.J. de Kock (ed.), *The Dictionary of South African Biography*, vol. 1. Pretoria: Human Sciences Research Council, 1968.

——."The Role of the Wesleyan Missionaries in Relations between the Mpondo and the Colonial Authorities." In Saunders, C. and R. Derricourt (eds.), *Beyond the Cape Frontier*. London: Longman, 1974.

Eldredge, E. "Sources of Conflict in Southern Africa, ca.1800-30: The Mfecane Reconsidered," *Journal of African History* 33, 1 (1992): 1-35.

Etherington, N. "Christianity and African Society in Nineteenth Century Natal." In A. Duminy and B. Guest (eds.), *Natal and Zululand from Earliest Times to 1910: A New History*, Pietermaritzburg: University of Natal Press, 1989.

——."New Wine in Old Bottles: The Persistence of Narrative Structures in the Historiography of the Mfecane and Great Trek." In Hamilton, *Mfecane Aftermath*.

Gladwin, F.P. "Historical Sketch of the Mpondomise Tribe as Taken from Vete, the Son of Umziziba." In Brownlee, *Transkeian Territories*.

Jolly, P. " Interaction between South-Eastern San and Southern Nguni and Sotho Communities c.1400 to c.1880." *South African Historical Journal* 35 (November 1996): 30-61.

Peires, J.B. "Matiwane's Road to Mbholompo: A Reprieve for the Mfecane." In Hamilton, *Mfecane Aftermath*.

Peires, J.B. "The Implosion of Transkei and Ciskei." *African Affairs* 91 (1992): 365-87.

Pridmore, J. "The Production of H.F. Fynn, c.1830-1930." In Edgecombe, et al. *Zulu Origins*.

Redding, S. "Government Witchcraft: Taxation, the Supernatural, and the Mpondo Revolt in the Transkei, South Africa, 1955-1963." *African Affairs* 95 (1996): 555-79.

Redding, S. "Sorcery and Sovereignty: Taxation, Witchcraft, and Political Symbols in the 1880 Transkeian Rebellion." *Journal of Southern African Studies* 22, 2 (1996): 249-70.

Stapleton, T.J. "Reluctant Slaughter: Rethinking Maqoma's Role in the Xhosa Cattle-Killing." *International Journal of African Historical Studies* 26, 2 (1993): 345-69.

Stapleton, T.J. "The Expansion of a Pseudo-Ethnicity in the Eastern Cape: Reconsidering the Fingo Exodus of 1865." *International Journal of African Historical Studies* 29, 2 (1996): 233-50.

Webster, A.C. "Unmasking the Fingo: The War of 1835 Revisited." In Hamilton, *Mfecane Aftermath*.

Wright, J. "Political Transformations in the Thukela-Mzimkhulu Region in the Late Eighteenth and Early Nineteenth Centuries." In Hamilton, *Mfecane Aftermath*.

Wright, J. "Making the James Stuart Archive." *History in Africa* 23 (1996): 333-50.

Wylie, D. "Proprietor of Natal: Henry Francis Fynn and the Mythography of Shaka." *History in Africa* 22 (1995): 408-37.

Theses and Unpublished Papers

Bramdeow, S. "Henry Francis Fynn and the Fynn Community in Natal, 1824 to 1988." MA thesis, University of Natal, Durban, 1988.

Cele, N. "A Mixed Inheritance: the Fynns and Land in No Man's Land in the 19th Century." Paper presented at the South African Historical Society, Pretoria, July 1997.

Cobbing, J. "Ousting the Mfecane: Reply to Elizabeth Eldredge." Paper presented at the Mfecane Aftermath Conference, University of the Witwatersrand, September 1991.

——"Rethinking the Roots of Violence in Southern Africa, ca.1790-1840." Paper presented at the Mfecane Aftermath Conference, University of the Witwatersrand, September 1991.

Cragg, D.G.L. "The Relations of the AmaMpondo and the Colonial Authorities 1830-1886. with Special Reference to the Role of Wesleyan Missionaries." D.Phil. thesis, Oxford, 1959.

Gamede, V.W. "The Oral History of the Bhaca of Umzimkhulu." MA thesis, University of Transkei, 1992.

Gorham, C. "Port Natal: A Blind Darkness; Speculation, Trade, the Creation of a Vortex of Violence and the Mfecane." Paper presented at the Mfecane Aftermath Conference, University of the Witwatersrand, September 1991.

Makaula, A.M. "A Political History of the Bhaca from Earliest Times to 1910." MA thesis, Rhodes University, 1988.

Pridmore, J. "Keep My Seat, I'm on My Way: The Fynn Family and Traditional Leadership in Southern Natal in the 1990's: A Preliminary Investigation." Paper presented at the South African Historical Society, Pretoria, July 1997.

Index